**GRADES K–3**

# Differentiating Reading Instruction for Success With RTI

Margo Southall

SCHOLASTIC

New York • Toronto • London • Auckland • Sydney
Mexico City • New Delhi • Hong Kong • Buenos Aires

I would like to thank the following reading specialists and teachers in Nashville, Tennessee who contributed to this book with photographs of their students at work: Susan Porter at Maxwell Elementary, Jacqueline Jones, Pennie Pulley-Sloan and Betsy Potts at Goodlettsville Elementary.

To my editor, Joanna Davis-Swing, thank you for your continual support and encouragement.

Editor: Joanna Davis-Swing
Copyeditor: Carol Ghiglieri
Cover Designer: Jorge J. Namerow
Interior Designer: Kelli Thompson
Cover and Interior Photos: Courtesy of the author

ISBN: 978-0-545-21486-5

# CONTENTS

**All featured forms are available on the companion CD.**

# INTRODUCTION

## The Purpose of This Book

Response to Intervention (RtI) is a model of instruction that has been adopted by school districts across the nation after it was introduced within the Individuals With Disabilities Education Improvement Act of 2004 (IDEA). The goal of RtI is to prevent reading difficulties by systematically assessing students and providing immediate support to those who demonstrate a need. At the core of any RtI program is high-quality, differentiated classroom instruction, which is supplemented by tiers of increasing support provided in small-group or one-on-one settings and targeted to student need. The benefit of RtI is that it provides a road map for coordinating intervention at the classroom and school levels.

I've spent the last eleven years working alongside teachers as an on-site literacy coach, supporting teachers in their efforts to differentiate reading instruction effectively. Much of this time I also had instructional responsibilities working with low-progress readers, so I know full well the realities of translating principles into practice. For the past four years, I have worked as a professional learning provider, helping schools implement workable RtI programs. Differentiating reading instruction within an RtI framework has implications for daily classroom instruction and for intervention programs. The process of planning and implementing a responsive, differentiated reading program with appropriate intervention support is a central challenge shared by both classroom and intervention teachers.

When it comes to differentiated instruction, I hear two questions from teaching colleagues over and over again:

**1:** How do I put it all together—planning for and teaching students with a range of needs and addressing the management issues of scheduling, organizing students in groups, and selecting materials?

**2:** What types of instruction work for specific types of low-progress readers?

In the following chapters, I address these critical questions, sharing a working guide to accomplishing the following goals:

- Streamlining the process of planning, implementing, and managing a differentiated reading program that aligns with the Response to Intervention framework.

- Meeting the needs of on-grade and low-progress readers within classroom core reading and intervention programs.

In the following chapters, I'll share the strategies, lessons, and tools that have made effectively differentiating instruction within an RtI framework a reality in the many schools I've worked with.

# How to Use This Book

To successfully differentiate reading instruction within the RtI model, we need to see both the big picture and the components that comprise it. To support you in this process of putting it—and keeping it—all together, in Chapters 1–3 we examine the *big picture*: what needs to be in place at the classroom and intervention level, and the typical issues that arise during the transition to differentiating instruction within an RtI framework.

**Chapter 1** describes how differentiated reading instruction and RtI impact our instruction in both the classroom core program and in our intervention programs, at each tier of implementation.

**Chapter 2** offers organizational tools for gathering and using assessment data for instruction. I show you how to create profiles of students as both readers and learners so you can design a responsive program for all your learners, including low-progress readers requiring Tier 2 and 3 interventions.

**Chapter 3** answers common questions regarding the daily implementation of differentiated instruction in the classroom (Tier 1). Here you will find teacher-friendly formats for differentiating the content, lesson structure, pacing of instruction, and reading materials in whole-class, small-group, partner, and independent contexts. In addition, you'll find supporting strategy charts, visuals, and other differentiation tools designed to give every child access to the knowledge, skills, and strategies they require on the path to literacy.

**Chapters 4–6** present lessons and templates of lesson sequences to address common areas of student difficulty, along with guided practice and independent activities for each component of reading: word solving, fluency, and comprehension.

## Chapter 4—Word Solving

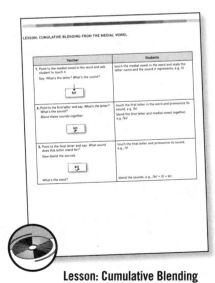

**Lesson: Cumulative Blending From the Medial Vowel**
Form 4.18 on the CD

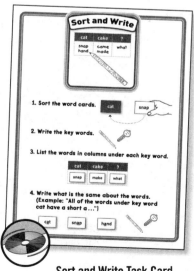

**Sort and Write Task Card**
Form 4.33 on the CD

## Chapter 5—Fluency

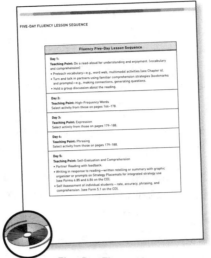

**Five-Day Fluency Lesson Sequence**
Form 5.5 on the CD

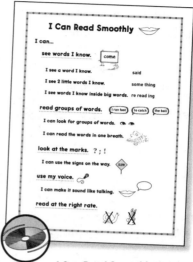

**I Can Read Smoothly Strategy Chart**
Form 5.2 on the CD

## Chapter 6—Comprehension

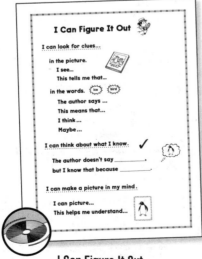

**I Can Figure It Out Strategy Chart**
Form 6.32 on the CD

**Strategy Placemat #1**
Form 6.85 on the CD

# DIFFERENTIATED INSTRUCTION AND RESPONSE TO INTERVENTION— WE'VE COME A LONG WAY

## Journey to Differentiation as a Classroom Teacher

I have been an elementary educator for nearly three decades. Before I worked as a reading specialist and special educator, I taught kindergarten through fifth grade. Over the years, I have participated in a series of initiatives that have moved my teaching toward differentiation. But lately I've noticed that I am constantly trying to beat the clock as I work to infuse every precious minute I have with powerful instruction.

Add to this the fact that few of us were offered training in how to implement differentiated reading instruction beyond grouping students by text levels. What's been missing is the framework that Response to Intervention (RtI) offers, a structure that links the assessed needs of our students with a focus on site-based professional learning and growth. Today, professional learning is part of our teaching day, beyond the (often very animated!) lunchroom discussions. Both classroom and intervention teachers actively participate in literacy teams, grade-level teams, and intervention team meetings where we consider how best to allocate our resources to better serve the needs of our students and devise research-based strategies to make our daily teaching more effective—*and* doable! A critical element in the success of the RtI initiative is that it requires both classroom and intervention teachers to collaborate on a coordinated approach for meeting the needs of their students.

To effectively differentiate instruction, provide multiple shared practice opportunities using interactive formats.

# Journey to RTI as an Intervention Teacher

In the late 1990's, I was a special education resource teacher who completed the preliminary assessments and referral processes for special education. The hope, of classroom teachers and children's families alike, was that once students were identified for special education services, they would finally receive the intensive teaching they needed to bridge the gap with their peers. Before a student was identified for these services, only meager interventions were available in the classroom. The risk of too little, too late hung over our heads.

With the advent of RtI, the approach to intervention changed. Instead of waiting for a student we know has reading difficulties to be identified for special education services, we now have a proactive plan that helps us provide intervention as soon as a student demonstrates a need. In my school, we use the following procedure to guide our interventions:

**Step 1:** Identify the areas of reading difficulty from assessment data.

**Step 2:** Determine what is *most* important for this student to learn next. This becomes the *instructional goal* for the student.

**Step 3:** Select teaching practices that target the skills and strategies that comprise the instructional goal and are appropriate for this student. This is the *instructional response*.

**Step 4:** Decide whether the classroom teacher or intervention teacher will deliver the instructional response and where it will take place; classroom and intervention teachers coordinate.

**Step 5:** Plan regular assessments to monitor and document student progress.

During our RtI intervention meetings, my colleagues and I review assessment data to identify the next steps in our instructional response for a particular student. We also correlate teaching practices and lesson formats to the area of student need and review available materials—such as leveled books, technology resources, and word study manipulatives—that best support the way a particular student learns. We use a log to maintain communication and consistency between classroom and intervention teachers, and we set up a schedule for administering assessments to monitor and document student progress.

This approach drives our daily planning for classroom instruction, not just intervention programming. Our grade-level team meetings often begin with a review of ongoing informal assessments to determine where we need to go next in our whole-class and small-group instruction. After identifying areas of need for the class as a whole, we can schedule units of study on skills and strategies and organize groups of students with a common need into strategy-based groups and record "next steps" for these students. Lastly, we pull from available resources, such as teacher guides, lesson plans, and student materials that can be found in our classrooms and school book rooms.

*Differentiating Reading Instruction for Success With RTI* © 2011 by Margo Southall • Scholastic Teaching Resources

Even with this procedure in place and interventions provided in a timely manner, students with pervasive reading difficulties continue to receive special education services, as is their right. But the numbers referred to special education *have been reduced*. I credit this reduction to our RtI program, which sparked a school-wide effort to reframe our thinking so that we ensure sufficient levels of instructional response at the first signs of difficulty and provide continued support, *whether or not the student qualifies for special education services*.

If schools follow the guiding principles of the RtI model, they can set in place a continuum of interventions offered to students as soon as they demonstrate a need, as we've seen in my school. RtI programs may assume different forms in different districts, but the principle that each child is allocated the resources he or she needs to bridge the gap, with monitoring mechanisms in place to revise instruction, remains the same.

This chapter describes the overarching structure of the Response to Intervention model and shows how it differs from traditional approaches to instruction and intervention. Chapters 2 and 3 provide the practical tools—record-keeping forms and ways to manage and organize your program to maximize student learning time—that you need to implement RtI.

## The Next Step—Response to Intervention

Traditional approaches to reading intervention have had limited success. The majority of students in intervention and special education programs never achieve the literacy rates of their peers (Pinnell & Fountas, 2009). This is not due to a lack of effort on the part of educators, but to the lack of a coordinated, responsive approach that aligns the intensity of instruction with student need.

"In many schools, instruction and time are constant—they do not vary on a student by student basis. RtI was designed as a way to encourage teachers to vary instruction and time to create a constant level of learning. A core assumption of RtI is that all students can reach high levels of achievement if the system is willing (and able) to vary the amount of time students have to learn and type of instruction they receive. Thus, RtI builds on the work done with differentiated instruction."

(Fisher & Frey, 2010, p. 15 ).

**What Makes the Difference?**

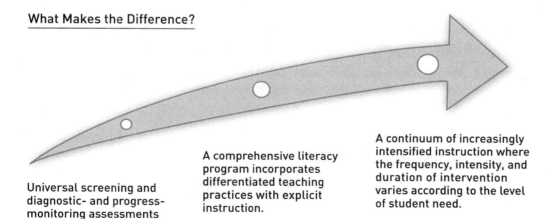

Universal screening and diagnostic- and progress-monitoring assessments guide instruction.

A comprehensive literacy program incorporates differentiated teaching practices with explicit instruction.

A continuum of increasingly intensified instruction where the frequency, intensity, and duration of intervention varies according to the level of student need.

Three Key Components of RtI That Distinguish It From Traditional Approaches to Intervention

What's different about RtI is the focus on establishing a working structure to ensure that students receive timely support when they demonstrate a need. By regularly screening students and administering diagnostic and progress-monitoring assessments, teachers can more easily identify when a student is falling behind and quickly move to address the problem area. Under the former discrepancy model of special education, support was sometimes delayed for several years until the discrepancy between a child's IQ and performance on a standardized test became large enough to qualify for special services; too often, students received no intensive intervention until this point. This system resulted in large numbers of students being placed under the special education umbrella, with identification seeming to be the end goal. The wording of the 2004 reauthorization of the Individuals With Disabilities Act (IDEA) supports states in using the RtI process rather than the traditional IQ discrepancy model for identifying students with learning disabilities. The concern has been that the discrepancy model may have led to insufficient monitoring and allocation of intervention resources to students before or after referral to special education services.

## IT'S A QUESTION OF EQUALITY

RtI is all about equality of access: access to the instruction a child needs to be successful, access to the same print resources as his or her peers, and access to information in a literate world. This access is denied to low-progress readers unless we recognize their need and provide an informed, coordinated instructional response.

# How Do Differentiated Instruction and Response to Intervention Work Together?

The principles of differentiated instruction are embedded in the framework of RtI to ensure that students who show signs of falling behind their peers will receive the necessary support in a timely manner. The chart on the next page summarizes how the two work together.

| Differentiated Instruction | + | Response to Intervention |
|---|---|---|
| Provides multiple pathways to learning a set of required skills and strategies, so these are accessible to all students. | + | Consists of timely, responsive intervention to prevent long-term academic failure. |
| Utilizes a teaching cycle of pre-assessment, instruction, assessment, and reteaching. | + | Involves continuous examination of the effectiveness of the core program and intervention for individual students. |
| Includes varied pacing. | + | Includes intervention and classroom instruction as part of an integrated instructional design. |
| Elicits active engagement of all learners. | + | Includes consultation between the classroom teacher and the intervention teacher. |
| Recognizes the importance of a student as a learner, addressing the "whole child." | + | Relies on more frequent use of informal assessments. |
| Entails flexible grouping of students by need and interests. | + | Includes requirements for ongoing progress-monitoring assessments at regular intervals. |
| Is fully inclusive. | + | Entails a problem-solving process involving teams of professionals. |
| Is student-centered. | | |

# How RTI Works: Common Models of Implementation

Across the country, you will find a variety of models for implementing RtI. The most familiar structure is the three-tier model (Haager, Klingner, & Vaughn, 2007) described in the following section. Fisher and Frey (2010) describe a model of RtI that integrates instruction and intervention, which they term RtI[2] (Response to Instruction and Intervention). This model of RtI places equal emphasis on regular assessment of student response to intervention and continuous examination of classroom instructional design. Whichever term we use, an over-emphasis on remediation efforts and under-emphasis on the role of core instruction in the prevention of reading difficulties will undermine the central goal of RtI. Ultimately it is the level of *responsiveness of the instruction and intervention to the needs of the student* that is the guiding principle of all RtI models, and this encompasses all aspects of the literacy program.

## THE THREE-TIER MODEL OF RTI: A CONTINUUM OF INCREASING SUPPORT

The tiers in RtI represent a continuum of differentiation aligned with the levels of student need. There are no rigid boundaries between tiers; rather, the intensity of instruction increases through the tiers. This continuum is

"All reading difficulties have explanations, but it is more productive to think about instruction that will help children overcome them."

(PINNELL & FOUNTAS, 2009, P. 31)

represented in the interconnected circles in the graphic below. Consistency is maintained across the tiers by using the same teaching terminology, prompts, and visual cues. Intervention is not merely more of the same skill or strategy as whole-class lessons, but tailored instruction determined by ongoing assessments (Dorn & Saffos, 2001). The tier system is not a hierarchy or separate steps where we move students toward an end goal, but integrated instruction on a continuum of differentiation.

## TEACHING ACROSS THE TIERS: INTEGRATED, SYSTEMATIC AND INTENTIONAL INSTRUCTION

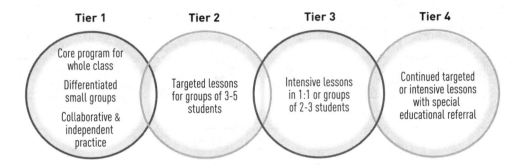

**Tier 1**
Core program for whole class

Differentiated small groups

Collaborative & independent practice

**Tier 2**
Targeted lessons for groups of 3-5 students

**Tier 3**
Intensive lessons in 1:1 or groups of 2-3 students

**Tier 4**
Continued targeted or intensive lessons with special educational referral

### Tier 1 Instruction: Differentiation for All

Tier 1 instruction includes the core reading program that is taught to all students. It encompasses whole-class lessons; differentiated, small-group instruction; and collaborative and independent practice opportunities. A comprehensive literacy program is another term for balanced literacy instruction.

### Tier 2 Instruction: Targeted Intervention

When students do not make adequate progress in Tier 1, more targeted services and interventions are indicated. This can occur as early as kindergarten. Targeted instruction at Tier 2 means adjusting the content, structure, and/or materials to meet specific student needs. Some students require only a short cycle (10–12 weeks) of intervention, while others may require two or three of these cycles to reach grade-level expectations. For some students the intervention occurs only once, while others may require additional boosts to their learning at different intervals during the elementary grades to maintain the same rate of growth as their peers.

Who implements Tier 2 instruction? Is this the role of the classroom teacher or the intervention specialist? The answer depends on the school. Does the school have enough intervention specialists to accommodate all Tier 2 students? If not, then teachers and administrators need to find strategies to

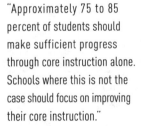

"Approximately 75 to 85 percent of students should make sufficient progress through core instruction alone. Schools where this is not the case should focus on improving their core instruction."

(Fisher & Frey, 2010, p. 24)

make it workable for classroom teachers to share this role. In some of the districts I work with, there are no intervention specialists at the Tier 2 level, and it is the classroom teachers who implement this second wave of more targeted instruction in the form of additional, daily small-group lessons. This book provides interventions, lessons, and management ideas to help teachers charged with implementing Tier 2 interventions. One teacher, for example, has an "after-lunch bunch," who meet with her every day while the rest of the students read from their book bag, complete literacy center tasks, or work on independent projects.

Another option in schools where classroom teachers and specialists share this responsibility is the W.I.N. (What I Need) model, where students are grouped across classrooms for an hour each day (sometimes in two 30-minute periods) based upon their learning goals; advanced and on-grade students meet in larger groups, and groupings for low-progress readers are smaller. Most of these schools also include teachers of physical education, science, social studies, art, and technology in the staffing of W.I.N. time, and these teachers often work with on-grade and above-grade-level students on project-based assignments. The services of speech-language pathologists may also be employed in small-group or one-to-one contexts to address student language difficulties.

Reducing the size of the Tier 2 groups to no more than five students is critical in order to achieve instructional goals and close the gap between current performance and grade-level expectations. This is where having enough teachers and intervention specialists who are scheduled to work with Tier 2 and 3 students makes a significant difference.

## Tier 3 Instruction: Intensive Intervention

For students who do not demonstrate adequate progress toward grade-level goals with Tier 2 interventions, intensive intervention practices are implemented along with additional minutes and either a smaller group size or one-to-one instruction. Intervention at this tier does not usually include special education, but precedes referral to these services. An interventionist, such as a reading specialist or special education teacher, works in collaboration with the classroom teacher at Tier 3. If students do not demonstrate adequate progress at this level, they may be referred for additional assessments and possibly for special education services, sometimes referred to as Tier 4.

In Chapter 2 we look at ways to increase the learning opportunities for students in Tiers 2 and 3 and how to design and revise our intervention to meet the varied needs of low-progress readers. In Chapter 3, we will examine how to plan and implement a responsive, differentiated reading program to successfully fulfill the principles of Tier 1 instruction.

"This intervention often takes the form of *additional* small-group instruction designed to complement the core instruction all students receive… It is estimated that 10 to 15 percent of students at one time or another require supplemental interventions in addition to the core instruction. Tier 2 supplemental interventions often last up to 20 weeks so learners can benefit from instruction that focuses on both short and long term goals."

(Fisher & Frey, 2010, p. 24)

"It is anticipated that 5–10% of students will require Tier 3 instruction for intensive intervention."

(Haager, Klingner, & Vaughn, 2007, p. 21)

## Summary of Key Principles

◈ RtI focuses on intervening as soon as students fall behind their peers.

◈ The three-tier system provides a roadmap for implementing a comprehensive core reading program and a continuum of intensified intervention.

◈ A continuum of tiers provides a guide to increasing the amount of instructional time, reducing the number of students in a group, adjusting the frequency of assessment, fine-tuning the responsiveness of the programming to student need, and drawing on specialized interventionists.

◈ The targeted skills and strategies, instructional terminology, prompts, and cues are consistent across the tiers to support the transfer of skills and strategies across multiple reading contexts.

*Differentiating Reading Instruction for Success With RTI* © 2011 by Margo Southall • Scholastic Teaching Resources

# 2

# PLANNING DIFFERENTIATED READING INSTRUCTION: ASSESSMENT IS THE KEY

This chapter describes how to compile the assessment information you need to plan efficiently and effectively for differentiated instruction. It is here we answer questions such the following:

- How can we ensure we are identifying and targeting each student's deficit skills and strategies?

- What are some teacher-friendly informal assessment tools that are informative enough to guide daily planning and teaching?

- Why is knowing the profile of a student as a reader and a learner important?

- How can we create an intervention plan? What does it look like?

- What can we do when a student is not meeting progress-monitoring goals?

- How can we organize our assessment data to facilitate collaboration and consistency within and across grade levels?

The first step is to prepare profiles of our students as readers and learners, as discussed in the following section.

# Students as Readers and Learners: Establishing Profiles to Guide Instruction and Intervention

To effectively differentiate instruction, we must first know our students. We need to assemble a profile of each student in our class, identifying how he or she:

- interacts with text or what strategic actions he or she employs, which comprises his or her *profile as a reader*.
- approaches learning within different social and physical contexts, which comprises his or her *profile as a learner*.

We can establish profiles of students as readers and learners by documenting their reading skills, behaviors, and attitudes over a specified period of time using both diagnostic assessment tools and observations. Together these profiles create a picture of each student as an individual with literacy strengths and needs. The information compiled in each of these profiles offers a window of opportunity for student learning, a chance to truly teach at the point of need in a way the child can benefit from. This chapter will walk you through the process of creating these profiles and then discuss how to use the information gathered to effectively differentiate instruction.

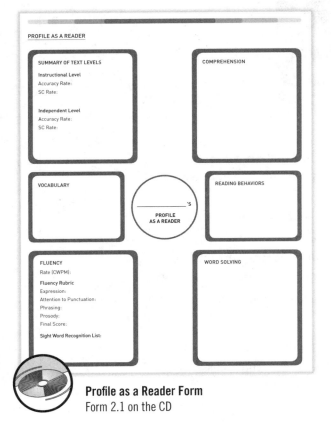

**Profile as a Reader Form**
Form 2.1 on the CD

## Profile: Student as a Reader

A student's profile as a reader (Form 2.1 on the CD) provides a place to summarize multiple assessments, each offering insight into how the student processes running text. On a single page, we can see information about a student's:

- Reading level
- Vocabulary knowledge
- Fluency rate
- Sight-word knowledge
- Comprehension strategy use
- Reading behaviors
- Word-solving skills
- Phonological awareness

In Part 1 of this chapter, we examine assessment tools that can help us collect information in each area of reading development: word solving, comprehension, and fluency. I also share a Student Reading Goals, Observation, and Instruction form (Form 2.3 on the CD) that helps you translate information in the profile into instructional plans. A completed example of each form can be found on pages 40 and 41.

### Profile: Student as a Learner

The second profile describes the student as a learner (see Form 2.2 on the CD and the example on page 41). This profile takes into account the student's self-esteem (affect), motivation, and engagement in addition to learning preferences. This information is collected through the Student Survey (Form 2.12 on the CD) in addition to observations you make during whole-class and small-group interactions and one-on-one reading conferences. An instructional approach that ignores this second dimension of students as learners will fail to tap their potential for success.

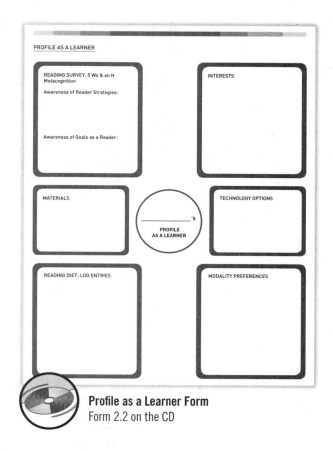

**Profile as a Learner Form**
Form 2.2 on the CD

## Part 1

# Students as Readers: Collecting the Data We Need

My colleagues and I have spent many hours selecting and administering multiple assessments and then examining these together to guide our daily lessons—all in an effort to gain an understanding of where our students are as readers. The following section discusses the range of assessment tools available and how to ensure you're using those that provide the data you need. There's no one "right" set of tools, but there is certain information you need to assess for. You'll summarize the data on students' reading skills in word recognition, fluency, and comprehension on the Profile as a Reader form, which you'll then use to plan instruction and intervention.

## Ongoing Assessment Tools

Until recently, there were relatively few formative assessment tools available for each component of reading, so we had limited information to help us adjust the content and pace of our teaching. Now we have a selection to choose from, which is important because different students will require different diagnostic assessments, depending on the area of difficulty and their developmental stage.

Using a variety of assessments is also important because one assessment tool can never provide sufficient information to plan a comprehensive instructional response. Over-reliance on one assessment tool may also lead to "teaching to the test" and narrowing

The observation forms and rubrics on the CD provide a record of students' strategy use.

the teaching of reading to a set of isolated skills. Ignoring other aspects of the reading process, especially integrated strategy use, actually hinders student progress.

## SELECTING ASSESSMENT TOOLS: WHAT DO WE NEED TO KNOW?

When selecting assessment tools, the first step is to review exactly what information your current screening tools do and don't provide, a form of gap analysis. Next, use a similar review to select the diagnostic and progress-monitoring tools you will need in addition to screening tools in order to plan and implement differentiated Tier 1–3 instruction and intervention. The elaborate data compiled from some district-wide screening tools can seem to have no relationship to the actual planning of daily instruction—spreadsheets of scores in isolated skills that leave your head swimming. Like me, you may have spent many hours analyzing these with colleagues to devise a school action plan addressing the areas of concern in student performance. We know screening tools help us to catch students before difficulties become pervasive. However, the information is not sufficient or specific enough for you to plan a year of differentiated Tier 1 instruction, and certainly not Tier 2 and 3 intervention. For that, you need assessments such as the ones in the table below, which help you identify what students need help with.

### What We Need to Know—and Assessment Tools to Use

| Area of Reading Development | What You Need to Know | Assessments |
|---|---|---|
| Reading Level | Independent Reading Level:<br>• Accuracy rate<br>• Self-correction rate<br>• Comprehension level | Running Record With Retelling and Benchmark Questions |
|  | Instructional Reading Level:<br>• Accuracy rate<br>• Self-correction rate<br>• Comprehension level | Running Record With Retelling and Benchmark Questions |
| Comprehension | Strategy Use:<br>Making Connections<br>Predicting<br>Asking Questions<br>Inferring<br>Visualizing<br>Clarifying and Self-Monitoring<br>Retelling<br>Summarizing | • Strategy Rubrics<br>• Observation Notes<br>• Running Records<br>• Benchmark Questions<br>• Checklist of Reading Behaviors<br>• Informal Reading Inventories<br>• Reading Responses |
| Vocabulary | Receptive and Expressive Vocabulary<br>Word-Learning Strategies | • Grade-Level List Test<br>• Writing Samples<br>• Oral Language |

*Differentiating Reading Instruction for Success With RTI* © 2011 by Margo Southall • Scholastic Teaching Resources

## What We Need to Know and—Assessment Tools to Use

| Area of Reading Development | What You Need to Know | Assessments |
|---|---|---|
| Word-Solving Skills | Letter-Sound Knowledge<br><br>Phonics Skills<br><br>Phonological Awareness | • Letter-Name Inventory<br>• Letter-Sound Inventory<br>• Phonics Inventory<br>• Writing Samples<br>• Dictated Sentences<br>• Phonological Awareness Inventory |
| Fluency | Rate<br>Expression<br>Attends to Punctuation<br>Phrasing<br>Prosody<br>Sight Word Recognition | • Running Record<br>• Fluency Rubric<br>• Timed Passage Reading<br>• One-Minute Probes (words per minute)<br>• Graded Sight Word Lists<br>• Word Identification Probe |

## DATA COLLECTION MADE SIMPLE

Once you've identified the tools you'll use to collect the data in each area of reading development, administer the assessments and record the data on the Profile as a Reader form (Form 2.1 on the CD). This will give you an at-a-glance look for each of your students' current levels and simplify the lesson-planning process. You'll update the form regularly with information from your progress-monitoring assessments.

In addition to the Profile as a Reader summary form, you'll find the following forms on the CD. These are tools I find most helpful for recording and tracking student progress and planning instruction.

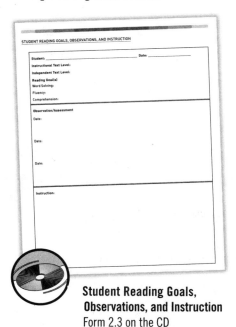

**Student Reading Goals, Observations, and Instruction**
Form 2.3 on the CD

Use Form 2.3 to record your observations during small-group lessons and reading-strategy conferences to help you identify the appropriate lesson focus for your students.

Use form 2.4 to plan lessons for groups of students who have common reading goals.

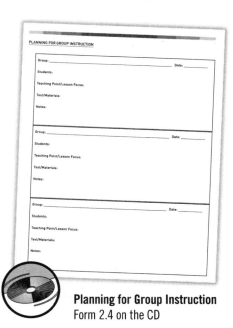

**Planning for Group Instruction**
Form 2.4 on the CD

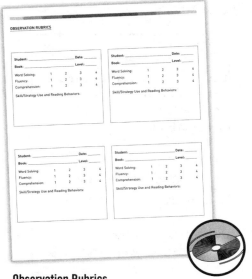

### Observation Rubrics
Form 2.5 on the CD
For on-the-run observations during whole-class and small-group lessons, print this form onto 4 x 3⅓ inch adhesive labels or use as a form. It has a rubric and space for anecdotal notes.

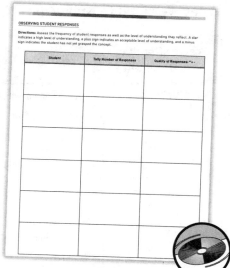

### Observing Student Responses
Form 2.6 on the CD
Assess the frequency and quality of student responses with this form. A star indicates a high level of understanding or strategy use; a plus sign indicates an acceptable level; a minus sign indicates the student has not grasped this concept.

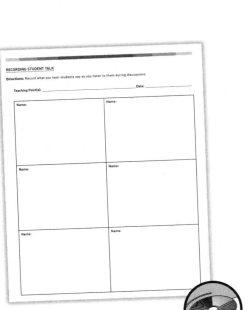

### Recording Student Talk
Form 2.7 on the CD
Record what you hear students say as you listen to brief turn-and-talk discussions at stopping points in the lesson. This gives insight into their understanding and application of the teaching point.

### Class Profile
Form 2.8 on the CD
See the class's independent- and instructional-text levels at a glance. In the Next Steps column, record reading goals and teaching plans to support students in reaching goals.

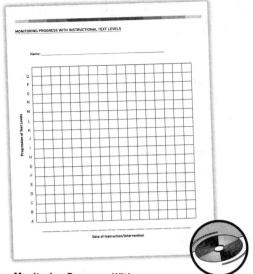

## Monitoring Progress With Instructional Text Levels
Form 2.9 on the CD
Establish the baseline text level and the target text level (progress-monitoring goal) for a student to achieve during an intervention cycle or scheduled benchmark assessment period. Plot the progress towards this goal at monthly intervals.

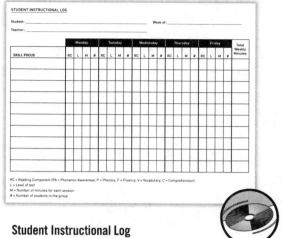

## Student Instructional Log
Form 2.10 on the CD
Document the skill or strategy focus and the frequency and intensity of small-group instruction for a specific Tier 2 or Tier 3 student with this form. It may be used as a communication tool between classroom and intervention teachers to ensure a coordinated response to student need.

## Intervention Group Log
Form 2.11 on the CD
Document the skill or strategy focus and the frequency and intensity of instruction for each Tier 2 or Tier 3 intervention group with this form.

## Student Survey
Form 2.12 on the CD
Check for continued engagement in reading and reading interests. You may read this form to the student and make notes or have them complete it independently, depending on their developmental level.

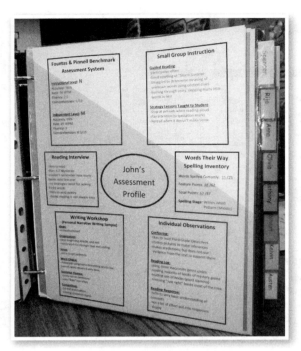

A data binder organizes essential information at your fingertips.

## MANAGING DATA TO STREAMLINE PLANNING: TEACHER DATA BINDERS

With all the documentation we collect in a year, we soon realize that we need to compile it all in an easily accessible resource. I use a Data Binder. I've tried to streamline the number of forms and samples I collect to make it more manageable, and I'll offer my suggestions below. Ideally, you and your colleagues will collaborate and determine common sections, forms, and assessments that will facilitate grade-level core and intervention planning.

Here is one option for data binder sections that has worked for me that may get you started. First, I organize the binder into the five sections described below using a set of labeled cardstock dividers (available from business supply stores). Sections in data binders may include:

1. **District or the Common Core State Standards for reading:** Include the scope and sequence of skills and strategies for your grade level, and the common skill and strategy statements you will use in instruction (see Common Strategy Statements in Chapter 3).

2. **Calendar of Assessments:** Include schedule with administering guides and master copy of the forms.

3. **Class Summary Sheets:** Include the Class Profile (Form 2.8 on the CD).

4. **Small-Group Reading Planning Forms:** List student groups and their current reading goals and teaching point(s), text levels, and reading materials. The Student Instructional Log (Form 2.10 on the CD) and Intervention Group Log (Form 2.11 on the CD) provide an ongoing record of both classroom (differentiated small-group) and intervention support.

5. **Individual Student Records:** Insert a plastic divider with pockets at the beginning of this section to store blank observation forms that you will need on hand during assessment conferences. Divide the rest of the section using an A–Z index of dividers and insert student names into the tabs. In each student's section, store copies of their summary profile sheets (Forms 2.1 and 2.2 on the CD), running records, and observation notes with current reading goal.

Organizing a data binder in this way allows you to store key information in an easily accessible format, and will save you time planning instruction and compiling student progress reports.

## TRACKING FOLDERS

Tracking folders provide a concrete way to use assessment data to form groups for instruction. Use a separate file folder for each reading component: word solving, fluency, and comprehension. Label the skills or strategies in sequence, leaving space below each one for sticky notes. Write student names on the sticky notes and place them under the appropriate skill or strategy statement. Look for students with similar needs and form groups.

The Folder Labels: Word Study Form 4.3 on the CD are used as a tactile way to organize groups of students by skill.

## RUNNING RECORDS: A KEY ASSESSMENT TOOL

One of the key assessment tools I rely on for assessing student understanding of the reading process is the running record (Clay, 2001), sometimes referred to as a reading record. The running record format is not new, but it's a well-proven, informative procedure that is also teacher-friendly and quick to administer, making it perfect to use during reading conferences and for on-the-run assessment as students read during a small-group lesson. Many teachers are comfortable using a blank form to record the notations, while others have embraced the next generation of running records in PDA formats on the market today.

For Tier 2 low-progress readers who are not reading at grade level, I administer and analyze a running record at least *every two weeks*, and for Tier 3 *every week*, to closely monitor any confusions or difficulties that may interfere with students achieving their current reading goals. For students who read at or above grade level, I administer running records individually every *four to six weeks*. This allows me to adjust the pace of instruction and to reteach skills whenever necessary so that my teaching is aligned with the rate of student learning. Running records provide information about a student's skills in all three areas of reading:

**Word Solving:** accuracy, error, and self-correction rate; word-solving knowledge; and strategy use

**Fluency:** rate, phrasing, and expression

**Comprehension:** self-monitoring strategies and reading behaviors; comprehension strategy use; and vocabulary knowledge

As you can see, running records can offer insight into every aspect of reading development; as such, they are invaluable assessment tools that should be a regular part of every teacher's repertoire. If you'd like more information on how to take and use running records, check out the resources in the box to the right.

### Running Record Resources

*Taking Running Records* (Shea, 2000)

*Running Records* (Johnston, 2000)

*Running Records for Classroom Teachers* (Clay, 2001)

# Progress-Monitoring Tools

The data you collect on students' reading development must be updated regularly to capture their reading growth. You can use any of the assessments from the chart on pages 18–19, but perhaps the simplest way is to use a running record and compare reading levels to benchmark levels.

## USING RUNNING RECORDS AND TEXT LEVELS AS PROGRESS-MONITORING TOOLS

A running record is often used to determine the appropriate level of text for instruction, as well as the appropriate level for independent reading. According to Pinnell and Fountas (2009), text the child can read with an accuracy rate of at least 90–94% is appropriate for instructional purposes. To guide the selection of texts for independent reading, they correlate students' accuracy rate to the complexity of the text. Thus, an accuracy rate of 95–100% is assigned to text levels A–K, and 98–100% for text levels L–Z. Independent reading levels will be at least one, if not two, text levels below the text level used in lessons. Familiar text from lessons may be added to independent reading selections when students demonstrate sufficient rates of accuracy and understanding. These accuracy rates for independent reading also take into account the level of comprehension that students demonstrate, with lower comprehension scores indicating the need for an easier text level. Administering and analyzing running records regularly provides insight into how students apply, or neglect to apply, practiced skills and strategies in authentic reading contexts (Clay, 2001).

A number of core and intervention programs incorporate regularly scheduled running record analysis to guide differentiated practice (Dorn & Saffos, 2011). When text levels are part of RtI progress-monitoring data, running records are a time-efficient tool to determine student progress. The chart below is used to determine whether students have met benchmark targets in school-wide screening that takes place three to four times a year.

### Text Level Expectations by Grade Level (Fountas & Pinnell, 2000)

|  | Baseline: Benchmark Text Level | Fall Benchmark Text Level | Winter Benchmark Text Level | Spring Benchmark Text Level |
|---|---|---|---|---|
| K |  | A | B | C |
| 1 | C | E | G | I |
| 2 | I | J | L | M |
| 3 | M | N | O | P |

*Differentiating Reading Instruction for Success With RTI* © 2011 by Margo Southall • Scholastic Teaching Resources

The form titled Monitoring Progress With Instructional Text Levels (Form 2.9 on the CD) can be used to track student progress in attaining their text level goal. *It is essential that comprehension scores—not just accuracy rates—are used to determine a student's progression through text levels.* For example, a student must achieve a minimum of 80%, or level 4, on a comprehension rubric before progressing to the next level. We must also take into account scoring differences between *fiction and nonfiction* text, or we will not gain a clear understanding of how students will read texts within their core program.

Text levels can be an informative part of our progress monitoring. The use of reading levels and running records is supported by current research for monitoring student progress within the RtI framework (Dorn & Saffos, 2012; Dunn, 2007). Text reading levels provide a valid measure for predicting future reading success and address the dual-discrepancy component of the RtI model (Fuchs, 2003). The first part of the dual discrepancy refers to the gap between the child's performance and grade-level expectations, comparing the child's achievement

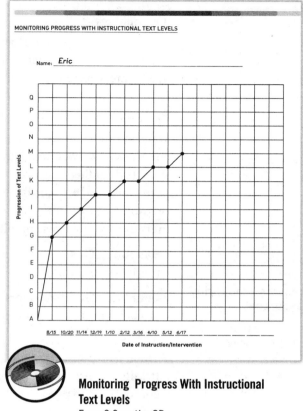

**Monitoring Progress With Instructional Text Levels**
Form 2.9 on the CD

with that of other children at the same grade level (child to grade-level peers). Using the text levels in the chart on page 24, we would compare the child's text level to grade-level text expectations for each benchmark assessment period (fall, winter, spring). The second part of the dual-discrepancy compares the child's baseline data to his or her own rate of progress toward benchmark goals (child to self). In the case of text levels, this would be the gap in the growth trajectory (from text level on initial assessment with running record) that would be necessary to meet target text levels within the designated time period or progress-monitoring goal. The example of a progress-monitoring graph on page 26 illustrates the dual discrepancy.

Identifying and tracking students' text-level performance provides the following:

1. **A beginning baseline for measuring growth over time.** Students who are below grade-level text expectations are organized into groups that receive increasingly intensive intervention, depending on the text level.

2. **A source of information that enables teachers to chart and compare a student's progression through text levels with benchmark levels.** These include text-level expectations for the designated schedule of school-wide assessments, such as September, November, February, and May. Some schools and districts select specific book titles for their benchmark assessments.

Having a target text level establishes a progress-monitoring goal that guides the duration of the intervention period based on how long it takes for the student to reach the target text-level goal toward grade-level performance. The *exit assessment, or cut score,* is the target text level, and this determines when the student no longer needs intervention.

## Progress-Monitoring Graph of Student Progress

You can track students' progress with instructional text levels using a graph like the one shown below. Simple graphs can be used to track student progress in specific skills, such as decoding words with a specific feature, recognition of sight words, and rate of reading (correct words per minute). You can use software such as Excel or other resources available online to generate customized graphs. Below are three key ingredients a progress-monitoring graph should include.

- **Baseline:** This is the assessment data gathered at the initial implementation of the intervention.

- **Goal line:** This represents the grade average or expected growth over time using peers as a reference point. This tells us when or whether the student is likely to meet grade-level expectations.

- **Trend line/Data line:** This line shows the achievement level during the intervention. It tells us the rate of progress and where the student's performance stands in comparison to peers (goal line).

### Monitoring Graph

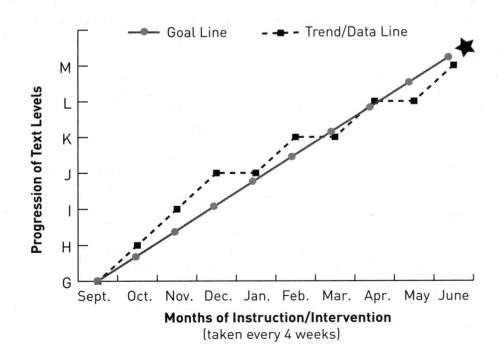

**Progress-Monitoring Resources**

For a comparison chart on the reliability of commonly available progress-monitoring tools, go to http://rti4success.org/progressMonitoring-Tools, the National Center for Response to Intervention Web site.

The Web site of the IRIS Center at Peabody College, University of Vanderbilt, provides case study examples and study modules for teachers: http://iris.peabody.vanderbilt.edu/resources.html (see Assessment; RtI: Progress Monitoring).

To generate customized graphs, go to www.studentprogress.org/; www.chartdog.com; or www.interventioncentral.org

*Differentiating Reading Instruction for Success With RTI* © 2011 by Margo Southall • Scholastic Teaching Resources

# Tier 2 and 3 Intervention Requirements:
# Text Levels as Entry and Exit Criteria

Progress-monitoring tools can help us determine when a student should be considered for Tier 2 or Tier 3 intervention, or when he or she should be discontinued from intervention. Text levels are one way to determine the criteria for entry and exit in and among the tiers of intervention. Here are some examples:

## Entry Requirements
**Tier 2:** Student is reading two text levels below grade-level expectations.
**Tier 3:** Student is reading three or more text levels below grade-level expectations.

## Exit Requirement
Student is within one text level of grade-level expectations.

## Moving From Tier 2 to 3
- Student has completed two to three consecutive cycles of Tier 2 intervention (each of 12 weeks) and is still two text levels below grade-level expectations as determined by monthly text-level progress-monitoring entries.
- Student has completed one cycle of Tier 2 intervention and the gap has widened so that the student is now three text levels below grade-level expectations
  *In both cases above, the instructional program itself should be reviewed.

## Moving From Tier 3 to Tier 2
- Student has completed a cycle of intervention (12 weeks) and is within two text levels of grade-level expectations.
- Student is able to maintain his or her rate of progress with Tier 2 support.

## When to Continue in Tier 3
- Progress predicts grade-level performance within a year.
- Inadequate progress indicates a need to modify or redesign the program.

## Professional Reading on Assessment-Guided Instruction/Intervention

*Checking for Understanding: Formative Assessment Techniques for Your Classroom* by Douglas Fisher and Nancy Frey

*Day-to-Day Assessment in the Reading Workshop: Making Informed Instructional Decisions in Grades 3-6* by Franki Sibberson and Karen Szymusiak

*Differentiated Assessment in the Reading Workshop* by Karin Ma and Nicole Taylor

*Intervention Strategies to Follow Informal Reading Inventory Assessment: So What Do I Do Now?* (2nd ed.) by JoAnne Schudt Caldwell and Lauren Leslie

*Test Talk: Integrating Test Preparation into Reading Workshop* by Glennon Doyle Melton and Amy H. Greene

*The Continuum of Literacy Learning: A Guide to Teaching* by Gay Su Pinnell and Irene C. Fountas

PDA format for running records available from: www.wirelessgeneration.com

# Using the Profile as a Reader to Guide Instruction and Intervention

In order to revise instruction for a particular student, we need to know the next teaching point for him or her in each of the core components of our reading program. To do this requires that we first synthesize and summarize assessment information in such a way that it informs our daily teaching. This is the purpose of the Profile as a Reader form; it enables us to see the status of student learning at a glance. The forms on pages 19–21 can also help you group students with similar needs and plan targeted lessons. You will find menus of lessons and independent practice tasks aligned with areas of need in each of the chapters on word solving, fluency, and comprehension and vocabulary. The lesson and practice tasks are appropriate for all tiers; simply vary the skills based on the individual assessment data of your students.

Intervention teachers continuously revise instruction in response to student progress.

During a week of Tier 1 lessons or a two-week Tier 2 or Tier 3 intervention plan, we include consecutive lessons on the skill or strategy that is most important for students to learn now— a specific teaching point (see an example of an Intervention Plan on page 43). To plan lessons in each component for differentiated small groups in Tier 1, and intervention in Tiers 2 and 3, we may identify a single teaching point or a dual focus, where two processes are reciprocal. Below are possible lessons in which two reciprocal processes provide a dual focus for our lessons.

- Phonological awareness and phonics (print concepts): isolating words in an oral sentence and recognition of word boundaries; one-to-one correspondence in the printed sentence.

- Phonemic awareness and phonics: segmenting and blending phonemes in words containing target vowel patterns.

- Word recognition: knowledge of spelling patterns and sight words within a lesson on accuracy and rate in fluency.

- Expression and intonation in fluency to support comprehension by inferring the intent of the character.

- Vocabulary and comprehension: using understanding of key words to clarify and repair understanding or use in a summary.

- Integrate multiple comprehension strategies: making connections and generating questions; predicting and inferring questioning and inferring, clarifying and inferring; questioning and retelling or summarizing.

*Differentiating Reading Instruction for Success With RTI* © 2011 by Margo Southall • Scholastic Teaching Resources

We use assessment data to revise our instruction so that it continues to respond to student progress. By *revise* I mean adjusting elements of our teaching to increase the level of support through the RtI tiers, as described in Chapter 1. There are six areas we examine in order to revise our teaching, summarized in the chart below.

| 1. Content | Focus the teaching point. Determine the knowledge, skill, strategy, or reading behavior that is the priority for this student based on current assessment data. Avoid a diluted, generalized approach that diminishes learning opportunities by presenting multiple skills simultaneously. |
|---|---|
| 2. Pace | Adjust the rate at which new concepts are introduced and practiced to match the rate of student learning. |
| 3. Instructional Sequence or Lesson Structure | • Break tasks into steps with a consistent format—e.g., teacher explanation of the skill or strategy (why and when it is used); demonstration (how to use it); student scaffolded practice; application to reading with coaching and feedback.<br><br>• Increase the number of student responses during a lesson. Students should respond every one to two minutes in an intervention session; two to three in the core program. We use two forms, the Observing Student Responses (Form 2.6 on the CD) and Recording Student Talk (Form 2.7 on the CD) to monitor student responses and determine if students are increasing both the quality and quantity of their responses.<br><br>• Increase the number of prompts and corrective or generative feedback.<br><br>• Use the same language for questions and cueing throughout core teaching and intervention.<br><br>• Extend time allocated to demonstration and scaffolded practice before independent application.<br><br>• Increase review and repetition of each skill. |
| 4. Frequency | Increase instructional minutes/intervention time if students are making progress, but at a slow rate. |
| 5. Group Size | Reduce group size—e.g., from five to three—when students are not making sufficient progress. |
| 6. Duration | Adjust the length of intervention, and/or the number of intervention cycles. |

## USE ASSESSMENT TO FOCUS THE TEACHING POINT

After you've constructed the Profile as a Reader, examine the information you've gathered. Identify and teach deficit skills: Have the student work on only those skills where he or she has identifiable gaps. For example, the student may not need to receive every lesson in sequence or review every phonics element. With regard to comprehension, assess to identify word knowledge, self-monitoring reading behaviors,

"Although the reasons children struggle vary from child to child, and we need to study the uniqueness of each child, *most are having trouble putting together the complex network of strategies needed to solve print and understand text.*"

(CLAY QUOTED IN JOHNSON, 2006, P. 20)

and specific strategies that are underdeveloped. That way you will not waste time. The use of informative assessment tools is key to maximizing instructional time. The goal of RtI is to increase or intensify instruction to close the gap, so more instructional time *and* more targeted instruction are both essential.

The multiple-tier support system described in Chapter 1 is an organizational system whose foundation depends upon our knowledge of student progress in specific skills and strategies. The effectiveness of differentiated practice in both the core program and intervention is driven by our continued awareness of student need. Aligning instruction and assessment avoids a mismatch of instruction so time isn't wasted and students can progress.

## Part 2

## Students as Learners: Rethinking Our Instruction

# Engagement: If Students Aren't "With You," They're Not Learning

"The assumption that just being more explicit will make for better instruction assumes that language is simply a delivery system for information, a literal packaging of knowledge. It is not... This is doubtless one reason why recent research (Taylor et al., 2002) has shown that the most accomplished teachers do not spend a lot of time in telling mode."

(Johnston, 2004, p. 8)

Students may cognitively and emotionally disengage from the instruction when educators ignore the aspects of individual differences beyond data scores. For example, in one intervention study where a highly structured intervention program was used, students were observed to disengage from the instruction after the third lesson, becoming passive and disinterested (Torgesen, 2005). There was nothing innately wrong with the program, but it was not going to work for some students, no matter how many repetitions of the content teachers went through. If students are not with you, if they are not applying themselves to the task and processing the information but simply echoing what you say and imitating what you do, then they are not learning. You will not see the progress you are hoping for. This is true for on-grade-level students as well. For these reasons, it's important to consider a student's profile as a learner. Use Form 2.2 to collect information about a student's interests, learning style, reading habits, and personal preferences for his or her learning environment.

### SIX WAYS TO MAINTAIN STUDENT ENGAGEMENT

#### 1. Incorporate Interactive, Multimodal Learning

Different students have different learning preferences. Some learn more easily by hearing a concept explained, while others need to see a diagram. Some learners need to be moving to process information, while others need quiet and time. We can increase the effectiveness of our lessons if we keep these differences in mind and plan a variety of experiences throughout the day. I've found that incorporating a variety of modalities within my lessons and activities maximizes my instructional time.

In each chapter, I offer multimodal lessons and activities; choose those that appeal to you and that you think will appeal to your students. Aim for variety, knowing that many of your students will have different learning preferences than you do. At the end of Chapters 4–6, I list sources for the materials you'll need to incorporate the multimodal activities.

Information on multimodal learning resources is included at the end of Chapters 4-6.

| Modality | Examples of Formats in Chapters 4–6 |
|---|---|
| **Visual** | • Picture-cued strategy icons, picture cards, charts, bulletin boards, and bookmarks, associative memory cues (meaningful associations for phonics generalizations and comprehension strategies<br>• Graphic organizers, storyboards and text maps<br>• Strategy-based reading response booklets<br>• Wall stories and concept murals |
| **Auditory** | • Peer turn–and–talk opportunities<br>• Dialogue journals<br>• Songs, raps, and rhymes with skill or strategy statements<br>• Group and class discussion<br>• Prompting for strategic actions |
| **Action** | • Hand motions to represent strategic thinking (letter sounds, comprehension strategies)<br>• Activities such as forming a shape or pointing with fingers<br>• Games and activities with movement |
| **Tactile** | • Cubes with strategic prompts<br>• Word and phrase sorts<br>• Sticky flags for marking thinking spots<br>• Strategy manipulatives<br>• Card games |
| **Role–Play** | • Picture-cued strategy visors or hats<br>• Character role cards<br>• Craft-stick strategy puppets<br>• Literature-based plays and Reader's Theater |

### 2. Offer Interesting Text Choices

Students are sitting in front of us because they have to. They did not choose the lesson, the book, or even their chair. We can offer a choice of reading materials in our core and intervention program for the guided and independent practice components. We can also invite students' opinions about the topic and the author's writing, both orally and in writing. The Student Survey (Form 2.12 on the CD) provides a starting point for helping students locate high-interest materials.

### At Their Fingertips All Day Long

To make interesting text choices possible, you need a wide selection of reading materials at students' *independent reading levels*. This means offering more than just the levels stated for your grade level; you need a rich selection of choices for low-progress readers as well. These texts should be high-interest with strong "kid appeal," available in both the core and intervention programs. The texts should be at students' fingertips throughout the day—in desks, book bags, seat sacks, or any place that's an arm's reach away. Minutes of reading make a difference, as we will see in Chapter 3.

Having independent reading materials within reach increases the minutes students read each day.

### A Balanced Reading Diet

A reading diet full of lots of short texts that students can successfully read builds confidence and stamina, and low-progress readers need to develop stamina in order to engage in the amount of practice they require. Graphic novels and other texts that are designed to include visual supports allow these readers access to the same issues, themes, and topics as their on-grade peers. We often hear of the importance of providing a balance of nonfiction reading materials, and in fact, nonfiction will account for 80% of the classroom reading by sixth grade. Some resources for nonfiction magazines include: *Zoo Nooz, Zillions, Ranger Rick, Time Magazine for Kids, Sports Illustrated for Kids* and *Wild Outdoor World*. A study by the National Assessment of Educational Progress (NAEP) demonstrated that fourth graders who read storybooks, magazines, and informational books have the highest proficiency in reading performance. High-achieving schools reported more reading of informational books by students than schools in the bottom third of the study, no doubt because between half and 75% of all items on standardized tests are based on nonfiction text (Moss, 2008).

*Differentiating Reading Instruction for Success With RTI* © 2011 by Margo Southall • Scholastic Teaching Resources

**Do Low-Progress Readers in Your School Have Access to Interesting, Independent-Level Text?**

| No Access | Limited Access | Fully Inclusive Access |
|---|---|---|
| Standard texts. No student choice. | Access to independent-level texts during part of the day. Some student choice of reading materials. | Access to a choice of independent-level, interesting texts throughout the day. |

## 3. Provide Visible Reminders of Reading Growth

To provide a tactile indicator of their recent progress, have students keep handy a copy of an individual strategy bookmark, or the integrated strategies bookmark, which depicts all of the strategies (see Chapters 4–6). Place a happy-face sticker next to the strategy icon when students demonstrate they have achieved this reading goal during reading strategy conferences. For older students, you can highlight the strategy statement achieved. The form My Reading Goals (Form 2.13 on the CD and page 34) provides feedback at each step of mastery.

## 4. Use Technology Tools: Do You Have the Apps That Make Text Accessible?

There is more than one way to gain access to books, as online book shoppers know well. From downloading digital text and listening to stories and songs on smartphones and iPods, new formats allow students ready access to books beyond their current reading levels, enriching their background knowledge, vocabulary, and familiarity with different genres and text structures. Larson (2010) describes how a second-grade teacher modeled the basic functions of the digital reader to her class with an LCD projector—such as inserting notes, changing the font size, and using the dictionary—then scheduled a student rotation with the two classroom Kindles.

Following are some advantages of digital readers, such as Kindles, Nooks, and Sony Readers:

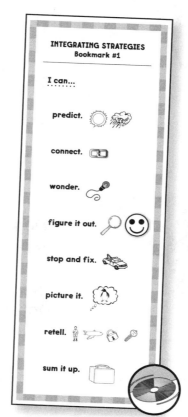

**Reading Strategy Bookmark**
Form 6.78 on the CD

"Recent studies of e-book reading and response behaviors suggested that e-book reading may support comprehension and strengthen reader response... Digital readers show promise in supporting struggling readers through multiple tools and features, including manipulation of font size, text-to-speech options, expandable dictionary, and note capabilities."
(Larson, 2010, p. 21)

# My Reading Goals

Name: _____

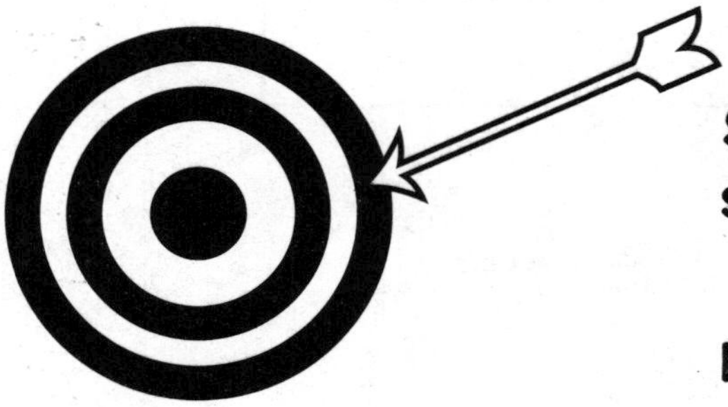

**Sometimes** I use the reading strategies listed on my bookmark.

Date: _____

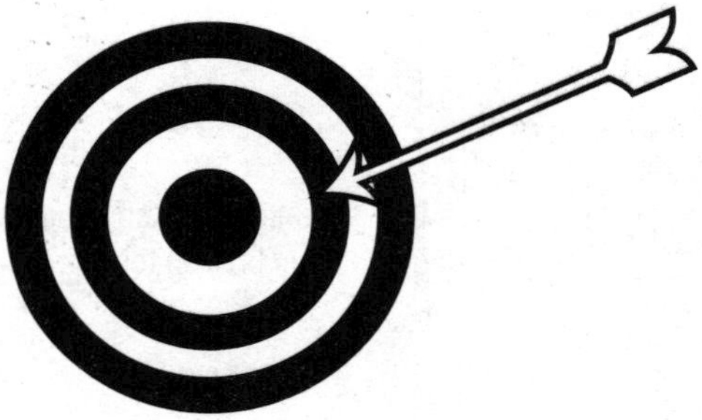

**Most of the time** I use the reading strategies listed on my bookmark.

Date: _____

I **always** use the reading strategies listed on my bookmark.

Date: _____

- A tool that enables digital note-taking supports interaction with the text while reading in a similar way to writing notes in a book's margins. Notes and markups can be saved for teachers to examine.

- A text-to-speech feature that enables students to listen to parts of the text, including words they find difficult to pronounce, or to "reread" a confusing or complex section of the text.

- Search features can be used to locate keywords or phrases.

- A dictionary provides access to the meaning of interesting and challenging vocabulary, reviews the phonetic spelling of words to help students decode them, and chunks multisyllabic words to aid in their pronunciation.

- Multiple books can be downloaded on a single device that is shared by students.

Author's Web sites are a source of digital storytelling. You may not be able to access YouTube at your school, but parents may view author storytelling sessions, as well as readings by other children. A site I recommend to parents is www.storylineonline.com, where well-known actors provide read-alouds for children. Often school or district technology specialists are a source of the latest tools to integrate into your teaching. For more information on how to use apps in the classroom, check out the latest books for teachers, such as *Teaching With the Tools Kids Really Use: Learning With Web and Mobile Technologies* by Susan J. Brooks-Young (2010).

## 5. Establish a Brain-Friendly Learning Environment

When we teach the way children learn best, and the way the brain processes and stores information most efficiently, children acquire skills with less repetition. This means they will be able to move on to more complex skills, catching up with their peers within a shorter timeframe.

### Kick-Start Language Processing With Brain Exercises

When I was working in my own classroom, one of my morning routines always included exercises to enhance whole-brain learning. These easy and fun exercises can be found in the books *Brain Gym* by Paul Dennison and Gail Dennison (1994) and *Making the Brain Body Connection* by Sharon Promislow (1998). The purpose is not only to increase students' ability to focus on the upcoming instruction, but also to enhance language learning with exercises specific to reading and writing skills, including comprehension, oral reading, spelling, and creative writing. The goal is to open pathways in the brain that allow learning to take place.

### Increase Focus and Reduce Inattention With Learning Placemats, Beanbags, Carpet Squares, and Literacy Labradors

These touchable tools may strike you as unnecessary—until you have to sit at a student's desk for hours at a time, which some of us have experienced at in-service meetings, longing to get up for a little stretch.

**Placemats:** We all like to personalize our own workspace. Many teachers have photographs of their families and other personal objects on their desks (somewhere under those piles of papers). In contrast, student desks and tables are often impersonal environments that lack any sensory or associative "Velcro" that encourages them to stay put and feel both relaxed and focused while there. Making desks inviting personal spaces can help reduce inattention and restlessness. One option is to provide desktop placemats from a choice of textured fabrics that provide sensory feedback. Some students find velvety textures quite soothing, while others prefer textures that are raised (Sprenger, 2008). You might opt for commercially produced placemats or create them as part of a class art project. It is common for students to decorate their own name cards for their desks, but placemats take this one step further in defining a space that is solely theirs within the larger classroom environment.

**Beanbags:** To simulate large muscle movement and produce a calming effect, provide beanbags, preferably covered with velvet, velour, or terrycloth, for students to manipulate. Adult versions—those squishy "stress balls"—are also available for teachers!

Stuffed animals become "study buddies" and an audience for student reading.

**Carpet Squares:** Try placing carpet squares under students' desks and allow children to take off their shoes and feel the texture of the rug underfoot. This is another way to support students during those stretches of time where they are expected to remain seated—especially kinesthetic learners and students with attentional difficulties. Even allowing students to stand at their desks with one knee on the chair can greatly assist students with high activity levels to remain focused.

**Literacy Labradors:** Marilee B. Sprenger (2008) describes how she brought in stuffed animals as study buddies for her students and found that when they signed "adoption" papers and named their critters, they demonstrated greater attachment to the animals and experienced an increased soothing effect. This was even successful with high school students. A "teddy bear for all" policy would certainly be conducive to a humanistic classroom environment.

### Eat, Drink, and Be Merry

We are all aware of the importance of students' having a good breakfast, keeping well-watered (water bottles on desks to hydrate the brain), and using humor in our teaching to increase attention and memory processes. Other ways to establish an environment conducive to learning include calming and motivating music linked to specific purposes and a colorful room with only hints of red (use red for short-term, high-energy activities and highlighting purposes [Howard, 2001]). The room should be 68 and 72 degrees Fahrenheit; temperatures above 74 degrees can negatively impact reading comprehension (Jensen, 2005). Classrooms can be stuffy, airless places, so go ahead—throw open that window and grab a sweater.

*Differentiating Reading Instruction for Success With RTI* © 2011 by Margo Southall • Scholastic Teaching Resources

## 6. Build a Sense of Empowerment With "Bibliotherapy"

Carefully selected books that reflect the struggles in the lives of our low-progress and behavior-challenged students can provide a venue for working through the frustration of struggling with the task of learning to read. These books provide a character who acts as a mentor or coach and encourages students to persevere when they feel like giving up. Select books that match the problems being experienced by the students and that are culturally relevant, and follow these steps.

1. Ask students to identify the theme or author's intent in writing the book. Explain the theme or author's point of view when necessary.

2. Encourage students to compare their experiences with situations in the book.

3. Build connections between the character's experiences and the students' experience. Provide prompts such as: *Why do you think she...? How do you think he felt? Has that ever happened to you? What would you do if you were...?*

4. Extend the theme and problem-solving discussions with role-play and art-related visualization strategy responses such as story walls, storyboards, and murals.

5. Provide time for personal responses to the reading in student-response notebooks. Students may write a diary entry from the point of view of the main character, a letter from one character to another, a Dear Abby letter, or they may craft a different ending in which they solved the problem in a different way.

## Resources

*Marvin One Too Many* by Katherine Paterson (reading difficulties)

*The Don't Give Up Kid* by Jeanne Gehret (Learning Disability)

*Timothy Goes to School* by Rosemary Wells (self-acceptance—feeling inadequate, making friends)

*Niagara Falls—Or Does It?*; *I Got a D* in *Salami*
and other books in this series by Henry Winkler and Lin Oliver (learning difficulties/differences with humor)

*Many Ways to Learn: Young People's Guide to Learning Disabilities* by Judith Stern (learning disabilities)

*Yes I Can* by Neil Smith: Struggles from Childhood to the NFL (learning disabilities)

*Thank You, Mr. Falker* by Patricia Polacco (overcoming reading difficulties)

*The Dot*; *Ish* by Peter Reynolds (self-concept, creativity)

*Through the Cracks* by Carolyn Sollman (importance of differentiating instruction)

## Case Study

## Using Jeff's Profile as a Reader and Profile as a Learner to Plan Instruction and Intervention

In my school, intervention plans and progress-monitoring data are reviewed by the RtI team every four weeks, which enables classroom and intervention teachers to tap into collaborative expertise of a group of educators rather than working in isolation. Jeff is a second grader whose case was examined by our RtI team during this past year. Jeff is a student whose history as a reader has included a continual struggle with print-based learning. He has a well-developed general knowledge, is sociable, and has many interests. Jeff is reluctant to read aloud in front of others due to self-consciousness about the "stumbles" in his reading, so he engages in avoidance behaviors.

In order to refer a student to the RtI team, classroom teachers are required to compile a summary of informal assessment data on students, including a recent running record, fluency probe, curriculum-based phonics inventory, and a graded sight word list. These are submitted prior to the RtI team meeting, so that the principal and reading specialist can review them before meeting with the classroom teacher at the scheduled monthly meeting. Jeff's teacher had summarized this information using the Profile as a Reader sheet; see page 40 for the completed form. So that the team could address the concern about Jeff's lack of focus in the core program, the Profile as a Learner was also included; see page 41 for the completed form. Jeff's teacher brought the original copies of the assessments (running record, etc.), selected samples of Jeff's work, and the completed Student Reading Goals, Observations, and Instruction Form (see page 42) for the team to examine at the meeting.

### JEFF'S INTERVENTION PLAN

After the team reviewed these assessments, it was evident that Jeff was experiencing difficulty in decoding, fluency (phrasing), sight word recognition, and self-monitoring for comprehension. He was already reading two text levels below his grade-level peers and was at risk of falling further behind. The next step in the process was for the reading specialist to administer diagnostic assessments, including an informal reading inventory, fluency probe and rubric, and phonological awareness and decoding assessments to provide more detailed information on Jeff's needs and identify instructional priorities. Jeff was provided additional support in one of the Tier 2 intervention groups where students shared similar reading goals. To ensure a high level of engagement and motivation, the reading materials and formats used in intervention would reflect the information on Jeff as a learner.

*Differentiating Reading Instruction for Success With RTI* © 2011 by Margo Southall • Scholastic Teaching Resources

# MONITORING JEFF'S PROGRESS IN TIER 2 INTERVENTION

To maintain a record of these teaching points and the instructional time devoted to each one, the classroom teacher completed the Student Instructional Log (Form 2.10 on the CD) and the reading specialist completed the Intervention Group Log (Form 2.11 on the CD). This enabled both teachers to maintain a record of their teaching points and the instructional time devoted to each one. Monitoring in this way allowed his teachers to adjust instruction as he met reading goals and new ones were identified, or as Jeff required more instructional time on current goals.

Jeff's progress was monitored with the tools you will find on his intervention plan on page 42. An example of Jeff's progression through text levels is on page 26. The Progress Monitoring Graph below is an example of the curriculum-based word identification assessment (graded high-frequency word list) that was administered every two weeks. Results of progress monitoring will be used to update the Profile as a Reader form and revise instruction. To ensure a high level of engagement and motivation, the reading materials and formats used in intervention would reflect the information on Jeff as a learner.

**Jeff's Progress-Monitoring Graph: Sight Word Recognition**

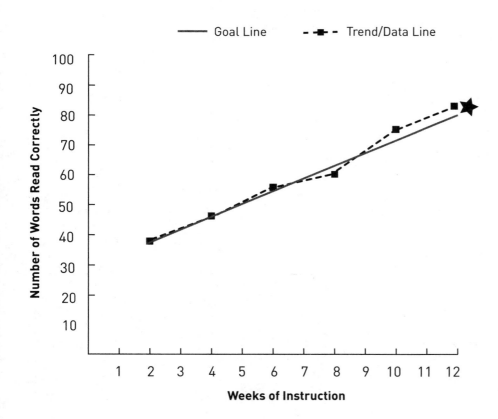

## Jeff's Profile as a Reader

### SUMMARY OF TEXT LEVELS

**Instructional Level:** G

Accuracy Rate: 91

SC Rate: 1:5

**Independent Level:** F

Accuracy Rate: 96

SC Rate  1:3

### COMPREHENSION

Retelling: 7/10
Benchmark Questions: 2/3

**Rubric Scores:** 5/5
Making Connections:               3
Asking Questions:                   3
Inferring:                               2
Monitoring/Fix-Up Strategies:   1
Synthesizing and Retelling:       3
Summarizing Information:          2

**Total Score:** 14/30

### VOCABULARY

Academic Vocabulary:

Score: 11/27

on grade level list

**JEFF'S PROFILE AS A READER**

### READING BEHAVIORS

- Reads on, seeks help
- Uses pictures and context cues
- Relies on background knowledge and familiarity with storyline or topic

### FLUENCY

Rate (CWPM): 54

**Fluency Rubric:**
Expression: 3/4
Attention to Punctuation: 2/4
Phrasing: 2/4
Prosody: 2/4
Final Score: 9/20

**Sight Word Recognition List:** 37/100

### WORD SOLVING

**Developmental Spelling Analysis:**
Stage: Letter Name
Feature: C (short vowels)

**Phonological Awareness Test:** (TBA)
Subtests:
Phonological Skills:
Graphemes:
Decoding:
Raw Total Score:
Standard Score:

*Differentiating Reading Instruction for Success With RTI* © 2011 by Margo Southall • Scholastic Teaching Resources

## Jeff's Profile as a Learner

**READING SURVEY: 5 Ws & H**
**Metacognition**

**Awareness of Reader Strategies:**
- Uses generalized language, without specific use of strategy terms
- Understands concept of making connections, generating questions, and retelling

**Awareness of Goals as a Reader:**
Can point to current goal on the strategy chart, but cannot always explain why it helps him as a reader

---

**INTERESTS**

Biographies of children

Animals—wants to be a vet

Humor—e.g., Roald Dahl read-alouds; books of jokes and riddles; humorous fiction series in graphic format (e.g., *Captain Underpants*)

---

**MATERIALS**

High-interest reading materials with graphic supports; nature, and science magazines

Manipulative word-study activities

---

**JEFF'S PROFILE AS A LEARNER**

---

**TECHNOLOGY OPTIONS**

Story mapping software

Digital text read-aloud formats

Listen to content material on CD

---

**READING DIET: LOG ENTRIES**

Brief questions or list of events/facts

Partner question/answer, group discussions support lengthier, conversational entries

Able to write about connections to other books and experiences using bookmark picture-cued prompts as an aid

---

**MODALITY PREFERENCES**

Looks for visual picture cues

Prefers active learning with movements

Engages in tactile activities

Enjoys music, but not singing

# Jeff's Student Reading Goals and Observations Form

**Student:** Jeff     **Instructional Text Level:**     **Independent Text Level:**

**Reading Goal(s):**

**Word-Solving:** consonant blends; transfer familiar vowel patterns to decode new words; discriminating vowel patterns with *e* and *i*

**Fluency:** sight words; phrasing; attention to punctuation cues to aid phrasing, expression, and understanding

**Comprehension:** clarifying and self-monitoring strategies

**Observation/Assessment:**

- Oral language overrides use of visual cues; may insert words that maintain the meaning of the passage, but lack visual correspondence.

- Miscues result from incomplete visual scanning of new words; neglects to attend to second consonant in consonant blend or digraph and word endings.

- Inconsistent use of familiar vowel patterns to decode new words; confuses sounds for *e* and *i* in short-vowel words. May skip unknown words. Will attempt with prompting.

- Pace of reading is slow, steady with little expression. Reads words one at a time or in two-word chunks. Inconsistent attention to punctuation resulting in run-on sentences. Pausing behaviors when this results in loss of meaning; reads on or seeks help.

- Reluctant to read aloud in front of peers. Self-conscious of miscues.

- Clarifying and self-monitoring strategies include use of picture clues.

- Demonstrates understanding of elements in a retelling; unfamiliar text or topics pose challenge to summaries.

- Regularly participates in class and group discussions to share connections and questions.

- Engages in off-task behaviors during independent practice.

**Instruction:** See Intervention Plan

Engage and check for understanding by:

- Cued verbal response

- Partner turn and talk with picture-cued strategy bookmarks

- Whiteboard responses, hold-up response cards

- Hand motions and actions for skills and strategies

- Prompt and coach for strategy use during reading – model, prompt, check

*Differentiating Reading Instruction for Success With RTI* © 2011 by Margo Southall • Scholastic Teaching Resources

# Jeff's Intervention Plan

**Student:** Jeff          **Teacher:** Ms. S.          **Implementation Period:** March 7–18

| Goals | Instruction/Intervention | Frequency #Sessions per Week | Monitoring Tool |
|---|---|---|---|
| **Word-Solving**<br><br>Increase accuracy reading words with consonant blends and digraphs<br><br>Apply known vowel patterns to decode new words | • Cumulative Blending with Initial Consonant Blends (see page 113)<br>• Explicit Six-Step Guided Word Sort for Low-Progress Readers<br>  • Feature: initial blends, short vowels e and i (see pages 126–127)<br>• No-Peeking Buddy Sort (see page 142)<br>• Recording Sounds in Sequence: initial blends (see page 117)<br>• Interactive Writing (see page 140))<br>• Dictated Word Sort (see page 151)<br>• Show What I Know (see page 144)<br>• Actions for (letter–sound correspondences, blends and digraphs (see page 132)<br>• Prompt to apply during reading | 2 | Weekly running record:<br>• accuracy rate<br>• miscue analysis<br><br>Graph of text level progression<br><br>Graph of success with phonological awareness and decoding subtests<br><br>Dictated word sort<br><br>Writing Samples |
| **Fluency**<br><br>Increase bank of known sight words<br><br>Develop use of phrasing<br><br>Attend to punctuation | • X-Ray Eyes activity (see page 172)<br>• High-Frequency Word Lesson #1 (see page 169)<br>• Step to the Beat: Phrase Walk (see page 186)<br>• Construct Phrase Pyramids (see page 182–183)<br>• Fluency with Humor (see page 181) and Reader's Theater passages with textual supports for punctuation, phrasing, and expression. Use colored pencils to circle end marks in repeated reading materials. | 1 | Graph of graded sight word list<br><br>Rubric |
| **Vocabulary and Comprehension**<br><br>Develop a set of self-monitoring strategies | • Stop and Fix strategy (see pages 253–264): review the picture cards for each fix-up tool; model and guide practice with fiction and nonfiction texts using the Pit Stop Game<br>• Prompt and cue to touch picture cues for each clarifying strategy on the I Can Stop and Fix bookmark to aid practice in thinking aloud at confusing parts in the reading | 3 | Weekly running record<br>• reading behaviors<br>• miscue analysis<br><br>Rubric of strategies |

*Differentiating Reading Instruction for Success With RTI* © 2011 by Margo Southall • Scholastic Teaching Resources

# Planning for Intervention: Different or Differentiated?

After a workshop I had presented to district literacy coaches, reiterating the importance of aligning instruction with varying profiles of readers, I heard this statement: *Oh, you mean **really** differentiated!* The district had adopted an intervention program for Tier 2 students. After the screening assessments, low-progress readers were placed in this program. This doesn't sound like a problem until you look more closely at the assessment profiles of these students and see that many of them have been earnestly working through a sequence of lessons that are not sufficiently aligned with their specific needs to generate significant progress.

## FLEXIBILITY WITH INSTRUCTIONAL PRACTICES: THE PHONICS EXAMPLE

The majority of early literacy phonics programs employ a synthetic approach to instruction, where students segment and blend phonemes to pronounce the word. I share an example of this approach in Chapter 4—cumulative blending (Beck, 2006), which is helpful for students with phonological memory difficulties who often find this abstract concept of blending difficult. What the quote above refers to, however, is the lack of differentiation inherent in the inflexible implementation of a singular approach to teaching phonics that is maintained even when a student continues to demonstrate a low rate of progress with this method. To revise our instruction, we have to reach into our teaching toolkit for practices that combine approaches. You'll find four approaches to teaching phonics in the word-solving lessons in this book (see Chapter 4).

"Failure in a synthetic phonics program (i.e., progressing from word part to whole words) does not mean that we must repeat the approach. Literacy leaders strive to learn analytic (i.e., progressing from whole words to word parts) and analogic (i.e., noting regularities between known and unknown words) phonics as alternative approaches that might be a perfect fit for some students."

(APPLEGATE, DEKONTY APPLEGATE, & TURNER, 2010, P. 211)

Different students benefit from different approaches to teaching phonics.

## KEY QUESTIONS TO DETERMINE THE EFFECTIVENESS OF OUR INTERVENTION

In order to assure that our instruction and interventions are addressing the needs of our students, we must ask ourselves these questions:

- Does the instructional approach meet the needs of this *profile of reader and learner?*

- Are we using a variety of diagnostic assessment tools to monitor progress?

- Do the instructional practices and materials support growth in this skill or strategy?

- How interactive are the lessons? How engaged are the students?

## IMPLEMENTING TIER 2 AND TIER 3 INTERVENTIONS

What is most important to move the student to the next step in his or her development as a reader? Students will need varying amounts of the three areas of reading instruction (word solving, fluency, and comprehension) at different times, based upon current assessments. An instructional diet needs to be guided by diagnosis. Similar to nutritional diets and fitness programs, an instructional diet will require larger portions of certain nutrients at different periods of literacy growth. Students will also need to perform more or less "reps"—that is, review lessons—depending on their progress. This adjustment on our part is what is meant by pacing our instruction. The chart on page 46 summarizes ten steps for designing and implementing Tier 2 and Tier 3 interventions.

## WHEN STUDENTS ARE NOT PROGRESSING: BEYOND MINUTES AND MATERIALS

Often in a quest to provide every possible resource to our students, we can overload them with myriad programs, academic terminology, and new concepts taught in different settings by different teachers. Tier 2 and Tier 3 students are already struggling to put the reading puzzle together, and in our well-intentioned efforts, we can actually made it harder for them. That doesn't mean we should simply reteach the same lesson, but it does mean we should continually check for consistency of terminology and approach throughout a student's day.

Scheduling intervention is also an issue, but we need to remember: intervention is an addition to the core program, so students should never be pulled out during whole-class read-alouds—these are their pathway to a knowledge of grade-level vocabulary, genres, and text structures. In shared reading, when the basal program is at students' frustration level, we have to question

# Ten Steps for Designing and Implementing Effective Interventions

**1** Assess each student with diagnostic tools targeting his or her deficit area(s).

**2** Observe and document transfer of skills and strategies during the reading of a short passage (running records, QRI).

**3** Analyze the data to determine what skill or strategy (the teaching point) is most important at this point of the student's reading development. This will become the current reading goal.

**4** Organize students into intervention groups based on data-based needs in a common skill or strategy (across classrooms and grade levels).

**5** Select classroom and any supplemental intervention materials that directly target the student's deficit skill(s).

**6** Write an intervention plan based on data for each group using their profiles as readers and learners to guide instructional decisions regarding structure of lessons.

**7** Schedule rounds or cycles of 10–12 week intervention periods (many students will need additional rounds either consecutively or at different times in their academic career). Maintain an intervention log recording the teaching point, instructional format, or approach used, text level, minutes of teacher demonstration and student practice, observations and recommendations for next step; you can use the Student Instructional Log (Form 2.10 on the CD) and Intervention Group Log (Form 2.11 on the CD) for this purpose.

**8** Incorporate all-student responses continuously during the lessons, including partner dialogue structures, to maximize student practice.

**9** Use the same terminology, visuals, prompts, and cues that are used in the core program.

**10** Review with progress-monitoring assessments every two to three weeks. Adjust lesson content, structure, and materials as necessary (see Chapter 1 for Tier 2 and Tier 3 schedule of assessment).

*Differentiating Reading Instruction for Success With RTI* © 2011 by Margo Southall • Scholastic Teaching Resources

if it is a good use of their time. Without a great deal of scaffolding, such as repeated shared and partner reading of short passages, which is not commonly a part of the program, shared reading is of questionable use to low-progress readers. Providing students with leveled texts on the same topic/genre/text structure and devoting less time to a whole-class text and more to instructional or independent level texts are options that may be more effective.

We must also be mindful of what students miss when they are pulled out for intervention, especially Tier 3 students, for whom intervention often does take place outside the regular classroom. If they are pulled out of class during content instructional time (social studies and science), then it's a great idea to incorporate leveled texts on the same topics as the reading materials for skill instruction. It's not fair that they should be unable to participate in class discussions and projects because they've missed out on the content.

The worst scenario for a low-progress reader is when he or she is expected to somehow catch up on what was missed when out for intervention. If students are expected to know the content due to district or state assessments in this area, *then give it to them*—the notes, the completed graphic organizers, the information on an audio CD, peer partners to review with, and so on. When children have processing difficulties, it just doesn't make sense to take up the space in their working memory needed to devote to learning to read. They certainly should have access to the grade-level content learning, but the teacher and peer scaffolds need to be in place for that to be a reality.

## A COORDINATED RESPONSE BY THE CORE AND INTERVENTION PROGRAM

To ensure our students receive a targeted, well-coordinated instructional response, consider the following questions:

1. How **aligned** are the lessons and materials with their assessed need (skills/ strategy use)? Do you need to "prune" lessons and activities that are not directly targeting deficit skills?

2. How many **minutes a day** are students reading connected texts at their instructional or independent levels?

3. How many **transitions** do students have in a day (classroom and intervention settings)?

4. Are the **different teachers** all working on the **same skill or strategy**?

5. Does each teacher use **consistent terminology, prompts, cues, and visuals**? (For more on this, see Chapter 3.)

6. How many **different reading programs or sets of materials** are used in a day?

7. How many **continuous minutes** are students in the **classroom** each day? Which subject areas do they **miss** during pull-out or push-in interventions? Are materials provided at their reading level in class? Are leveled content materials used in intervention?

8. What is the priority for each student—the most important skill or strategy he or she needs to grow as a reader? How is this reflected in the student's schedule and instruction?

9. Are students aware of their goal(s) as readers?

10. Do they see visible evidence of their progress on a daily or weekly basis?

Each of these ten questions makes for good discussion between administrators, classroom teachers, and intervention teachers. Some of the issues, such as scheduling, may require a school-wide change, involving collaborative efforts of both administrators and teachers. All require communication and coordination between classroom and intervention teachers, so that the pieces of the reading puzzle come together for our students. This will require careful prioritizing of what skills we teach, the way we teach, and the pace at which we teach. But, as you know, the rewards of watching a struggling reader blossom and grow under your care far outweigh the effort it takes. As teachers, we know that the leap in our heart we feel when we see the light come on in a struggling reader's eyes and hear them say "Oh, now I get it" makes it all worth it. It may be lesson 23, but they get it!!!

## Summary of Key Principles

- Use ongoing informal assessment tools to determine the focus of instruction and intervention

- Revise your instruction based on the profile of the student as a reader (rate of progress).

- Rethink your instruction based on the profile of the student as a learner (learning preferences and interests).

- Incorporate practices designed to maintain student engagement.

*Differentiating Reading Instruction for Success With RTI* © 2011 by Margo Southall • Scholastic Teaching Resources

# 3

# ORGANIZING AND MANAGING A DIFFERENTIATED READING PROGRAM

In Chapter 2 we discussed how to collect, organize, and align our assessment data with instruction and intervention. In this chapter, we examine the day-to-day implementation of classroom instruction and intervention. The issues surrounding the scheduling and management of whole-class, small-group, and independent learning can seem overwhelming. While we are all aware of the need for differentiation and understand the rationale for RtI, it is the unanswered *how* (teaching practices), *when* (scheduling), and *with what* (materials) questions that all too often get in the way of effective implementation. This chapter addresses these essential questions.

## Chapter Overview

In **Part 1** (pages 51–61) we take a practical look at organizing groups of students for differentiated instruction (Tier 1), targeted intervention (Tier 2), and intensive intervention (Tier 3).

**Part 2** (pages 61–72) provides practical ways to implement differentiated independent practice tasks for the "rest of the class," alongside small-group instruction.

**Part 3** (pages 73–81) looks at the teaching practices that make grade-level texts accessible to low-progress readers: inclusive teaching structures; incorporating all-student responses; using common visuals and language.

In **Part 4** (pages 81–82) we look at ways to increase the minutes students are practicing reading skills with instructional-and independent-level text.

Organize students with a common learning goal in Tier 1 differentiated small groups.

# Why Small-Group Instruction Is Essential

We know that even the most effective basal-based program will meet the needs of, at best, 75–80% of students (Allington, 2009; Fisher & Frey, 2010; Haager et al., 2007). This necessitates that we assess students and then selectively use a variety of instructional materials. This process of aligning student data and reading program materials is especially productive within collaborative teacher teams of grade-level colleagues. In schools where I work as a professional learning consultant, when we plan lessons together, we examine student progress data in order to identify appropriate supplemental resources and materials that target deficit areas of student performance. While basal programs have certainly improved in the last decade and now offer a guide for comprehension think-alouds, vocabulary-development activities, and graphic organizers, they are still simply a foundation to build upon with differentiated practice. We know that the basal is designed for breadth, to cover a set of grade-level concepts in 30–36 weeks. It is not intended to go into depth on any one strategy. The RtI framework encourages teachers to backtrack, to expand upon, and move ahead to specific units through the basal based on student assessment data (Walpole & McKenna, 2009).

Knowing that there is no one single program that meets the needs of every student, we need to expand upon our current basal with teaching practices and supplemental materials. For example, in kindergarten through third grade we often use a supplemental phonological awareness, phonics, or word-study program to support differentiation and provide sufficient depth of study. To ensure that students are able to successfully apply comprehension strategies to a range of genres, we integrate quality literature within daily read-alouds and think-alouds and schedule sufficient time for independent practice with instructional- and independent-level text. *The framework of RtI, with its focus on differentiation, empowers teachers to use assessment data to adjust the content, lesson structures, materials, and pace of instruction.*

Providing small-group instruction only to students who demonstrate difficulty isn't enough. If our goal is to *give every child full access to his or her potential to learn— the advanced as well as the low-progress reader*—we need to move toward responsive teaching, and small-group instruction is a necessity.

To determine if you should teach a particular lesson to your whole class, use assessment to identify the proportion of students who would benefit from it. *If 60% of your students would benefit, then it is appropriate to teach the skill or strategy to the whole class* (Vaughn, Bos, Shay, & Schumm, 2002; Massi, 2007). Otherwise, your students probably do not have the foundational skills and understanding at this point to benefit from the lesson. Teach it later in the year, or in small groups to students who demonstrate the prerequisite skills.

## Part 1

# Organizing Small Groups for RtI

## Tier 1 Grouping Options

When it comes to forming small groups in your classroom, the method you choose will depend on your teaching point and student reading goals. The chart below summarizes two of the most common grouping strategies for Tier 1 differentiated instruction. Each is discussed in detail below.

| Types of Groups | Instructional Purpose |
|---|---|
| Skill- or Strategy-Based Groups | • Focus on one or two skills or strategies throughout the lesson.<br>• Students' reading levels span two or three text levels.<br>• Lesson structures and sequence vary according to the teaching point and student need—e.g., word-solving and comprehension lessons will use different formats and materials. |
| Guided Reading Groups | • Focus on integrated strategy use.<br>• Students are all at the same reading level; students progress through a leveled set of materials.<br>• Same lesson structure for each session—e.g., introduce book, discuss strategies (may be extended with a mini-lesson on a relevant teaching point with this book), read, and so on. |

## DIFFERENTIATED SMALL-GROUP STRUCTURES

### Strategy- or Skill-Based Groups

After examining student data, you may identify students who share a common need in a specific skill or strategy. Text level does not drive membership in these groups. Simply select a text that is at the instructional level for the group member at the earliest stage of decoding. Students benefit from the strategy instruction and practice even if the text is at their independent level. If the text level is too simple to use for more complex strategies (such as inferring), you can work with a higher-level text by using a shared reading or read-aloud/think-aloud format. For fluency training, you can have each student reading a different book, one at his or her independent level. (See Southall [2009] for more information on strategy-based groups.)

Demonstrate how and when to use the skill or strategy.

The lessons will not sound or look the same for each group because the teaching point varies according to student need. If you scan Chapters 4 through 6 of this book, you will see a variety of lesson formats and student practice options designed to support specific skills and strategies. Strategy- or skill-based groups are often used for students who are approaching or below grade-level expectations and require a sequence of lessons that directly target their need. However, these groups *are not just for low-progress readers*. On-grade and advanced students also require focused practice on specific teaching points to continue to develop as readers.

Students practice the skill or strategy with teacher support.

### Guided Reading Groups

When students require support in applying previously taught strategies to texts of increasing complexity, guided reading groups are often used. Membership in these groups is based on a common text level. Students are guided to apply decoding and comprehending strategies through a progression of text levels.

### Use a Combination of Structures

In a differentiated reading program, both strategy-based groups and guided reading groups offer flexible structures for organizing students for instruction (Kosanovich, Ladinsky, Nelson, & Torgesen, 2006).

To provide effective differentiated small-group reading lessons, we vary each of the following:

- Content: the skill or strategy based on assessment data
- Lesson structure or teaching sequence
- Materials: the materials used, such as leveled text or word sort manipulatives
- Pace of instruction: the number of lessons in each skill or strategy
- Frequency of instruction: the number of times we meet with each group
- Intensity: the number of students in the group

In each of Chapters 4–6 you'll find a section on Grouping Students for Instruction, which discusses how to strategically group students for word solving, fluency, and comprehension.

*Differentiating Reading Instruction for Success With RTI* © 2011 by Margo Southall • Scholastic Teaching Resources

# Organizing Groups of Students for Targeted Intervention (Tier 2 and 3)

Strategy- or skill-based groups are the most common grouping arrangement for Tier 2 students, who require targeted lessons on skill deficits over a sequence of sessions. Intervention programming in Tiers 2 and 3 is differentiated based on specific profiles of student need. No one program will meet the varied needs of low-progress readers. The teaching focus, lesson sequence, and materials used will vary according to their profiles as readers and learners.

When attempting to replicate the results of a researched intervention program, keep in mind the number of students in the group and the number of minutes of instruction students received in the study. It is important to note that there is a lack of research supporting the effectiveness of intervention with groups of more than five students, resulting in the recommended intensity within the RtI framework for Tier 2. Larger groups of students mean more diluted instruction and a slower rate of student progress. Students who continue to demonstrate difficulty after working in a Tier 2 group of three to five students require a Tier 3 level of intensity—one-to-one tutoring, if possible, or at least a group of only two or three (Vaughn & Roberts, 2007; Torgesen, 2005). Therefore, if we wish to replicate the results of research studies and close the achievement gap using the same approach, we need to replicate the level of intensity (number of students).

> **Small-Group Requirements for Tier 2 and Tier 3 Interventions**
>
> **Tier 2**
> - 20–30 minutes (in addition to Tier 1 instruction)
> - Five or fewer students per group
>
> **Tier 3**
> - 45–60 minutes (in addition to Tier 1 instruction)
> - Three or fewer students per group

If you have ever taught students with pervasive reading difficulties (Tier 3), you know that each student demonstrates a unique profile as a reader and learner that can challenge a school's capacity to respond with sufficient intensity to achieve an accelerated rate of progress. This challenge is the catalyst for continually seeking ways to revise and rethink our intervention program. For Tier 3 students to make sufficient progress and close the gap between current performance and grade-level achievement, one-to-one, or at least groups of no more than three students is not just preferable, it's a necessity. This is a reality we need to address in scheduling and, at the administrative level, in budgeting for highly trained intervention teachers. I still see much larger groups of students in intervention and special education programs and am deeply concerned for these students. At my presentations and school visits across the country, teachers regularly share their frustration about this issue, and it is evident that we still need to advocate for adherence to the RtI guidelines for group size and number of instructional minutes.

In terms of group structure, I have grouped Tier 2 and Tier 3 students using a variety of teaching structures, each of which has a specific focus (see chart below).

| Tier 2 and Tier 3 Groups | Instructional Purpose |
|---|---|
| Early Literacy | • Phonological awareness, concepts of print, alphabet recognition, letter-sound relationships |
| Skill/Strategy | • Word-solving and/or fluency skills, vocabulary-building or comprehension strategy<br>• Application of skills and strategies to fictional texts and content-learning materials (social studies and science texts)<br>*used across all tiers |
| Guided Writing | • Interactive writing<br>• Craft of writing using mentor texts (leads, endings, expanding main events with detail and description)<br>• Traits of writing in composition and revision (generating ideas, organization, sentence fluency, word choice—each within writer's workshop approach)<br>• Genre writing—e.g., informational text, personal narrative |
| "Booster" Groups | • Weekly intervention-group session may continue for three to six weeks when exiting Tier 2 intervention (at or approaching grade-level expectations).<br>• Support transfer of previously taught skills and strategies to classroom materials. |

## Allocating Minutes for Small-Group Instruction

RtI impacts every teacher's schedule, and this may mean adjusting the minutes spent in each component of our reading program: read-alouds, shared reading, guided reading or strategy groups, book clubs, partner reading, and independent reading. Tier 1 instruction includes time for differentiated small-group instruction for all students, with an additional 20–30 minutes of targeted intervention four to five times a week for students in Tier 2. So, what proportion of your total minutes for reading instruction is allocated to small-group instruction? In responsive, differentiated teaching, whole-class reading instruction should take no more than 45 minutes daily. Depending on your literacy block, this leaves a remaining 45–75 minutes for small-group

"The organization of instruction is another important factor in how responsive the general education classroom lessons are to the needs of struggling readers... The more whole-class teaching offered, the lower the academic achievement in that school."

(ALLINGTON, 2009, P.35)

instruction, literature circles or book clubs, partner reading, and independent reading. The chart below shows how you might allocate the minutes you have. Remember, this time is for reading instruction (word solving, fluency, and comprehension) and does not include writing workshop.

| Total Minutes | Minutes in Whole-Class Lessons | Minutes in Small-Group Lessons |
|---|---|---|
| 90 | 30–45 | 45–60 |
| 120 | 45–60 | 60–75 |

# Scheduling Small–Group Reading Lessons in the Core Tier 1 Program

RtI guidelines describe daily small-group differentiated instruction in Tier 1, and providing this is certainly our goal. This is where the mathematics of reading instruction begins. Because the requirement for Tier 1 stipulates group sizes of no more than six students, we often face a logistical challenge when trying to implement daily small-group instruction for every student in the time available. This is especially true when your class size is more than 20 students and where there is a high number of low-progress readers—for whom daily small-group lessons in the core program and additional minutes in Tier 2 and Tier 3 intervention groups are essential. I know this reality very well, having taught grades 1–3 with 25 or more students and in Title 1 profile schools. If you teach in a district that requires daily small-group lessons for every student within a 60-minute block of dedicated time, then your lessons are going to have to target one or two complementary teaching points within a short session—for example, you'll meet for 15 minutes with four groups.

As skills and strategies in each reading component become increasingly complex in grades 2 and 3, small-group lessons may become longer. The time frames on page 56 for each grade level are intended as a general guide for scheduling your time for small-group instruction. The accompanying diagram illustrates time allocations for the four parts of your lesson: modeling the teaching point; guided interactive practice; coaching students to apply the strategy on their own; and reviewing the teaching point, where we encourage further practice during independent reading. It is essential to carefully plan your time for each part of your lesson so as not to spend too much time on the demonstration or leave out the review of the teaching point. You want students to be able to verbalize the concept (their reading goal) when they leave the teaching table. When scheduling 20-minute

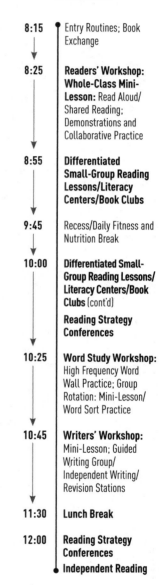

## Timeline

**8:15** Entry Routines; Book Exchange

**8:25** **Readers' Workshop: Whole-Class Mini-Lesson:** Read Aloud/ Shared Reading; Demonstrations and Collaborative Practice

**8:55** **Differentiated Small-Group Reading Lessons/Literacy Centers/Book Clubs**

**9:45** Recess/Daily Fitness and Nutrition Break

**10:00** **Differentiated Small-Group Reading Lessons/ Literacy Centers/Book Clubs** (cont'd)
**Reading Strategy Conferences**

**10:25** **Word Study Workshop:** High Frequency Word Wall Practice; Group Rotation: Mini-Lesson/ Word Sort Practice

**10:45** **Writers' Workshop:** Mini-Lesson; Guided Writing Group/ Independent Writing/ Revision Stations

**11:30** **Lunch Break**

**12:00** **Reading Strategy Conferences**
● **Independent Reading**

lessons within a 45- to 60-minute time frame, low-progress students will receive daily small-group lessons and other students will have three or four weekly sessions.

### Plan Your Time for Each Part of the Lesson

**Kindergarten:** In Tier 1, it is preferable that beginning readers receive daily small-group instruction. In kindergarten this means scheduling daily 10- to 15-minute early literacy skill group lessons for every student to prevent gaps in achievement and confusions in the building blocks of reading—mastery of phonemic awareness skills and letter-sound relationships. Without ongoing small-group instruction, the gap will widen as the year progresses.

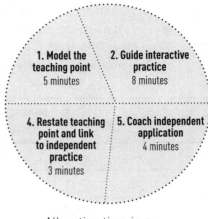

Allocating time in a small-group lesson

**Grade 1:** In first grade, we schedule 15–20 minutes per session, working with three or four groups within the 45- to 60-minute time frame. Allow five minutes between groups to check in on the rest of the class and have students indicate to you the center/station or core task on the class menu that they're working on next (see Implementing Differentiated Independent Practice, page 61).

**Grades 2-3:** In second and third grade, it is preferable to schedule 20 minutes for each lesson in order to have sufficient time to model and coach students to apply comprehension (higher-level thinking skills) and word-solving strategies. This will mean working with three groups in a 60-minute time frame, allowing for transition time and checking in with the rest of the class—in fact, 70 minutes is more realistic. If structural constraints beyond your control prevent this time allocation, you will have to work with two groups a day for a total of 45 minutes, including transition and check-in time, or reduce the lesson time to 15 minutes.

**Support Staff:** If you are fortunate enough to have push-in support from a Title 1 teacher, reading specialist, or special educator, then two groups can receive instruction simultaneously, making daily small-group instruction possible for all students. However, the reality often is that support staff are already committed to providing the second small-group lesson to Tier 2 or "triple dose" to Tier 3 students and therefore may not have time in their schedules to support differentiated small-group instruction at the Tier 1 level in the classroom. Keep in mind the expectation in RtI that classroom teachers work with every student in small-group instruction and the intervention minutes are in addition to this.

### Classroom Example

In the following classroom there are four differentiated reading groups and a total of 60 minutes of small-group instruction. Groups are numbered in order of their priority for daily instruction, with Group 1 consisting of Tier 2 low-progress readers and Group 4

*Differentiating Reading Instruction for Success With RTI* © 2011 by Margo Southall • Scholastic Teaching Resources

consisting of more advanced students. If you have more than 60 minutes available, the number of weekly sessions can be increased, so that all students receive four or five sessions a week. Note that groups are continually formed based on a common need, and the numbering system is purely for teacher planning purposes; students do not "belong" to a specific group, and membership is constantly changing as student reading goals change.

### Common Scheduling Formula for Small-Group Lessons

Number of Students: 22

Total Minutes of Small-Group Instruction: 60

Number of reading groups: 4

Minutes for Each Lesson: 20

| Number of Sessions per Week | Monday | Tuesday | Wednesday | Thursday | Friday |
|---|---|---|---|---|---|
| Group 1 x 5 (M–F) | Group 1 | Group 4 | Group 3 | Group 1 | Group 1 |
| Group 2 x 4 (M, T, W, F) | Group 2 | Group 1 | Group 1 | Group 3 | Group 2 |
| Group 3 x 3 (M, W, Th) | Group 3 | Group 2 | Group 2 | Group 4 | Group 4 |
| Group 4 x 3 (Tu, Th, F) | | | | | |

### Flexible Groups ... Flexible Scheduling?

Perhaps you're not inclined to have a rotation schedule such as the one above, and would rather fluidly pull groups based upon current needs. Either way, you will need to allocate 45–60 minutes daily for small-group instruction, with more of this time devoted to teacher-directed strategy groups for low-progress students than more advanced students over the course of your instructional cycle.

If 45 minutes seems like a long stretch for your students to work independently, even when they do come to the teaching table for a session every day, you can alternate whole-class and small-group sessions, so that students come together for whole-class input after each rotation of small-group lessons and independent practice (centers). Using this approach, the schedule for a 90-minute reading block in which the teacher meets with three reading groups each day would look like the flow chart. If time allocated to whole-class lessons seems too short, keep in mind that independent practice at the centers is connected to whole-class (multilevel center tasks) and small-group lessons (differentiated center tasks). This means less time is needed for whole-class lessons, and these will consist of teacher demonstrations and collaborative interaction. The upcoming pages provide more detail on how this works. Keep in mind that a rotation schedule will always vary based upon the number of groups you meet with and the total minutes in your reading block.

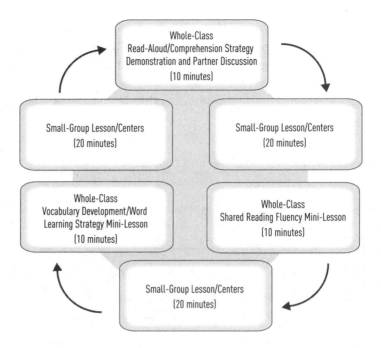

## Assessment and Conferences

To incorporate time for ongoing informal assessment and conferences, work with two or three groups for a total of 40 to 50 minutes and schedule two student reading conferences each day—one during small-group instruction, and a second conference during whole-class independent reading time. At times when your conferences do not include informal assessments, such as running records, you can meet with more students.

## Minutes in Each Component of Your Program

Create a visual time guide for yourself to represent the key formats in your reading program; see the sample on page 55. This can help to plan the best use of the minutes you have and ensure sufficient time is given for teacher demonstration and student practice within a framework of differentiated instruction.

| Format | Monday | Tuesday | Wednesday | Thursday | Friday | Total |
|---|---|---|---|---|---|---|
| Whole Class | | | | | | |
| Differentiated Small Groups (homogeneous) | | | | | | |
| Literature Discussion Groups (heterogeneous) | | | | | | |
| Partners—Book Buddies | | | | | | |
| Independent Practice | | | | | | |

## FINDING MORE MINUTES—SCHEDULE TIME SAVERS IN TIER 1

RtI may require more minutes than you are currently scheduling for small-group instruction, so how can you find those minutes? While certain factors are out of your control, some changes can be easily incorporated into your reading block:

- Integrate reading and writing workshop; students can read and write the same text structure using a common mentor text.

- Integrate phonics and spelling into whole-class and small-group word-solving lessons; have students decode and spell the same words, discuss their meanings, and so on, rather than scheduling separate phonics and spelling lessons.

- Use sharing circles rather than having individuals share their work with the entire class; each student shares a piece of writing or presents a one-minute reading review to three peers.

- Incorporate a "Floating RtI Schedule" where each grade level has a daily RtI block of at least 30 minutes, in addition to the core 90 minutes. Share students across classrooms during the RtI block so that some teachers will work on enrichment with larger groups of students (up to 20), and others will work with students who are on or approaching grade level within strategy groups. The remaining teachers take on an interventionist role with smaller groups. This distribution of students is made possible when no grade levels overlap their RtI time, which allows interventionists (reading specialists, Title 1 teachers, and special education teachers) to be part of the RtI team, working with small groups of students. The floating RtI schedule saves teachers preparation time because they only have to plan for specific profiles of students, and it facilitates intervention schedules. Sharing data on student progress in bimonthly meetings and common assessments is key to the success of this model.

### Streamlining Preparation for Multiple Groups

The skills and strategies you teach in small-group lessons are not new to you. No doubt you have taught them at some point before, but teaching them intensively may be new. What you first need is a set of lesson templates for skills and strategies for each component of reading (word solving, fluency, and comprehension) for the range of reading stages in your classroom. This will mean access to skills from one to two grade levels below the grade you teach in order to meet the needs of low-progress students. In Chapters 4–6 you will find lesson templates and sequences in common skills and strategies taught in grades K–3. For example, once you have become familiar with the teaching sequence for a comprehension strategy (see Chapter 6) or a guided word sort (see Chapter 4), you can use these formats with materials that represent multiple levels of complexity. Pull in some multimodal tools to keep students focused and you have a teacher toolkit at your fingertips that will streamline your preparation.

In my book *Differentiated Small-Group Reading Lessons* (2009), I provide a set of lesson templates along with interactive tools such as picture-cued bookmarks and strategy charts. A number of schools are busy compiling notebooks of lesson plans for each

## Do You Have What You Need to Differentiate Your Reading Program and Successfully Implement RtI?

| | |
|---|---|
| Scope and sequence of reading skills and strategies | • A record of the history of the student as a reader, in which learning to read is viewed as a continuum of skills, strategies, and behaviors (across grade levels) and used as a guide to plan next steps in reading instruction (Fountas & Pinnell, 2008). |
| School-wide consistency in terminology for skills and strategies | • A common language of instruction, including shared terminology for concepts, skills, and strategies across classrooms. Common visuals are used for strategies. |
| Formats/lesson structures | A set of lesson sequences for skills and strategies aligned with assessment data and designed to meet the needs of specific profiles of readers and learners. |
| Schedule | Time is allocated for: <br>• Differentiated small-group instruction for all students. <br>• Tier 2 targeted lessons when the classroom teacher instructs intervention groups. <br>• One-on-one reading conferences on a daily basis for two to four students. <br>• Students to read independent level text <br>• Reading connected text; additional time for low-progress students. <br>• Intervention that is scheduled *across* classrooms where students are grouped by a common need in specific skills and strategies (student-driven) to ensure targeted instruction at the point of need. |
| Range of leveled reading materials, interactive tools and other resources | • A sufficient range of leveled text, both fiction and nonfiction genres. <br>• Leveled texts available for each grade-level content topic, including accessible social studies and science materials. <br>• Flexibility in the use of mandated materials—for example, adjusting the pace and content in response to student data-based need. The number of lessons may be increased for more complex strategies and areas of student need; not all accompanying practice materials are used in order to allow time for small-group instruction. <br>• Interactive tools. |
| Informal assessment and progress-monitoring tools | • Informal assessment tools for daily use in comprehension, fluency, word-solving strategies, and self-monitoring metacognitive strategies. <br>• A common assessment notebook with sections for scope and sequence, standards, a guide to administering assessments, and sections for records of each student (see Chapter 2). |
| Collaborative support from peers and administrator(s) within grade-level teams and school-wide structures | • Teacher teams, such as literacy teams and RtI intervention teams, include teacher representatives, a literacy coach, a reading specialist, and intervention teachers who collaborate to make informed instructional decisions for low-progress students. <br>• Administrative support for differentiation: funding for materials and professional learning, scheduling for an uninterrupted reading block, and grouping students for intervention across classrooms. |

(*for grades K–3)

*Differentiating Reading Instruction for Success With RTI* © 2011 by Margo Southall • Scholastic Teaching Resources

reading component so that teachers will have access to a set of relevant resources. Making an inventory of what reading materials and programs are already in your building is a good place to start. Work with your grade-level team to construct an alignment chart listing the skills and strategies you teach in each reading component and supporting resources. This will greatly help reduce time spent continuously searching through instructional materials.

## Part 2

# Implementing Differentiated Independent Practice— So You Can Teach Small Groups

In my earlier book *Differentiated Literacy Centers* (2007), I set out to address the management issues that arise when we teach multiple small groups each day and to provide a set of differentiated materials for independent practice. Independent practice does not have to occur at a physical location, but the terms "centers" or "stations" are used to represent tasks within each reading component—for example, the comprehension center. When teachers hear the word center or station, they can feel overwhelmed with concerns about having to create new activities every week and the many hours of preparation this requires. The focus in this section is on how to make independent practice an effective use of time for all students with a minimum of teacher preparation—

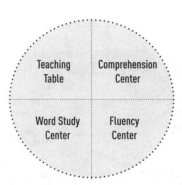

Small-Group Instruction + 3 Centers

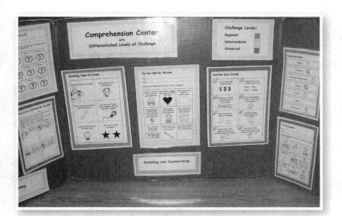

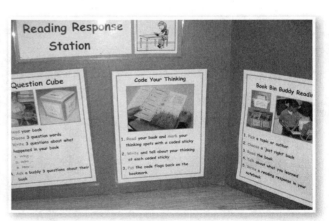

Students read independent-level text and complete a reading response from the comprehension center.

to implement independent practice in centers that are doable and sustainable all year long. To achieve this we will examine how to:

- **Provide differentiated practice for each component of reading instruction** with the resources in Chapters 4–6 (word solving, comprehension, and fluency).

- **Incorporate a menu of core tasks** for each center that will provide students with consistent formats throughout the year.

- **Maintain on-task behaviors** with visuals and routines that provide clear expectations for student work, including rotation systems and picture-cued, step-by step posters for completion of core tasks.

## PLAN DIFFERENTIATED LITERACY TASKS

### Incorporate Reading Components in Three or More Centers

In the section on rotation systems (pages 65–72), you will see how we can schedule our independent practice program so that students have an opportunity to work on skills and strategies in all areas of reading. First, let's look at a summary chart (see page 63) that shows how we differentiate the independent practice for each component at the centers and the types of resources provided in Chapters 4–6 to support you.

Note the expectation that students will not only read independent-level text at the comprehension center, but also write in response to reading in their journal to extend their strategic thinking, which has the added benefit of creating a record for monitoring their growth.

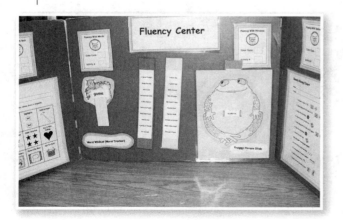

Tic Tac Toe menus provide multisensory practice of skills.

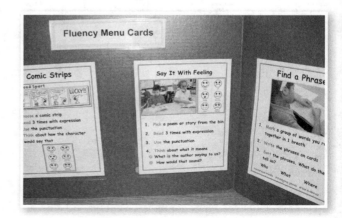

Fluency center task cards with photos and picture cues are displayed on a project board.

| Center | What do students do and how is it differentiated? | What resources are available? |
|---|---|---|
| **Word Solving**<br>**Chapter 4 and Vocabulary section in Chapter 6**<br>ABC WORD STUDY | Students engage in multisensory practice tasks using tactile materials, such as games and picture and word sorts.<br><br>Each group of students works with materials at the appropriate complexity of letter-sound relationships or word patterns based upon assessment.<br><br>Students work on recognizing their group's high-frequency words. | Build and Blend Domino Game (page 109)<br><br>Picture-cued independent practice task cards (page pages 141–150)<br><br>Guided and independent practice tasks in Chapter 4 |
| **Fluency**<br>**Chapter 5**<br>FLUENCY | Students read familiar text independently or collaboratively; use technology-assisted reading programs to read/reread instructional- or independent- level text.<br><br>They work on reading rate, phrasing, and use of expression. | Shared reading texts, such as poems, big books, charts, songs, short passages; technology-based reading passages<br><br>High-frequency phrases (see Resources on page 190)<br><br>Guided and independent practice tasks in Chapter 5 |
| **Comprehension**<br>**Chapter 6**<br>COMPREHENSION | • Students practice their comprehension reading goal (teaching point in small-group lesson) with text at their independent reading level.<br><br>• They complete a strategy-based written or oral response at the appropriate level of challenge (see Label the Tasks on page 64). | Graphic organizers and strategy booklets<br><br>Guided and independent practice tasks in Chapter 6<br><br>Manipulatives and mentor texts (see Resources on page 296)<br><br>Leveled texts in your classroom library and/or school bookroom |

## Vary the Level of Challenge

Provide differentiated tasks so students are always working at the appropriate level of challenge that engenders growth. For instance, at the comprehension center, I provide tasks that require students to apply the same strategy we have been working on as a class to their independent reading material, and then to produce an oral and/or written response. To make the strategy accessible to all students, I provide both an easier and a more complex task. So even though students are working on the same strategy, different students will be working on a different level of challenge or complexity.

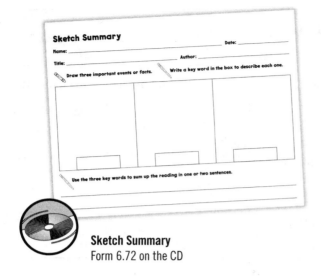

**Sketch Summary**
Form 6.72 on the CD

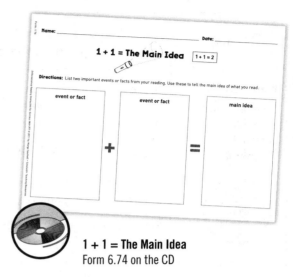

**1 + 1 = The Main Idea**
Form 6.74 on the CD

### Label the Tasks

So students know which task to complete, label the folders or bins with colored stickers—for example, green, yellow, or red. These same colors are on their tracking sheets alongside each center (see Provide Student Notebooks and Picture-Cued Task Cards on pages 68–69). Some teachers use different geometric shapes to label differentiated tasks. Whether you rotate students by reading group or have heterogeneous center teams consisting of students from different reading groups, your labeling system will ensure they will all know what to do.

### Provide Multilevel Tasks Based On Whole-Class Experiences

Open-ended, multilevel tasks based on shared class experiences are also included at the centers, such as author studies and poetry the class has enjoyed together. All students can work on these tasks regardless of their reading group. I code these multilevel tasks with a blue sticker.

### Differentiate Both Tasks and Materials

We can differentiate both the tasks and the materials at the centers—scaffolding student practice and application of the skill or strategy. For example, at the comprehension center provide an easier and a more challenging task together with leveled text. At the word-solving center, all students  might follow the format for word sorting (task), but the word cards (materials) would reflect different levels of complexity in letter-sound relationships and spelling patterns, based upon assessment.

## CONNECT THE INDEPENDENT PRACTICE TASKS TO SMALL-GROUP LESSONS

The fundamental purpose of independent practice centers is to provide opportunity for students to link the demonstrations in lessons and guided practice to their own reading—the transfer step. The practice at centers is not separate from instruction; the same skill or strategy you teach to each small group has an application to independent reading. Independent practice is always a part of the lesson planning cycle, so the tasks are an integral step in the teaching and learning process.

For students to value center work and maintain motivation, it is essential they see this purpose—how the practice tasks will help them grow as a reader and writer. During the last section of your lesson in which you review the teaching point, show students the link between what they are learning together in small-group lessons and tasks they will perform at the center. Verbally reaffirm the importance of having time to practice their comprehension, fluency, or word-solving strategy goal on their own, saying something like:

> *Learning how to use fix-up strategies as you read is your current goal as a reader. Practicing with different books at the comprehension center will help you achieve this goal and be a stronger reader. Remember, as you read, keep a picture in your head. If your navigation screen goes blank, use a fix-up strategy so you will understand what you are reading.*

The same is true for multilevel tasks based upon whole-class lessons. Here we also link new learning by modeling how to go about applying this useful skill or strategy "on your own" as an independent reader.

**I Can Stop and Fix Strategy Chart**
Form 6.44 on the CD

## Keep It Simple With a Set of Weekly Core Tasks

Consistency in formats and routines saves you and students learning time. Select a set of core practice tasks for comprehension, fluency, and word study. For example, I always have a read-and-respond task at the comprehension center. The strategy varies, and so do the texts students read, but the reading and responding formats are consistent, so students know how to record the response in their notebook and use the strategy bookmark, chart statements, or other support materials. The comprehension strategy booklets described in Chapter 6 are an example of an ongoing set of tasks students can complete during the reading of a book using multiple strategies.

At the word study center, there is always a set of core word-sort tasks and high-frequency word tasks that all students complete using the words their group is currently studying.

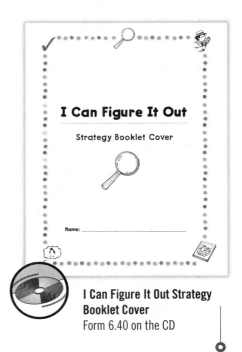

**I Can Figure It Out Strategy Booklet Cover**
Form 6.40 on the CD

You can make task cards of these core activities by copying the task cards in Chapter 4 or the graphic organizers and strategy sheets in Chapter 6 onto 8½" x 11" cardstock. Display at the center in a portable tub with the supporting materials. Supplement these core tasks with a variety of multimodal activities throughout the year to maintain engagement.

## CREATE AN ENGAGING TIC TAC TOE MENU OF CORE TASKS

Another way to provide a set of core tasks for students is the Tic Tac Toe format. The word-solving Tic Tac Toe menu displayed below is an example of how to use the icons for the independent practice tasks described in Chapter 4 to provide a rotation of selected tasks each week for word solving. There are several ways to display the menu in the classroom.

Word-Solving Tic Tac Toe Menu

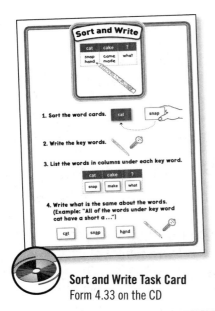

**Sort and Write Task Card**
Form 4.33 on the CD

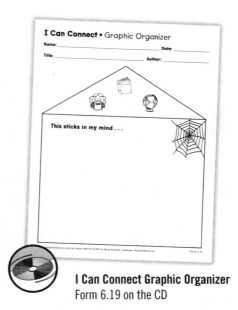

**I Can Connect Graphic Organizer**
Form 6.19 on the CD

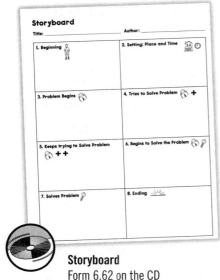

**Storyboard**
Form 6.62 on the CD

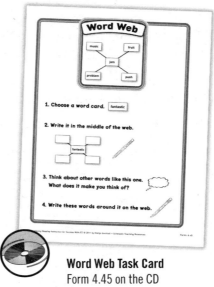

**Word Web Task Card**
Form 4.45 on the CD

Core tasks may include one from each reading component.

- Paste the icons onto posterboard arranged in Tic Tac Toe game board format.
- Arrange individual icons in the pocket chart.
- Photocopy individual menus and have students paste them into their reading response or word-solving notebooks.
- Copy onto 8½" x 11" cardstock to make task cards and display at the center.

This menu of independent practice not only streamlines your planning but also maintains student motivation: students get to choose three tasks to complete in a game-like format. A variety of tic tac toe menus to support skills in word recognition, fluency, and comprehension are available in *Differentiated Literacy Centers* (Southall, 2007).

## Sort and Write

1. **Sort** the word cards under the headings
2. **Write** the headings. List the words in columns under each heading

Task cards with photos of what the procedure looks like in action can keep students on track.

For second-and third-grade students, make a photocopy of Tic Tac Toe menus in a task card format for students to keep in plastic sleeves in their center notebook, or paste at the front of a spiral notebook. For each task, it's helpful to complete an example together as a class or in a small-group session, depending on how open-ended the task is, so students can refer to the model while working independently.

## USE PHOTOS TO MAKE STEP-BY-STEP POSTERS

The classroom management tool I have found most useful for keeping students on task is to take digital photographs of students as they complete our core practice tasks. Together, we discuss what the task should look and sound like as I take photos of each step. Then I paste the photographs on posterboard along with the related skill or strategy icons and label each step with the language we used during our discussion. Then, if a student is off track, I refer him or her to these photographs, which clearly depict what the task should look and sound like and ask, "What should we see? What should we hear? What do you need to do to get back on track?"

For example, the steps in the Sort and Write independent practice task in Chapter 4 would include some variation on the following:

1. Put the key words at the top of the mat.

2. Read each word card and compare it to the key words.

3. Sort the word cards on the mat.

4. Write the key words.

5. List the words under each key word.

6. Write a sentence telling what you noticed about each group of words.

## PROVIDE STUDENT NOTEBOOKS AND PICTURE-CUED TASK CARDS

Make sure each student has a reading response notebook or journal and a word study notebook to record the work they do at centers. These two notebooks are the same ones students use to record their work during whole-class and small-group lessons. In this way, students will have a model to refer to when working on their own at the centers. For example, to practice and apply the comprehension strategy you are teaching to a group, have them complete a strategy sheet or use their strategy bookmark cues as sentence starters to write in response to the reading in their notebook. You can also copy the strategy sheets and graphic

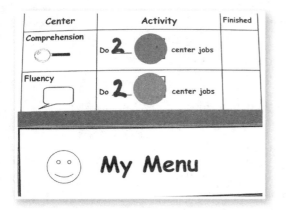

| Center | Activity | Finished |
|---|---|---|
| Comprehension | Do **2** center jobs | |
| Fluency | Do **2** center jobs | |

☺ **My Menu**

Center Tracking Sheet (Form 3.1 on the CD)

organizers onto cardstock and use these as task cards at the center or have students paste them inside their notebooks. Or you can have students paste Tic Tac Toe menus inside their notebooks for ready reference.

Providing simple prompts supports students in making authentic responses to reading. It also requires them to reread a section or, in the case of short text, the entire passage and process it with strategic thinking in order to respond. Have students bring their spiral notebooks to the small-group lessons for feedback and accountability.

You may use the Center Tracking sheet (Form 3.1 on the CD) to set the number of required tasks and level of challenge (color-coded green, yellow, or red) for each student.

## Maintain On-Task Behaviors

### Display the Group Rotation Visual

Now that we have examined the menu of center tasks and toolkits students will require, it's time to consider a rotation system. A rotation system—where all students move systematically through the centers—ensures all students have equal time to work on each reading component and equal access to classroom materials. You do not need a separate physical location for each center. Use the tables or clusters of desks where students now sit and label these for each center (comprehension, fluency, and word study).

To rotate students through the centers, use a visual planning board, such as a pocket chart or bulletin board with center icons. Here are two different methods:

- Rotate groups of students to specific centers after each small-group lesson. The pocket chart example above shows how this would look with four groups and three small-group rotations each day. Students "move" to the next center under their group card at each rotation. The teacher moves the group card in the pocket chart to the right on the next day.

- Allow students to choose the order in which they work on each center while still moving to a different center after each small-group lesson. You can use the Center Tracking sheet (Form 3.1 on the CD), as well as the class check-in routine (described below) to ensure they balance their use of time at each center. In addition to the center icons, you might display a poster of the core tasks and a Choice Board for fast finishers (see page 70).

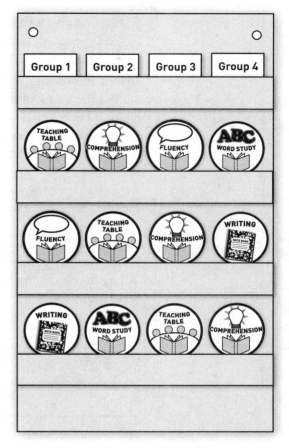

Center Rotation (teacher-directed)

Core Tasks (student-driven)

### Class Check-In Routine

Teach students to read the center rotation or task board and respond as you ask them to identify which center they will be working on next. You can number the centers so that students show the same number of fingers, or have students respond by orally stating the name of the center. When scheduling time for small-group instruction, allow three minutes of transition time between groups to allow for checking in on the status of every student.

### The What-Ifs

As a class, generate a two-column chart of what-if situations and brainstorm ideas on how students or the group materials managers can take care of the problem themselves. Examples might include when students can't find a material or when a classmate won't share. Next, list the exceptions—critical situations that warrant interrupting the small-group lesson and seeking teacher assistance, such as a student falling ill. Place a marker (a carpet square or masking tape X) on the floor near your table indicating where a student should stand if he or she needs to see you in one of these exceptional circumstances.

| What if . . . | I can . . . |
|---|---|
|  |  |

## Avoid the Dreaded "I'm Done" With a Choice Board

Once students are familiar with center rotations, they will be able to work independently in such a way that enables you to use this time to teach small-group lessons.

Having a Choice Menu keeps fast finishes productively engaged.

There will, however, always be students who finish faster than their peers and will find other things to do that were not on the planning board! We need a menu of choices from which they may select.

If you have a set of regular tasks that are completed each week, such as the Tic Tac Toe menus, you may wish to select certain practice activities as part of a Choice Board. Choice Boards comprise activities that are not part of this regular rotation, but provide options for those who have completed the required activities. Having a choice of four to six tasks can certainly help to avoid any issues of "nothing to do." It is important that students receive additional credit for these tasks so they are not seen as

*Differentiating Reading Instruction for Success With RTI* © 2011 by Margo Southall • Scholastic Teaching Resources

extra work. In this way you can plan ahead for fast finishers, who can select from the Choice Board when they truly do finish their work. Some teachers dedicate a time for Choice Board tasks, especially on Fridays, so that all students have an opportunity to work on them. Here are some suggested tasks for each of the six Choice Board icons (Forms 3.2–3.4 on the CD). Possible activities for each one are described on page 72.

**Choice Board Icons**
Form 3.2 on the CD

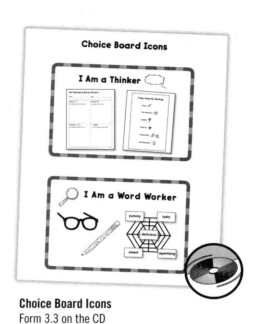

**Choice Board Icons**
Form 3.3 on the CD

**Choice Board Icons**
Form 3.4 on the CD

| I Am a Reader | I Am a Writer |
|---|---|
| **Tasks:**<br><br>Read from individual book bag, author-study books, theme reading materials, classroom library, digital text with interactive features for noting responses (e.g., Kindle); listen to audiobooks (online or CD). | **Tasks:**<br><br>Record ideas from read-alouds, other reading materials, and discussions for future writing; make lists of possible topics to write about. Write stories and information in notebook; complete a research project—"All About" flap book of facts; write a script for Reader's Theatre based on a reading; write a news report, brochure, blog entry by a fictional character, a real person (e.g., a scientist in informational text or from a biography) or an author; write a text message from one fictional character to another. |
| **I Am a Thinker** | **I Am a Word Worker** |
| **Tasks:**<br><br>Write opinions, ideas, connections, personal responses to the reading; make a set of Flip Up cards (concentration) or game board; complete a thinking map—for example, a concept web, flow chart, Venn diagram; make a cube where each side represents an event or fact; make a riddle booklet with questions and answers on the topic or story. | **Tasks:**<br><br>Find interesting words to add to the class Word Watcher chart and record in notebook; make word cards with illustration and a description of what the word means to you; read jokes and riddles with wordplay. |
| **I Am a Picture Maker** | **I Am a Partner** |
| **Tasks:**<br><br>Create a cartoon or comic strip, picture dictionary, illustrated timeline, accordion or flap booklet, quilt squares, storyboard or windowpane sequence (4–8 frames with pictures and words to retell or compose a new story), trading cards with three facts and picture. | **Tasks:**<br><br>Book Buddies format: Read the same book or a different [leveled] book on the same topic as a partner, discuss and share ideas, important points, and personal connections.<br><br>Listen to a buddy read a book or their word cards. |

*Differentiating Reading Instruction for Success With RTI* © 2011 by Margo Southall • Scholastic Teaching Resources

**Part 3**

# Making Whole-Class Lessons Work for Every Student

We have examined ways to provide differentiated instruction within small groups to teach at the point of need, but whole-class lessons can still have value for low-progress students. We know that incorporating quality literature that is at and above grade level in our read-alouds offers both low-progress readers and on-grade-level students opportunities for building background knowledge, vocabulary, and familiarity with a wide range of genres; developing higher-level thinking skills; and much more. Literature provides essential material for teacher demonstrations of the thinking processes required for comprehension strategies and word-solving and fluency skills. Low-progress readers often consume a diet of controlled texts, but their diets need to be enriched or the achievement gap will only be reinforced.

As mentioned, many teachers use a basal program that is written at grade level in their core program for whole-class lessons. In order for these texts to be accessible to our low-progress readers so they are able to participate alongside their peers, we need to ensure certain scaffolds are in place. Because the text is at frustration level and they cannot read it independently—or even in a typical guided reading format—the traditional model of assigning the reading and assessing with the end-of-unit tests will not be an effective practice for these students. So let's look at three workable options to guide our weekly plans; we'll examine each in turn.

> **What Makes Grade-Level Concepts Accessible**
>
> - Inclusive structures—e.g., shared reading and fluency formats such as echo reading, choral reading, and repeated reading
> - Sets of alternative books on the same topic or theme
> - Multimodal learning tools
> - All-student responses with time to process new concepts
> - Common visuals and language

## Inclusive Teaching Structures

By referring to structures, I mean the lesson formats and the sequence of teacher input and student interactions. Below I'll present three ways to scaffold access to text.

### Implement the Wide-Reading Approach
(Kuhn & Stahl, 2003)

This approach emphasizes the need to extend the reading mileage of students with different texts over the course of a week. Studies have demonstrated that both repeated readings and wide-reading approaches result in similar gains in fluency development (Kuhn & Stahl, 2003). The focus is not just fluency but comprehension and word recognition as well. In her research, Kuhn (2004) describes how the wide-reading approach supports low-progress readers in applying decoding skills to connected text. Note the *balance of basal and trade books* in the students' reading diet.

Students "share" the reading of the practiced passage.

**Day 1:** The teacher introduces the basal passage or article (story 1) and reads it to the class. The class discusses the story and the teacher may develop a graphic organizer using student input. Students complete a basal activity; then they read self-selected text at their independent reading level for 15–30 minutes, in class or at home.

**Day 2:** The class echo reads the basal passage or article (story 1), with the option of partner reading. Students read self-selected text at their independent reading level.

**Day 3:** The teacher assigns an extension activity, such as writing in response to reading. Students read self-selected text at their independent reading level. The teacher may administer running records with individual students.

**Day 4:** The class echo or choral reads a new passage from a trade book or article (story 2). Alternative options include partner reading of story 2 and an extension activity, such as writing in response to reading. Students read self-selected text at their independent reading level.

**Day 5:** The class echo or choral reads a new passage from a trade book (story 3). Students partner read story 3, and the teacher has the option of introducing an extension activity (e.g., writing or a performance reading). Students read self-selected text at their independent reading level.

## USE SETS OF ALTERNATIVE BOOKS/MATERIALS ON THE SAME THEME OR TOPIC

To offer students access to the same content, provide reading materials on the same theme or topic at varying reading levels. Here's the general procedure.

**1.** Introduce the theme or topic.

**2.** Provide books for students to read at two or more reading levels on the same theme or topic so that all students have instructional-level text.

**3.** Work with low-progress readers in a flexible group—read to them, echo read, and/or choral read the text. Other students may read with a partner or independently.

**4.** Gather the class together for comprehension-oriented discussion and extension activities around the theme or topic.

## PROVIDE DIRECT SUPPORT WITH SHARED READING

In this model, the teacher provides a passage or text at a single reading level. The teacher works with low-progress readers much as she does in step 3 of the model above, as a prelude to whole-class discussions and extensions. Other students complete partner and independent reading with responses.

### Resources

- Graphic novels, such as those found on www. scholastic.com/graphix

- Digital leveled texts, such as those found on www.pebblego.com

- *Scholastic News*, *Time for Kids*, and other magazines

- *National Geographic Explorers* (provides two levels on same topic)

- Graphic nonfiction, such as that found at www. rosenclassrom.com

# Multimodal Learning Tools

In Chapter 2 we briefly examined the range of multimodal tools that can be integrated into class lessons. These are described in detail in Chapters 4–6 for each component of reading. By incorporating one or more of these tools, we make concepts and skills accessible to students who learn in different ways.

# Incorporating All-Student Responses

Keeping all students actively engaged is a common dilemma for most teachers. We find ourselves teaching a lesson where a few students are doing all the thinking—and all the learning. Every class has a group of eager learners, the students who always respond to questions, while the rest of the group sits back.

Plan all-student responses at regular intervals in lessons to allow students to process the information.

The good news is that there are some simple, time-efficient ways we can incorporate all-student responses into whole-class and small-group lessons to keep all students thinking and responding throughout the lesson. Scheduling time for these responses is a critical step in lesson planning. We can get so caught up in getting through a long list of skills that we end up taking up too much airtime and not allowing our students the processing time they need to gain understanding. When students remain engaged, the minutes where learning (not just teaching minutes) takes place are increased, regardless of the core program or intervention materials you use. For a whole-group lesson, plan an all-student response every three to four minutes; for small-group work, have one every two to three minutes. Use an organizer like the one on page 76 to ensure a balance of teaching and processing time.

| | Teaching Minutes [Teacher] | Processing Minutes [Student] |
|---|---|---|
| Read-aloud | | |
| Shared reading | | |
| Small-group lesson | | |
| Content learning | | |

## TIPS FOR INCREASING STUDENT PARTICIPATION AND LEARNING

Use these strategies to boost student response.

### Partner Formats

### Partner Turn-and-Talk (30-60 seconds)

Ask a question, then have students share their answer or response with a partner first. Call on one of the partners to share their thinking. If students have trouble managing this type of conversation, tape cards with the number 1 or 2 onto student desks or count off before coming to the rug. Then prompt for either student number 1 or 2 to begin the turn-and-talk conversation. This prevents issues of who talks first. Having cards taped on their desks saves preparation time for future discussions.

### Think-Pinch-Share Bookmarks

Picture-cued strategy bookmarks such as those in Chapter 6 (see also Southall, 2009) for each skill and strategy scaffold the turn-and-talk activity in a focused, structured way. Each bookmark depicts how to apply a particular skill or strategy step by step. The corresponding statements can be used as sentence starters to support students as they verbalize their strategy use.

### Best Idea

Students record their partner's best idea in their notebooks. This process trains them for active listening and encourages piggybacking off the ideas of others to extend learning. Circulate around the class and record students' ideas on the whiteboard as they are sharing with their partners.

### Summary

Students record everything their partner can remember about the reading or discussion and tally the facts, events, or ideas. Then partners switch roles and repeat. Finally, they compare records to find what is the same and different in their notes, using check marks and minus signs.

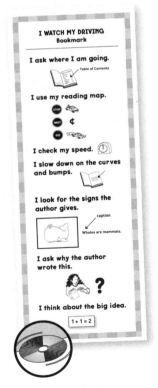

**I Watch My Driving**
Form 6.51 on the CD

## Jot-Pair-Share

Pose a higher-level question to the class. Students record their response in the Think section of a form such as the one shown below, talk with a partner, then summarize their sharing in the Pair section. Have partners share one main idea with the class. Decide on partners beforehand, and have students change partners to share with more than one.

| Think | Pair |
|-------|------|
| (individual response) | (summary of responses) |

Students jot their predictions at planned stopping points in the reading.

## Making Sense of New Information

These brief, focused activities will enable students to integrate new information with what they already know

### Build Connections and Activate Prior Knowledge

- **Free Write:** Students record whatever ideas or information come to mind for a specific time—for example, three minutes.

- **Sketch and Label:** Students sketch a pencil drawing that represents the events or information they have heard in a read-aloud or read in their small-group or independent reading material. Plan spots to pause in the reading to allow for students to cumulatively add more detail to their sketches and integrate new information.

- **Journal or Learning Log:** Students may reflect on their learning during a component of the literacy block and/or write about their personal responses to a read-aloud, shared reading, or independent reading material.

- **What Do You Know About . . . ?** Students turn and talk for one minute about previous knowledge and connections. You may wish them to record this information on an index card or in their notebook to gauge class levels of background knowledge and guide future lesson planning.

## Processing New Information

Plan all-student responses during the lesson and in the last few minutes of the lesson so students can have time to synthesize and summarize new learning. Use these ideas:

- **Listen-Stop-and-Write:** In this note-taking technique, you alternate three-minute bursts of instruction with two-minute writing periods on index cards or in notebooks.
- **Response Cards:** Students show a card, such as yes or no, or word cards from word-solving lessons, in response to your prompt.
- **The 10-Minute Rule:** After ten minutes of teaching, pairs of students summarize what they have learned, orally or in writing.
- **Fast Five Facts:** Students share and/or record the most important things they learned by describing five important facts.
- **Quick Write/Stop and Jot:** Students take one minute to describe three important facts from the lesson or reading.
- **Structured Note-Taking:** Students use a two-column format, listing main ideas and facts on the left and key words on the right.

| Main Ideas/Facts | Key Words |
| --- | --- |
|  |  |

## Nonverbal Cues and All-Student Responses

Using a nonverbal cue to indicate a timed all-student response gives students an opportunity to indicate their level of understanding in a physical manner and increases their attention and engagement.

## Questioning

Ask a question or prompt students for a response, then give a timed, nonverbal cue to provide think time. At the end of the think time, students respond in unison. For example, hold up one finger at a time until you get to five, then say, "Everyone..."

## Checking for Understanding

Use these quick, nonverbal ways to check students' understanding during a lesson.

- **Whiteboards:** Students hold up whiteboards and show a word, statement, question, or answer written in response to your prompt.

*Differentiating Reading Instruction for Success With RTI* © 2011 by Margo Southall • Scholastic Teaching Resources

- **What Color Is Your Understanding?:** Provide students with a colored paint wheel or strip where colors increase in intensity. You can also make a stoplight signal with colored sticky dots on a strip of cardstock. Students touch the color that indicates their level of understanding as the teacher circulates and offers support: red (strongest intensity of color) indicates "I don't get this, and I need help"; yellow (medium intensity of color) indicates "I'm a little puzzled; stop by when possible"; green (least intense color) indicates "I get it; there's no need to stop by."

- **Arm Gauge:** Students place their hand along their arm in such a way that shows their level of understanding. Placing a hand on their shoulder means "I don't get it"; a hand on the elbow means "a bit tricky"; and a hand on the wrist means "I understand this."

- **Fist of Five:** Students show the a number of fingers that indicates their level of understanding. Five indicates they understand completely, four shows that there's one part they're not sure of, three indicates some confusion, two expresses the need for help, and one means "I cannot understand any of this."

# Using Common Visuals and Language

In Chapter 2 we noted the importance of consistency in terminology in teaching low-progress readers. Consistent, student-friendly statements are used in the strategy charts, bookmarks, and other visual and tactile tools you'll find in Chapters 4–6 as well as in lessons and demonstrations and in directions for student tasks. Reinforcing these concepts in an integrated way scaffolds the learning process.

### Strategy Charts

Copy charts on cardstock for use at the teaching table during small-group instruction to ensure that the dialogue structures are accessible for every student. Place the chart on a tabletop stand and clip a clothespin alongside the focus skill or strategy to cue students' strategic thinking processes.

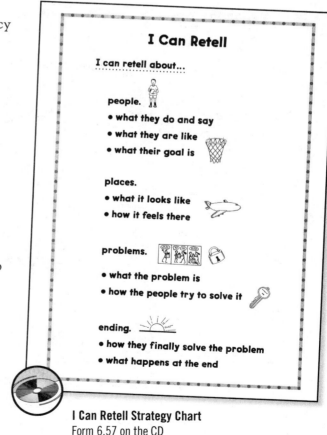

**I Can Retell Strategy Chart**
Form 6.57 on the CD

### Class Bulletin Board

Display the strategy statements on Forms 3.5–3.12 on a class bulletin board. Print the statements on sentence strips and illustrate with the icons or enlarge on a photocopier. You may also have students illustrate sentence strips with an icon that is meaningful to them based on a class discussion.

# Classroom Bulletin Board

| WORD SOLVING | FLUENCY | COMPREHENSION |
|---|---|---|
| I can read the words. | I can read smoothly. | I can understand what I read. |
| I can sound and say. | I see words I know. | I know interesting words. |
| I can chunk the word. | I read groups of words together. | I can connect. |
| I can use what I know. | I can look at my marks. | I can predict. |
| I can switch the vowel. | I use my voice. | I can wonder. |
| | I can read at the right rate. | I can figure it out. |
| | | I can picture it. |
| | | I can stop and fix. |
| | | I can retell. |
| | | I can put it all together. |
| | | I can sum it up. |
| | | I can rate it. |

Forms 3.5–3.12 on the CD

*Differentiating Reading Instruction for Success With RTI* © 2011 by Margo Southall • Scholastic Teaching Resources

Display the statements with icons under the corresponding area of reading instruction: Word Solving, Fluency, or Comprehension. Add the statement strips to the bulletin board as you teach each skill or strategy so that is it cumulatively constructed during the year. As you introduce and teach the skill or strategy, touch and read the statements. This provides a visual reminder to students of their reading goals. Goals are reviewed during small-group instruction and individual conferences. The same icons and statements are on the students' bookmarks that are kept at their fingertips as a form of nonverbal prompt for strategic actions during reading.

## Part 4

# Increasing the Minutes of Practice With Accessible Text

We have examined ways to maximize our teaching time and student learning within whole-class and small-group lessons, as well as organizing independent practice tasks. Now we take a closer look at the time low-progress readers are actually engaged in reading instructional- or independent-level text over the course of a day and a week. Lack of attention to this aspect of a reading program can explain why some students are not making sufficient progress. The 40–60 minutes of small-group lessons for Tier 2 and 65–80 for Tier 3 still only represent a fraction of students' learning time. Both Allington (2009) and Fisher and Frey (2010) point out the importance of examining our curriculum with an eye to increasing the minutes students are practicing and applying their newly learned skills and strategies. The chart on page 82 shows an example in the typical day of a low-progress reader. What do you notice?

"The current situation in many schools is that struggling readers participate in 30 or 60 minutes of appropriate reading intervention instruction and then spend the remaining five hours a day with texts they cannot read, cannot learn from, cannot learn science and social studies from ...In other words, most struggling readers find themselves spending most of the school day in learning environments that no theory or empirical evidence suggests are likely to lead to substantial learning"
(ALLINGTON, 2009, P. 29)

Student progress depends upon how much access they have to instructional- and independent-level text in the core and intervention program.

| Teaching/Learning Structure | Average Daily Minutes Tier 2 & 3 Students Have Access to Books They Can Read | Core Program and Intervention Materials |
|---|---|---|
| Read-Aloud (15 minutes) | 0/15 | Quality literature above their reading level/grade level. |
| Shared Reading (40 minutes) | 0/40 | Frustration [grade] level passages (less than 90% accuracy) from core text (basal), charts, overhead, SMART Board; may increase accessible minutes with scaffolds where teacher reads/students read text multiple times in different formats (choral, partner, etc.) |
| Small-Group Lessons (50–70 minutes) | Tier 2–50/50 minutes reading (includes 20 in Tier 1 + 30 in Tier 2)<br><br>Tier 3–70/70 minutes reading (includes 20 in Tier 1 + 50 in Tier 3) | Instructional level (90–94%) accuracy or independent level (95–100%) accuracy where students are applying skills to the reading of connected text |
| Independent Reading (15 minutes) | 15/15 | Independent level (95%+) |
| Content Learning (60+ minutes) | 0/60+ | Math, Social Studies, Science materials at frustration level (less than 90%) accuracy |
| | Total minutes daily that Tier 1 and Tier 2 students read at their independent and instructional levels:<br><br>**A. Not Including Content Areas:**<br>Tier 2 – 65/120<br>Tier 3 – 85/140<br><br>**B. Including Content Areas:**<br>Tier 2 – 65/180+<br>Tier 3 – 85/200+ | |

As you can see, out of the total minutes scheduled for reading instruction, not including content-area reading, Tier 2 and Tier 3 students are actually reading less than half of the time allocated for this purpose. After examining this example, discuss with your colleagues how you can increase the reading minutes in your schedules.

*Differentiating Reading Instruction for Success With RTI* © 2011 by Margo Southall • Scholastic Teaching Resources

# Ten Key Principles for Implementing a Differentiated Reading Program

**1** Implement screening tools three or four times a year to identify students at risk and who are a priority for differentiated small-group reading lessons (use an objective tool, not a chapter test provided with a commercial reading series).

**2** Assess each student regularly with informal assessment tools at intervals of six to nine weeks, and more frequently for students demonstrating difficulty. Include an assessment that requires reading of a short passage (running records, QRI, etc.) to determine strategy use (comprehension, fluency, decoding). Analyze the assessments to determine the teaching points for whole- and small-group lessons

**3** Examine the scope and sequence of the content for your grade level. Schedule and plan sequences based on class data and adjust the content and pace of instruction based on observed and documented level of understanding demonstrated in student work and informal assessment tools (what they say and do).

**4** Review instructional materials available to meet the range of student reading levels and for think-aloud demonstrations, including basals, literature sets, leveled books, and trade books.

**5** Scaffold access to content by using consistent, concise language to refer to each skill or strategy. Include visuals of these strategy statements and refer to them regularly. Support students in verbalizing their individual goal as a reader and how this helps them understand the intent of the reading material.

**6** Differentiate reading response tasks in whole-class lessons with multilevel menus and/or provide independent practice with differentiated literacy centers.

**7** Incorporate interactive tools consistently during instruction (such as turn-and-talk discussions) to allow time for students to process the content.

**8** Ensure students have access to reading materials at their independent level throughout the day and examine how to increase the minutes devoted to reading accessible text, especially for Tier 2 and Tier 3 students.

**9** Organize students into small groups based on data-based needs in a common skill or strategy, i.e., their reading goal. Meet with all students each week and with low-progress readers four or five times a week.

**10** Include heterogeneous grouping formats to provide access to higher-level thinking for low-progress readers—for example, literature discussion groups or "book buddies" (book club partners) in which there is a structured choice of reading materials (for instance, choosing from a set of three titles or two book bins).

# 4

# DIFFERENTIATING WORD-SOLVING INSTRUCTION

This chapter addresses all-important questions about planning and implementing effective word-solving instruction and provides a menu of lessons, guided practice activities, and tools that you can use to develop students' word-solving abilities.

## Chapter Overview

In **Part 1** of this chapter, Organizing Word-Solving Groups (pages 87–108), we look at common profiles of student need, followed by the steps required for planning, assessing, and differentiating a word-solving program, including options for organizing students for small-group instruction and independent practice.

In **Part 2**, Lessons for Guided Practice (pages 108–140), we examine the lesson sequences for letter-sound relationships, vowel patterns, and affixes along with reading and writing activities to extend student learning.

In **Part 3**, I share independent practice activities (pages 141–150) that provide students needed practice and allow for teachers to work with small groups.

In **Part 4**, Assessment (pages 150–155), I discuss assessments you can use to guide your word-solving instruction and I show how all the pieces come together in a seamless cycle of instruction.

## What Does Word-Solving Instruction Entail?

The concept of word solving in this chapter includes four areas (Pinnell & Fountas, 2009):

1. **Phonics:** using relationships between individual letters (such as *a, m, s*), letter clusters (such as *tr, ch*), and sounds

2. **Spelling Patterns:** recognizing larger units within words such as the consonant-vowel-consonant [CVC] pattern in *cat*, consonant-vowel-consonant-silent e [CVCe] pattern in *lake*; rimes such as *_ail, _ean*

3. **Word structure:** breaking down words into syllables and word parts, such as affixes *-ed, -ing, -er; un-, re-*

4. **Word-solving strategies:** using a set of strategic actions to problem solve new words during reading

Ideally, the knowledge, skills, and strategies these four areas of word solving require are taught using an integrated approach, where students read and spell the same sets of words, which facilitates the transfer of skills between reading and writing and maximizes our teaching time.

For word-solving instruction to be effective, students require a foundation of phonological awareness skills such as isolating words in a sentence, discriminating and producing rhymes, and segmenting and blending words first by syllables and then individual phonemes. The lessons in this chapter explicitly teach phonemic awareness skills while developing students' knowledge of word boundaries and larger units within words.

In grades K–3, I use the term "word-solving groups" rather than "word study groups" because the lessons do not include vocabulary other than incidental conversations on the meanings of words used in the lessons. Vocabulary is taught alongside comprehension (see Chapter 6). In grades K–3, phonemic awareness, phonics, and vowel patterns are the main focus. In grades 4–8, the focus shifts to "word study" as the instructional sequence of word features progresses to a focus on the meaningful parts of words, such as affixes, base words and roots, along with syllable patterns, rather than phonics.

I have fine-tuned this differentiated approach to word-solving instruction in my own classroom for over a decade and, along with my colleagues, have identified many questions along the way that needed to be addressed in order for differentiation to work in our classrooms:

- How can you differentiate phonics instruction to meet a range of student developmental stages and target the needs of low-progress readers?

- What are the common student profiles of need and what are the telltale signs of difficulty?

- What content can you teach the whole class and what should be taught in small-group lessons?

- Which visuals, interactive tools, and materials make the difference for low-progress students?

- Where do word sorting approaches fit in? Are they explicit enough?

It is the practical responses to these questions that we will now examine, so that your students too can benefit from differentiated word-solving instruction.

## Journey to Differentiation in Word Solving

Traditional phonics instruction is done with the whole class, with teacher demonstration and worksheet practice taking up the bulk of instructional time. Typically, students respond in chorus to the teacher's prompts, but whether each one has fully grasped a concept is difficult to monitor; echoing their neighbor is a common coping strategy for low-progress students. Phonics features are generally taught in lockstep sequence, regardless of which concepts students have already mastered or "missed" along the way. When we taught phonics this way in my school, the high percentage of students being referred to intervention due to decoding issues was an ongoing concern. It became clear that we needed a better way.

In an effort to differentiate, I had already begun to incorporate making and sorting words as a regular part of my guided reading lessons (Cunningham, 2000). I read *Words Their Way* (Bear, Invernizzi, Templeton, & Johnston, 1999) and *Word Journeys* (Ganske, 2000), which outlined a roadmap for assessment-based instruction. As I implemented this new approach for differentiating my instruction, I learned over time what worked for my students and what routines I needed to have in place. My goal in writing this chapter is to give you the teaching tools you need to make differentiated word-solving effective for your students and doable for you, so you can focus your teaching energy where it counts—on your interactions with the students.

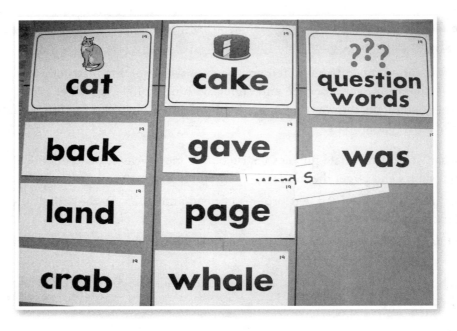

Word sorting is an effective practice that focuses on recognizing categories of words by their common features.

## Part 1

# Organizing Word-Solving Groups

The first part of this chapter examines how to get started organizing for differentiated word-solving instruction. We begin by examining profiles of common student needs and linking these to assessments. Then we cover how to differentiate word-solving instruction through engaging demonstrations and think-alouds and how to organize small groups. The graphic below provides an outline of Part 1 of the chapter.

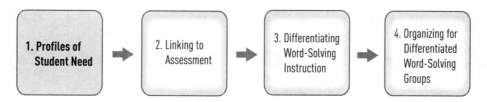

## Profiles of Student Need: Word Solving

The goal of word-solving instruction is for our students to be able to solve new words in running text while maintaining fluency. Common difficulties students experience in acquiring word-solving strategies include the following:

- blending sounds
- recognizing vowel patterns and knowing the sounds they represent
- using what they know to read new and complex words

Students who have these decoding difficulties often fit one of these profiles:

- **At-a-Glance Readers:** They scan words ineffectively and do not attend to the successive elements in the word, such as final and medial sounds. They often use only initial letter cues.

- **Huffers and Puffers:** They experience difficulty blending letter-sounds in words accurately and fluently. They may not yet be able to hold a sequence of sounds in their phonological memory in order to pronounce the word.

- **Over-Analyzers:** They often rely on smaller units of sound to decode (e.g., phonemes) rather than larger units, such as vowel patterns and affixes. They over-analyze even familiar words.

- **Word Callers:** They have not acquired the self-monitoring strategies required when solving new monosyllabic and multisyllabic words. They may substitute a nonsense word or omit words. These students do not use patterns in familiar words to decode new words (analogy).

- **Isolationists:** They do not transfer or apply their phonics knowledge in different contexts (e.g., from small-group lessons to independent reading) or to the reading of new text.

- **Solo-Strategy Readers:** They are unable to integrate strategy use to solve more complex words.

The lessons in this chapter address these common difficulties and help all students develop their skills. The chart below summarizes the lessons you'll find.

| WHEN the student profile of need is: | THEN provide these lessons and tasks | Page Number |
|---|---|---|
| At-a-Glance Reader, Huffer and Puffer, Over-Analyzer, work on<br>• Attending to initial, medial, and final sounds<br>• Blending letter-sounds | • Cumulative Blending With CVC Words<br>• Cumulative Blending With Initial Consonant Blends<br>• Blending From the Medial Vowel<br>• Word Building for Medial Vowels<br>• Sorting for Medial Vowels<br>• Recording Sounds in Sequence Lesson and Form<br>• Build and Blend Dominoes | 113<br>113<br>114<br>114<br>115<br>117<br>109 |
| Word Caller, work on<br>• Recognizing vowel patterns and affixes<br>• Using patterns in familiar words to decode new words (analogy)<br>• Identifying patterns in multisyllabic words | • Five-Step Guided Word Sort<br>• Six-Step Explicit Guided Word Sort<br>• Extending on the Lesson Activities<br>• 1-2-3-Show the Key! | 122<br>126<br>130<br>138 |
| Isolationist, Solo-Strategy Reader, work on<br>• Applying phonics knowledge and word-solving skills to new text<br>• Integrating strategy use to solve new words | • Training-for-Transfer Lessons and Game Formats<br>• Journal Writing<br>• Independent Practice Tasks | 135<br>140<br>141–150 |

Many phonics programs focus only on knowledge and skills and neglect the strategic aspect. Without practice applying their knowledge of phonics and decoding skills to actual texts, students do not transfer their abilities to reading. We need to give students training in how to operate strategically on text to effectively solve words. Word-solving strategic actions are the in-the-head operations that we need to make overt. Just as we model comprehension strategies through think-alouds, we can demonstrate how we solve new and complex words through think-alouds. In this way, students can build a self-monitoring and extending system for independent word-solving during reading.

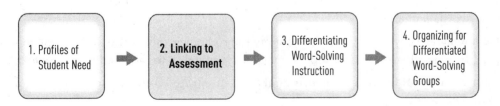

1. Profiles of Student Need → **2. Linking to Assessment** → 3. Differentiating Word-Solving Instruction → 4. Organizing for Differentiated Word-Solving Groups

# Linking to Assessment

Before the principles of differentiated instruction and RtI were adopted, if a child did not grasp a phonics concept, the only response was to provide more practice time on that same concept, rather than assessing and teaching within the child's instructional zone. We now know that phonics is developmental. We need to go beyond assessing student reading levels to determining where students are in their phonics knowledge, skills, and strategies. The chart on page 90 summarizes the developmental sequence of phonics concepts; this chart is also available as Form 4.1 on the CD.

Assessment in word solving focuses on students' knowledge of phonics, decoding skills, and ability to transfer knowledge and skills to reading.

In Chapter 2 we identified several assessment tools to use as a guide for lesson planning in whole-class and small-group contexts. These include three categories of assessments relevant for planning word-solving instruction:

1. Phonics inventories that help us determine level of *phonics knowledge and ability to use decoding skills to read words in isolation.*

2. Spelling inventories that help us determine ability to apply *generalizations (rules) for common spelling patterns and word structures to writing new words.*

3. Analysis of student miscues on running records to *assess transfer of phonics knowledge, skills, and word-solving strategies to reading new words within connected text.*

Together, these assessments provide valuable insight into which concepts, skills, and strategies are most important for students to acquire now.

You will find several assessments on the CD that I use to informally assess, track, and record student progress; see the box on page 91 for a summary of what is available. These are designed to accompany the guided word sort lessons found in Part 2 of this chapter. In Part 4, you will also find an explanation of how to use each assessment to monitor student understanding.

## Developmental Progression of Phonics Knowledge in Grades K–3

- **Initial Consonants**: *l* as in *like*, *m* as in *me*, *c* as in *can*

- **Final Consonants:** *g* as in *bag*, *p* as in *hop*, *m* as in *jam*

- **Initial Consonant Blends:** Two or more consonants with separate sounds, such as *l*-blends (*plan*), *r*-blends (*frog*), *s*-blends (*stop*)

- **Consonant Digraphs:** Two consonants with one sound, such as *ch* (*chat*); *sh* (*ship*), *th* (*that*), *wh* (*when*)

- **Short Vowels:** *a* as in *ran*, *e* as in *ten*, *i* as in *win*, *o* as in *dog*, *u* as in *bug*

- **Final Consonant Blends:** *st* as in *best*, *mp* as in *camp*, *nk* as in *pink*, *nt* as in *tent*, *sk* as in *ask*, *ft* as in *craft*

- **Final Consonant Digraphs:** *sh* as in *cash*, *ch* as in *rich*, *ng* as in *sing*, *th* as in *path*

- **Long Vowel-Consonant-e:** aCe as in *lake*, eCe as in *these*, iCe as in *nice*, oCe as in *hope*, uCe as in *cute*

- **R-Controlled Vowels:** Patterns where *r* follows a vowel or team of vowels, such as *ar* (*car*), *are* (*share*), *air* (*chair*), *er* (*her*), *ear* (*hear, learn*), *eer* (*deer*), *ir* (*girl*), *ire* (*fire*), *or* (*corn*), *ore* (*more*), *oar* (*roar*), *ur* (*turn*), *ure* (*cure*)

- **Other Common Long Vowels:** Most are vowel digraphs (two vowels representing one sound), such as *ai* (*rain*), *ay* (*day*), *ei* (*eight*), *e* (*she*), *ee* (*feet*), *ea* (eat), *ie* (*piece*), *igh* (*night*), *y* (*fly*), *i*-CC (*child*), *oa* (*boat*), *oe/o* (*toe, go*), *o*-CC (*cold*), *ow* (*blow*), *ew* (*chew*), *ue* (*blue*), *ui* (*juice*)

- **Complex Consonants:** including digraphs such as *qu* (*quick*); digraph blends (a consonant digraph with another consonant making a separate sound) such as *shr* (*shrimp*) and *thr* (*throw*); triple letter blends such as *scr* (*scrape*), *spl/spr* (*splash, spray*), and *str* (*stray*); final consonant patterns that sound alike such as *ck* (*back*), *ke* (*joke*), and *k* (*week*); sound-alike consonant and vowel units such as *ge* (*cage*) and *dge* (*badge*); soft consonants *g* (*germs*) and *c* (*cent*); silent consonants *gn/kn* (*gnaw, knee*) and *mb/wr* (*climb, wrap*)

- **Abstract Vowels:** Most are two vowels that form a diphthong (sound produced when one vowel glides into another) such as *ew/ou* (*new, soup*), *oy* (*toy*), *oi* (*coin*), *ou* (*out*), *ow* (*cow*), *au* (*sauce*), *aw* (*paw*), *al* (*ball*), *wa* (*walk*)

**Form 4.1 on the CD**

In addition, the Study Guide on the CD addresses these frequently asked questions about implementing differentiated word-solving instruction:

- If we adjust our pace of instruction based on the assessment of where students are on the continuum, how will we ever get through the grade-level curriculum?

- My students don't consistently use the phonics patterns we practice in their reading and writing. How can I get them to transfer their skills to reading?

- Our grade-level team has found that our basal is not explicit enough, and we need to supplement our program in order to differentiate effectively. What materials should we use?

- How will I align the skills in the basal with supplemental activities?

- We teach phonics and spelling separately, and the programs don't focus on the same skills at the same time. How can we integrate phonics and spelling in this case?

- Our spelling program focuses mostly on high-frequency words. How can we integrate this with our word-solving program?

- We don't have a scope and sequence of phonics instruction at our school. Can you recommend one?

- I differentiate by giving the groups easier or more challenging words with the same pattern based on our assessment. Isn't that enough differentiation?

**Word-Solving Assessment Resources on the CD**

- Developmental Progression of Phonics Knowledge (Form 4.1 on the CD)

- Assessment Record: Word Study (see Form 4.2 on the CD)

- Folder Labels: Word Solving (see Form 4.3 on the CD)

- Hearing and Recording Sounds in Sequence (see Forms 4.12–4.15 on the CD)

- I Can Use Words I Know (see Form 4.26 on the CD)

- I Can Read and Write New Words (see Form 4.27 on the CD)

- Dictated Word Sort Form (see Form 4.49 on the CD)

Provide multimodal guided and independent practice that helps students learn to use what they know to read new words containing the same pattern.

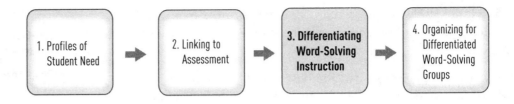

1. Profiles of Student Need → 2. Linking to Assessment → **3. Differentiating Word-Solving Instruction** → 4. Organizing for Differentiated Word-Solving Groups

# Differentiating Word-Solving Instruction

Word-solving instruction should be integrated into whole-class, small-group, and independent practice contexts. Teaching phonics and spelling solely to the whole class just doesn't address the reality of the range of student developmental levels. It is highly likely that we have at least three or four groups of students at similar developmental stages in decoding who can be grouped for instruction. All students deserve this differentiation or we restrict their opportunity for growth and prolong academic inequality. Within RtI it is expected that *all students in the core program receive small-group instruction, and not just in fluency or comprehension.* Students not demonstrating grade-level progress will be provided with additional small-group time when data indicates an ongoing challenge for the reader. All students benefit from independent practice in which they work on targeted tasks to consolidate their skills.

## WORD-SOLVING CYCLE OF INSTRUCTION

We have looked at linking assessment to instruction and the progression of phonics knowledge as a guide to planning our teaching. In Part 4 of this chapter, on page 150, we examine ongoing assessment tools that accompany the rotation of lessons and independent practice. The graphic below illustrates this cycle of instruction, a continuous process of assessing and teaching.

> "Struggling readers often find it difficult to grasp a mini-lesson principle that is pitched to the majority of a class, because they do not have the prerequisite understandings. For example, if you do not know quite a few of the consonant letters and related sounds, it will be hard to understand consonant clusters (blends and digraphs)."
>
> (PINNELL & FOUNTAS, 2009 P. 242)

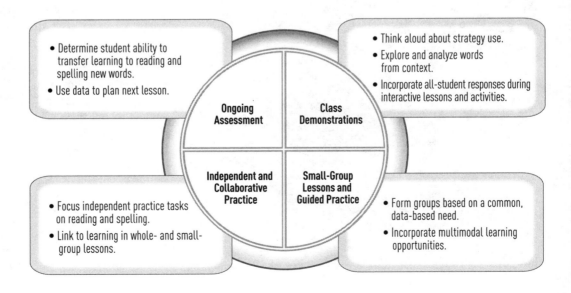

**Ongoing Assessment**
- Determine student ability to transfer learning to reading and spelling new words.
- Use data to plan next lesson.

**Class Demonstrations**
- Think aloud about strategy use.
- Explore and analyze words from context.
- Incorporate all-student responses during interactive lessons and activities.

**Independent and Collaborative Practice**
- Focus independent practice tasks on reading and spelling.
- Link to learning in whole- and small-group lessons.

**Small-Group Lessons and Guided Practice**
- Form groups based on a common, data-based need.
- Incorporate multimodal learning opportunities.

## INTENTIONAL TEACHING

Above all, your word-solving instruction should be *intentional*. Provide direct instruction in specific skills and strategies, according to a systematic plan. Offer scaffolding as necessary and integrate concepts whenever possible.

### Common Elements of Intentional Teaching

- Curriculum is *systematic* and follows a sequential set of phonics elements or word structures.

- Instruction focuses on a *specific teaching/learning point*.

- Concepts are *explicitly* taught and include related practice.

- Teacher *scaffolding* is provided within small-group sessions.

- Letter-sound relationships are taught that build toward whole words.

- Students practice blending the sounds of words.

- Guided practice includes using phonics to read real words in connected text.

- Word-solving instruction is *integrated* with continuous review of previously taught concepts.

- Practice materials support application of phonics concepts to both reading and writing.

- Phonics and spelling are presented simultaneously within lessons.

"Highly systematic and explicit approaches were characterized by direct teaching, high-level student engagement, and individual accountability."

(Mesmer & Griffith, 2006, p. 375)

## USE BRAIN RESEARCH

Incorporating the principles of brain research along with interactive learning opportunities can boost student engagement and have a positive effect on students' rate of progress (Lovett, Lacerenza, & Borden, 2000). Research by Maryanne Wolfe (2000) provides a guide to just which processes are critical for students to store and retrieve words. To support these processes, we need to analyze words in three ways, by their:

1. **Sound** (phonological memory)

2. **Spelling** (orthographic or visual memory)

3. **Meaning** (semantic memory)

The importance of these three processes and the teaching of strategies to facilitate transfer is reflected in Dorn and Saffos's (2001) framework for early intervention that includes five categories for word-solving instruction: sound analysis, visual analysis, pattern analysis, analogies, and vocabulary development, all of which are incorporated into the lesson sequences in this chapter.

The lessons in Part 2 of this chapter integrate these processes. For example, in the Six-Step Explicit Guided Word Sort on page 126, students discriminate the sounds in a key word and then are shown its visual image (addressing phonological and orthographic memory). As the teacher presents the word cards with the focus feature, the meaning of each is discussed before continuing the activity (addressing semantic memory).

## SELECT APPROPRIATE TEXTS

Students should apply their skills in each and every lesson by reading authentic text, even if it is just a shared reading of a sentence for students at the earliest stages of development. This immediate application of new skills is crucial for low-progress readers, who often experience difficulty linking learning from one context to another.

To select an appropriate text, consider its reading level and features. Students in a word-solving group are typically reading text at their *instructional level* (90–94% accuracy), so there are some words to figure out, but not too many. You'll want to ensure that the text contains examples of the phonics feature you're studying. You might use a familiar shared reading text that students can read from memory; you can pull words from the text and examine them for the targeted feature, as long as the word itself is of appropriate complexity and not a multisyllabic word or an uncommon word that is not useful for vocabulary building.

Decodable texts are also a source you can draw from. Low-progress readers and early literacy groups may certainly benefit from reading multiple texts containing the same features. However, you don't want to limit students' choices of independent reading to these instructional materials. Some of the newer series of books that are designed to support word solving are less contrived than they were a decade ago. There are also a number of books of poems that are particularly suited to a word-solving focus. I have listed some of these books and reading series in the Resources section at the end of the chapter.

## IDEAS FOR INTRODUCING AND DEMONSTRATING WORD-SOLVING STRATEGIES

Can students tell you how they figured out that tricky word? If not, they either have not grasped the concept and/or they do not have access to the language to express how they figured it out. Let's look at how we can offer students access to both the process and the language of word solving in our lessons, whether in a whole-class or small-group setting.

*Differentiating Reading Instruction for Success With RTI* © 2011 by Margo Southall • Scholastic Teaching Resources

## Word Sorting

Word sorting is an essential component of word study. By comparing and contrasting letter patterns and categorizing words based on their patterns, students learn about our sound-spelling system. Through modeling and guided practice, students learn how to use this knowledge to decode and encode new words. The lessons and practice activities in this chapter have students actively sorting words, talking about the patterns and categories they find, and applying this knowledge in reading and writing.

## Use Strategy Statements, Visuals, and Interactive Tools

To successfully think aloud about word-solving strategies, be sure to use the terminology you use in your word-solving lessons. Refer to your class strategy charts and bulletin boards to show students how to use them as resources. The strategy charts I use for word-solving instruction are shown below. Encourage students to talk with a partner about what you did, giving them the opportunity to verbalize the strategy independently. If word-solving instruction is to be truly interactive and student-centered, the supports need to in place for students' participation, so ensure strategy charts with visual cues, consistent verbal prompts, and peer interaction are a part of all lessons and guided practice. Interactive tools go beyond the inclusion of tactile materials to allow students time to talk about their learning in a focused, structured way, with visual tools at their fingertips, should they need them.

**Sound and Say Strategy Chart**
Form 4.4 on the CD

The Sound and Say Strategy Chart provides a step-by-step visual for segmenting and blending sounds in a word.

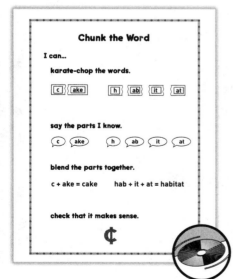

**Chunk the Word Strategy Chart**
Form 4.5 on the CD

The Chunk the Word Strategy Chart guides students through the process of breaking a word into pronounceable parts using vowel and consonant letter patterns.

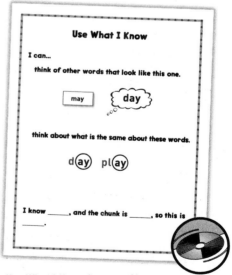

**Use What I Know Strategy Chart**
Form 4.6 on the CD

The Use What I Know Strategy Chart illustrates the steps in recognizing familiar parts of words and using these to decode.

# Sound and Say

**I can...**

**sound out the letters.**

r a n       r-a-n

**blend the sounds together.**

r + a + n = ran

**say the word.**

ran

**check that it makes sense.**

# Chunk the Word

**I can...**

**karate-chop the words.**

**say the parts I know.**

**blend the parts together.**

c + ake = cake        hab + it + at = habitat

**check that it makes sense.**

*Differentiating Reading Instruction for Success With RTI* © 2011 by Margo Southall • Scholastic Teaching Resources

## INCORPORATE THINK-ALOUDS

Think-alouds in comprehension instruction have become commonplace, but the same technique is rarely used to model the process of decoding and figuring out the meaning of a new word. Plan on an extended think-aloud about a word-solving strategy at least once a week during a regular whole-class read-aloud, in addition to your small-group demonstrations. The strategic focus of the whole-class think-aloud will be primarily on word solving as a way to make meaning from a text.

For example, you can use a whole-class think-aloud to analyze a word from context. Brainstorm with students and list what they know about the target word in the form of a web—e.g., consonant clusters, vowel patterns, affixes, and so on. Link what they know about other words containing these same features to the target word, which models how to apply their word-solving skills and knowledge during the reading process.

How many **beaches** have you seen on our lake?

**Word Web**

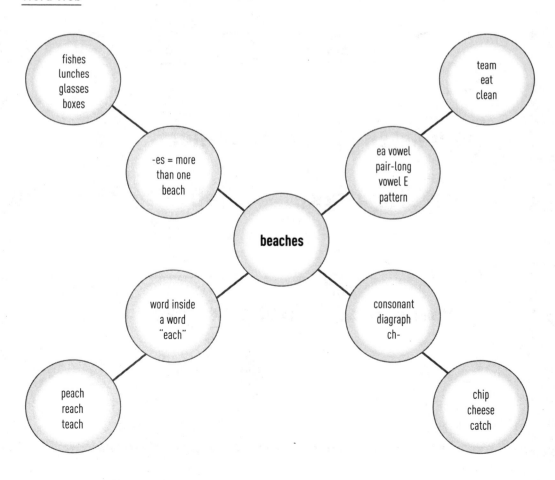

## Picture Cues and Drawing

Use alphabet cards designed to help students discriminate letter formations and remember letter-sound correspondences. You can find cards that use familiar animals or objects to represent the letter and sound, and/or cards that associate a story or motion with the letter-sound; see Resources on page 156. You can also have students create and illustrate their own alphabet books.

## Environmental Print

Display wrappers or labels that contain target letters or patterns on a bulletin board.

## Chunking Word Wall

Create a word wall with labels for the five vowels. Display key words for each vowel pattern according to the first vowel in the pattern. Use the chunking wall to demonstrate and practice the analogy strategy; students verbalize how to use a key word on the wall to solve a new word: *Is there a word we know that can help us? Let's check the Chunking Word Wall. We know* seat, *and the chunk is* eat, *so this word is* wheat.

## Word Wall

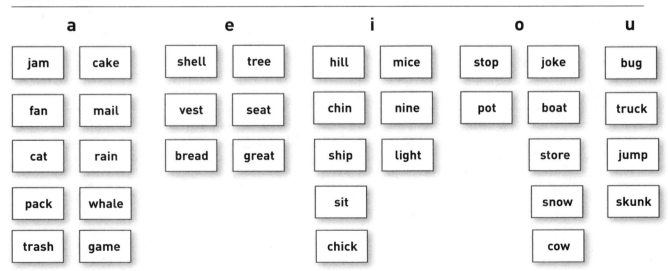

| a | | e | | i | | o | | u |
|---|---|---|---|---|---|---|---|---|
| jam | cake | shell | tree | hill | mice | stop | joke | bug |
| fan | mail | vest | seat | chin | nine | pot | boat | truck |
| cat | rain | bread | great | ship | light | | store | jump |
| pack | whale | | | sit | | | snow | skunk |
| trash | game | | | chick | | | cow | |

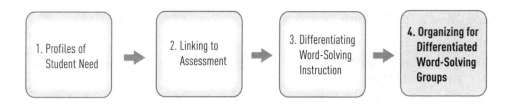

| 1. Profiles of Student Need | → | 2. Linking to Assessment | → | 3. Differentiating Word-Solving Instruction | → | 4. Organizing for Differentiated Word-Solving Groups |

## Organizing for Differentiated Word-Solving Groups

Differentiating word-solving instruction benefits students immensely. Don't be overwhelmed by the idea of managing even more small groups—you don't begin by teaching three differentiated word-solving groups. You begin by teaching your class the analytical thinking processes needed to recognize patterns in sets of words in a whole-group word sort. Then you build from there. I have been through this implementation process and now continuously coach teachers to find their own starting points and build from there. Here is one example of the process: In the first approach, word solving is taught within the context of reading strategy or guided reading groups (Fountas & Pinnell, 1996; Joseph, 2000). In the second option, groups are formed for the sole purpose of word-solving instruction (in addition to reading groups) according to their data-based needs (Bear et al., 2008; Pinnell & Fountas, 2009; Walpole & McKenna, 2009).

Different groups of students work with different sets of words, based upon their assessment.

### Implementation Process

| Step 1 | Step 2 | Step 3 | Step 4 |
|---|---|---|---|
| Model and practice word sorting with your students in a whole-class activity using words from your basal, literature, or content reading material. | Model and practice the partner and independent tasks. | Work with one word-solving group while the rest of the class completes the same task independently. | Work with two or three word-solving groups while the rest of the class completes independent tasks with their group's word sort words. |

Once you're ready to begin differentiated word-solving instruction by teaching small groups, you have two options.

Two Options for Teaching Word-Solving in Small Groups

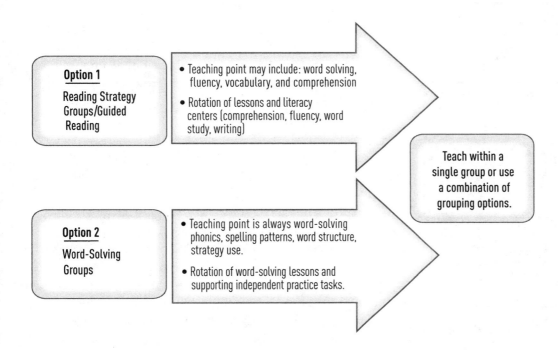

**Option 1**
Reading Strategy Groups/Guided Reading

- Teaching point may include: word solving, fluency, vocabulary, and comprehension
- Rotation of lessons and literacy centers (comprehension, fluency, word study, writing)

**Option 2**
Word-Solving Groups

- Teaching point is always word-solving phonics, spelling patterns, word structure, strategy use.
- Rotation of word-solving lessons and supporting independent practice tasks.

Teach within a single group or use a combination of grouping options.

## OPTION 1: ONE GROUPING—READING STRATEGY GROUPS (OR GUIDED READING)

In reading strategy groups, students are grouped by a common need in a specific skill or strategy (see Tier 1 Grouping Options on pages 51). In a typical word-solving lesson in this type of group, teachers demonstrate a useful problem-solving strategy, such as recognizing familiar vowel patterns in new words, then guide students' interactive practice, and coach them to apply the strategy during reading. In guided reading groups, teachers may also provide a mini-lesson to address challenges students encountered or are likely to encounter during reading.

You will need to teach more than one lesson per word-solving teaching point in this setting—one to introduce it and a second to coach for application, with more sessions for low-progress readers. To organize this type of schedule, use the independent practice tasks on pages 141–150 to extend the interactive guided practice from the reading strategy group lesson at the Word Study Center (see also Plan Differentiated Literacy Tasks on page 62).

"In research on reading programs that have included a combination of phonemic awareness, phonics instruction, blending letter sounds to decode words, and reading the words in short stories and books, 5–10 minutes of decoding for each 30 minutes of instruction has generated strong reading gains for young children."

(O'CONNOR, 2007, P. 65)

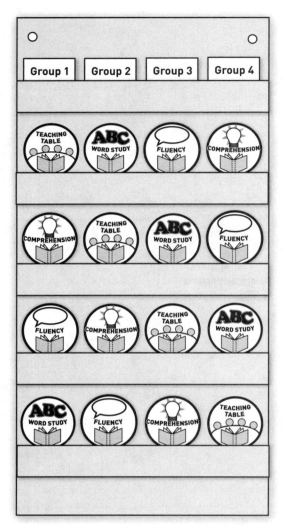

Each day groups rotate through strategy group lessons and independent practice tasks.

## Advantages

- Students have an opportunity to practice skills and strategies with connected text immediately following teacher demonstration.
- One daily rotation schedule of small-group lessons for teaching all components of reading—word-solving, fluency, vocabulary, and comprehension, as opposed to two scheduled timeslots for small-group lessons—one for strategy groups and one for word-solving groups.

## Disadvantages

- The schedule of strategy group lessons must take into account varying student needs in word-solving, fluency, vocabulary, and comprehension.
- For most students in grades K-3, when strategy group lessons must include a balance of all the components of reading, the number of lessons dedicated to word-solving may not be sufficient for them to achieve mastery of basic skills and strategies. Having a separate timeslot dedicated to word-solving groups allows more time for the other components of reading to be taught in strategy groups.
- For low-progress readers, the time allocated for small-group word solving lessons will not be sufficient to close the gap with grade-level peers.
- For all students, additional time will still need to be scheduled for intentional word-solving instruction. Before RtI was implemented, this often took place in whole class contexts, where the complexity of the skill was not differentiated to meet varying student needs. In many schools, this time is now used for differentiated small-group teaching and more targeted instruction. Whole class think-alouds for modeling word recognition strategies with read alouds (see page 98) are still incorporated, but specific skills, such as consonant and vowel patterns are taught in a small group context.

## OPTION 2: TWO GROUPINGS—READING STRATEGY GROUPS *AND* WORD-SOLVING GROUPS

In this option we schedule a separate time for:

● Reading strategy groups together with rotation of literacy centers (see rotation chart in Option 1).

*and*

● Word-solving lessons with related independent practice tasks. Twenty to 30 minutes daily is devoted to word-solving group lessons, such as the Guided Word Sort on page 122, together with a rotation of partner/independent practice tasks found on pages 141–150. The Rotation Cycle for Option 2 (shown below) illustrates the organization of student groups during this time.

Option 2 requires two distinct times in the schedule, rather one time slot as in Option 1, but Reading Strategy Groups (or Guided Reading) and Word-Solving Group rotations may certainly follow one another consecutively in a classroom literacy block. For example, I plan 45–60 minutes of Reading Strategy Groups and 20–30 minutes for Word-Solving Groups (see pages 105–107). Again, the independent practice tasks later in the chapter also support this option.

### Sample Five-Day Rotation of Lessons and Independent Practice

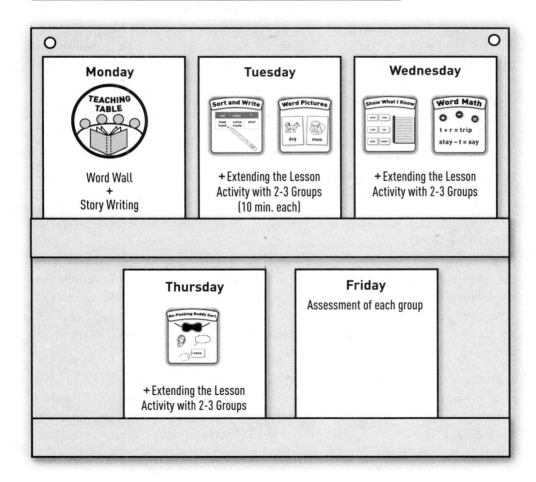

### Advantages

- Allows sufficient time to meet the needs of students at different stages in their development (phonics, spelling patterns, structural analysis, and problem-solving strategies).
- Allows more time to teach other components of your reading program—fluency, vocabulary, and comprehension—within reading strategy group lessons.
- Framework meets the required minutes of small-group instruction in Tier 1, 2, and 3. All students are more likely to have the opportunity to participate in small-group lessons every day.
- Uses time once allocated to whole class phonics and spelling to provide differentiated instruction and practice.

### Disadvantages

- Scheduling of time for two types of groups within the literacy block.
- Requires teachers to implement a second rotation of independent practice dedicated to word solving, in addition to a center program during reading strategy group rotation (see Rotation Cycle for Option 1 on page 102 and Option 2 on page 103).

### So What Works Best and for Whom?

Ultimately, at any grade level and with any reading program, it will be the degree of student need that dictates our instructional response, including the scheduling and pacing of instruction. Most importantly, word-solving strategies must always be reinforced and practiced within reading strategy groups to facilitate transfer of skills, as we continue to coach students to problem solve new words encountered in running text.

## Implementing a Rotation of Word-Solving Groups

In the following section, we look at how to organize students in a schedule where word-solving groups are taught separately from reading strategy groups (Option 2 in the previous section), starting with the scheduling and management of group rotations.

### FINDING TIME

If you choose to have separate word-solving groups—as I highly recommend from the latter half of first grade on—there are two options you can use to schedule the lessons. In each type of schedule, groups of students who are not working with the teacher rotate through practice tasks as described on pages 141–150. I schedule 20–30 minutes for this rotation, training my students to complete the independent practice tasks before I begin (see pages 141–150).

If finding the time to schedule another rotation of groups just doesn't seem possible, keep in mind that we are maximizing our time by teaching both phonics, word structure, word-solving strategies, *and* spelling patterns in integration. Traditional approaches to teaching spelling require a separate time slot in our schedules, whereas here we expect students to read *and* spell the same sets of words and no longer schedule spelling as a separate "subject" in our literacy block.

"The children understand why I am meeting with them … and they know that they must apply what they're learning to their own reading. Word study [word-solving] groups are effective only to the extent that children see these connections."

(TABERSKI, 2000, P. 117)

## MANAGEMENT AND MATERIALS

Owing to the hands-on, interactive nature of the tasks, students are engaged and on-task, making this an enjoyable and effective use of our time. Having students all complete the same set of core independent tasks, but with words that are differentiated by complexity, keeps it simple and doable for me—I'm using the same routines and lessons, but with different materials. Limited access to materials does not pose a problem, as inexpensive, reproducible word sort materials, tactile letters, phonics poems, and chart stories are readily available (see list of resources at the end of the chapter). Interactive SMART Board phonics resources are also becoming popular, such as the one developed by Wiley Blevins (2011).

## GROUP SIZE

If you have already met the required daily minutes in small-group instruction for Tier 1 within your reading strategy group rotation, with groups of no more than six students, then the word-solving groups can vary in size from four to ten students. The reality is that students do not cluster nicely in groups of six along the developmental progression of phonics knowledge (Form 4.1 on the CD), so the group size usually varies. This would mean most classrooms would have no more than three word-solving groups. If you are just starting out, you might begin with just dividing your class into two groups based on levels of achievement, then progress to three groups as you gain a comfort level with this approach.

## SCHEDULING THE GROUP ROTATIONS

There are two options for scheduling a rotation of word-solving groups.

### Schedule A: Students Complete the Same Task on the Same Days

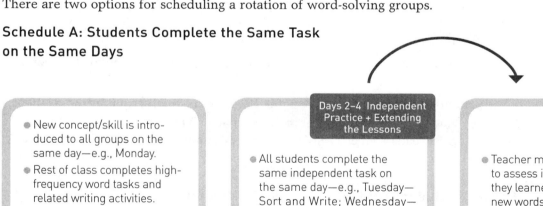

**Day 1: Group lessons**
- New concept/skill is introduced to all groups on the same day—e.g., Monday.
- Rest of class completes high-frequency word tasks and related writing activities.
- Requires 45–60 minutes on Day 1 to meet with three groups.
- There are no Reading Strategy Groups scheduled on Day 1 to allow for this time.

**Days 2–4 Independent Practice + Extending the Lessons**
- All students complete the same independent task on the same day—e.g., Tuesday—Sort and Write; Wednesday—Show What I Know; Thursday—No Peeking Buddy Sort (see tasks on 141 to 150).
- Teacher works with groups on extension activities.
- Requires 20–30 minutes daily.

**Day 5: Assessment**
- Teacher meets with groups to assess if they can use what they learned to read and spell new words (see Assessment, page 150).
- May dictate words to each group simultaneously.
- Requires 20–30 minutes daily.

### Day 1: Introduce Feature/Skill/Strategy to All Groups on Same Day (45-60 Minutes)

- Students all receive an "input" lesson on the same day, often Monday, allowing all students to participate in a small-group lesson on the first day of the cycle.
- No small-group reading instruction is scheduled for this day to allow time for three or four word-solving group lessons.
- Students rotate through the teacher station for the input lesson.
- While the teacher works with a small group, the rest of the class completes independent practice activities, writing activities, and high-frequency word activities.
- During the lesson, students are given the word cards they will work with that week.

All students participate in an input lesson and one or more "extending-the-lesson" activities each week.

### Days 2–4: Students Complete Practice Tasks (20–30 Minutes)

- All students complete the *same task on the same day,* but each group will be working with their group's word cards.
- All students receive a second, briefer (10-minute) small-group lesson at the teacher station for one or more of the extension activities (see pages 130–140). Low-progress readers receive three of these "extending the learning" sessions over a five-day sequence.

### Day 5: All Students Are Assessed (20–30 Minutes)

- All students have a common assessment day. You can pull each group in turn to the teacher table and present new words for them to read and spell (see Step 5 in the Guided Word Sort lesson sequence on page 123), or you can use a dictated word sort (see page 151), dictating words simultaneously to each group—for example., *Group 1, your word is... Group 2 your word is . . .*

### Schedule B: Students Complete Different Tasks on Different Days

This scheduling option is designed to address situations where you are not able to implement Reading Strategy Groups on four days a week, and use a fifth day to introduce the new word-solving concept/skill to each Word-Solving Group, so that they can all begin the cycle on the same day (see Day 1 of Schedule A on page 105).

The first implication of this is that when you first begin, you will need to stagger the input lessons over three days for the three groups to get them up and running. During this time, the rest of the students can complete a follow-up to a whole class lesson or work on high frequency word and writing tasks. The second implication is that groups of students will be working on different tasks simultaneously, as they complete the sequence of the cycle on different days. For this reason, I highly recommend Schedule A wherever possible, especially for first grade students, as it is the simplest for them to follow, and easiest for you to track and manage.

Once you have begun, students will work through their group's independent and partner practice activities (pages 141-150). These activities are common to each group and can be practiced with the whole class first using vocabulary from a read aloud.

You can vary the length of this instructional cycle so you have time to meet with your small groups two or three times. The cycle usually lasts five or six days.

Daily: 20–30 minutes

- Meet with one group each day for an input lesson, where you teach each group its set of words for the cycle. You will spend the first two or three days of a cycle on input lessons, depending on the number of groups you have.

- After each group has its input lesson, for the rest of the days in the cycle, pull one or two groups for "Extending the Lesson" activities with you at the teacher table.

- When groups are not meeting with you, they rotate through the tasks you have prepared for them to practice applying their strategies. They may do one or two tasks per day. All groups work on a different activity each day with their group's set of words.

- Groups are assessed on the last day of the cycle for their group—for example, Day 6 in a 6-day cycle. They complete the same assessments as in Schedule A.

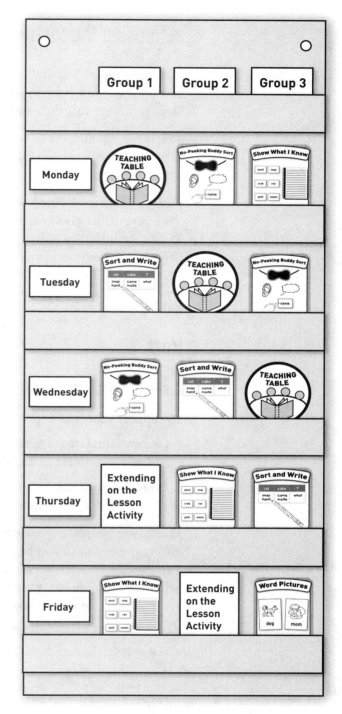

In a 6-day cycle, all 3 groups will participate in an input lesson at the Teaching Table and Extending on the Lesson Activity with the teacher. In a 5-day cycle, 2 groups participate in 2 small-group lessons and complete 3 independent practice activities, while 1 group will participate in 1 lesson and complete 4 independent/partner practice activities.

## Increasing the Instructional Minutes for Tier 2 and 3 Students

No matter which scheduling option you choose, low-progress readers will need extra small-group work in addition to their group's weekly input lesson. Here are some ideas for increasing their instructional minutes.

- Increase the number of review lessons according to student need. Pull groups of students to the teaching table for additional instruction while others are completing the practice tasks.

- Offer Tier 2 and Tier 3 students three or four days of small-group work while the rest of the class works through a rotation of collaborative and independent tasks. In addition to the Extending on the Lesson activities at the teacher station, low-progress students benefit from partner practice activities, such as the No-Peeking Buddy Sort (page 142), which can be completed independently or with teacher scaffolding.

## Part 2

## Lessons for Guided Practice

To support your instruction and student learning, in this section you'll find:

1. **Lesson Templates:** sequences for introducing and teaching letter-sound relationships and vowel patterns in small groups

2. **Extending the Lesson Activities:** activities that help students transfer new learning to reading and writing tasks

The lesson templates provide examples of lessons and an at-a-glance guide to refer to during lessons until you have sufficient practice and no longer need to refer to them. Full descriptions of word-solving lesson demonstrations and guided practice are provided in my book *Differentiated Small-Group Reading Lessons* (2009). The lessons are organized into two areas of word-solving instruction:

- Letter-Sound Relationships
- Vowel Pairs, Rimes, and Other Spelling Patterns

## Letter-Sound Relationships

The lessons are designed to develop the following skills:

- Cumulative blending with CVC words
- Cumulative blending with initial and final consonant blends
- Blending from the medial vowel

- Discriminating medial vowels (minimal pairs)
- Hearing and recording sounds in sequence to spell (encode)

## OVERVIEW OF THE LESSONS

### Cumulative Blending With CVC Words • Cumulative Blending With Initial and Final Consonant Blends

In the two lessons on page 113, we use the cumulative blending approach, where the student is required to identify the initial consonant and then blend it onto the medial vowel to form what's called a bigram. In a bigram, the initial consonant of a CVC word is blended with the vowel—for example, /s/ + /i/ = /si/. Finally this bigram is blended into the final consonant (/si/ + /p/ = /sip/).

Students build and blend words using manipulatives.

The same process is followed with *consonant blends,* whether in the initial or final position (*stop, post*). In words with *consonant digraphs*, we touch and say both letters without sounding them, then pronounce the sound they both represent, such as /ch/ or /th/ (*chop, both*).

## CUMULATIVE BLENDING GUIDED PRACTICE

### Build and Blend Dominos

Guide student practice of cumulative blending with this simple game that reinforces cumulative blending with CVC words.

Copy the game cards from the CD (Forms 4.7 through 4.11) onto cardstock and cut apart. To match the two domino cards and build a word, students take a beginning sound card, which contains an initial consonant and vowel, such as *hi*, and combine it with a final consonant card, such as *p*. The game is played in two stages.

### Stage 1

Follow the same steps as the lesson for cumulative blending with CVC words on page 113. Model the following procedure:

1. Pick up the first card; say the sounds of the initial consonant and then the vowel, blending these together (/h/, /i/ - /hi/).

2. Pick up the second card; say the sound of the final consonant (/p/).

3. Blend these together to pronounce the word (/hi/ + /p/ = /hip/).

Have students take turns to use this process to build a word.

### Stage 2

Once students no longer need to sound and blend the initial consonant and vowel, and this has become automatic, have them:

"Sometimes I see teachers asking children to imitate the teachers' rendition of stretching out the sounds. Imitation is a good first step, but instruction has to go further if children are to learn to apply blending independently ... The problem with final blending is that one has to keep three meaningless phonemes in short-term memory and then blend them. Three is hard enough, but think how hard it is to keep four or five meaningless phonemes in memory. It is virtually impossible for a beginning reader. In contrast to final blending, I strongly recommend successive blending (which I have sometimes called cumulative blending)."

(Beck, 2006, p. 49-50)

1. Say the sounds represented by the letters of the first card and then blend with the sound represented on the second (/hi/ + /p/ = /hip/).

2. Take turns flipping over two cards to see if they can make a word.

When students have sufficient practice with this format, integrate it into your word study center, where they can play it as a solitaire concentration game by turning over two cards from the two sets of cards (initial bigrams and final consonant).

*Example:*

**Beginning Sound Cards**

| mi | ha |

**Final Sound Cards**

| x | s |

BUILD AND BLEND DOMINO GAME: VOWEL *e*

**Beginning Cards**

| be | he | je |
| le | me | ne |
| pe | te | we |

**Ending Cards**

| b | d | g |
| g | ll | n |
| n | t | t |

**Build and Blend Domino Game**
Form 4.7 on the CD

Word-solving manipulatives and game formats are key to differentiating instruction.

## Blending From the Medial Vowel

When students are continually confusing the medial vowel, beginning with this element can address their difficulty. The lesson on page 114 also uses the cumulative blending approach, but the student is required to identify the medial vowel first and then blend it onto the initial consonant, finally blending this bigram (initial consonant + vowel) onto the final consonant in a CVC word (/i/, /si/, /sip/).

## Discriminating the Medial Vowel: Word Building

*Minimal pairs* are words that differ by one speech sound or phoneme, such as *cat* and *mat* (Moats, 2000). Much of the focus of word-making activities is substituting the onset or the rime, but low-progress readers often struggle with the discrimination of the medial sound, typically a vowel in one syllable words (*cat, cot*). Word-building activities that focus on substituting the medial vowel is an effective teaching practice and easily introduced into your current word-solving sequence. The lesson template on page 114 outlines the process. It is important that students have the opportunity to use tactile letters—tiles or magnetic letters—and not just write them on a whiteboard. The multimodal learning that takes place in word building (and sorting) is more likely to be processed and retained.

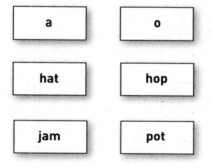

... instruction that focused on blending letter sounds to pronounce words and then changing just one letter and blending again helped students learn to decode words and attend to all the letters of the word in sequence. After several sessions with this kind of blending instruction, students became much less likely to guess the pronunciation of words and more likely to rely on letter by letter decoding. Older poor readers (mainly second and third graders) learned to decode rapidly with this approach, which is also called Word Building."

(BECK AND HAMILTON, 2000 IN O'CONNOR, 2007, P. 64)

## Word Sorting for Medial Vowels

A sample lesson of a word sort for medial short vowels can be found on page 115. An illustrated summary of this sequence for a guided word sort lesson can be found in the second section on vowel patterns on pages 122–123. Students can sort words by their medial vowels. Use a ready-made set of word cards or a reproducible word sort that students can cut apart and sort (see List of Resources on page 156).

The same format can be used when teaching initial and final consonants, as well as consonant blends and digraphs. Simply coach students to attend to the feature you are studying.

| s**a**t | s**i**t | s**e**t | | b**a**g | b**i**g | b**u**g |

As we teach students and listen for letter-sounds they know how to spell, an effective practice activity is to have them indicate where a target sound is in a word by using a physical cue, such as a marker or finger. The following activities help students discriminate sound-spellings in initial, medial, or final positions.

### Physical Cues to Indicate the Position of Sounds in Words

To help students discriminate the location of sounds within a word, use this process. Say the target word, such as *dog*. Then ask students to listen for a particular sound within the word, such as /o/, and to indicate when they hear it by turning their thumb to the left for initial, pointing the thumb straight up for medial, or turning the thumb to the right for final. Say the word again slowly; students point their thumb in the appropriate direction when they hear the target sound.

### Recording Sound-Spellings

You can also provide students with cards or Forms 4.13–4.15 on the CD for working with initial, medial, and final sounds, and have them record the letter-sounds they hear. Students can write the letter of the target sound in the box that corresponds with its position in the word. To modify this activity, students can place a counter or bingo chip on the line to indicate the position of the sound/letter in the word. See the sample lesson on hearing and recording sounds in sequence on page 117.

**Sounds in Sequence: Initial and Final Sounds**
Form 4.13 on the CD

This form focuses on recording initial and final sounds.

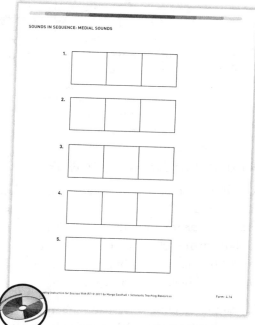

**Sounds in Sequence: Medial Sounds**
Form 4.14 on the CD

This form focuses on discriminating medial vowels.

## Sample Lesson: Cumulative Blending With CVC Words

| Teacher | Students |
|---|---|
| 1. Point to the first letter in the word. Ask students to touch and say the first phoneme. Say: *What's the letter? What's the sound?*<br><br>`mop` | touch the first letter in the word and state the letter name, then the sound it represents, e.g., /m/ |
| 2. Point to the second letter and ask students to do the same. Say: *What's the letter? What's the sound?*<br><br>*Now blend these sounds together.*<br><br>`mop` | touch the medial letter in the word, say it, and pronounce its sound<br><br>blend the first letter and medial vowel together, e. g., /mo/ |
| 3. Point to the final letter. Say: *What sound does this letter stand for?*<br><br>`mop`<br><br>*Now blend the sounds. (/mo/ + /p/) What's the word?* | touch the final letter and pronounce its sound, e.g., /p/<br><br><br><br>blend the sounds, e.g., /mo/ + /p/ = mop. Say the word, e.g., *mop.* |

## Sample Lesson: Cumulative Blending With Initial Consonant Blends

| Teacher | Students |
|---|---|
| 1. Point to the first consonant and say: *What's the letter? What's the sound?*<br><br>`plan` | touch the first letter in the word and state the letter name and sound it represents, e.g., /p/ |
| 2. Point to the second consonant and say: *What's the letter? What's the sound?*<br><br>`plan`<br><br>Then say: *Blend these sounds together.* | touch the second consonant in the word and state the letter name and the sound it represents, e.g., /l/<br><br>blend the consonants together, e.g., /pl/ |
| 3. Point to the medial vowel and say: *What's the letter? What's the sound?*<br><br>`plan`<br><br>Then say: *Blend these sounds together.* | touch the medial vowel in the word and pronounce its sound, e.g., /a/<br><br><br><br>blend the consonants and medial vowel together, e.g., /pla/ |
| 4. Point to the final letter and say: *What sound does this letter stand for?* Then say: *Now blend the sounds.*<br><br>`plan`<br><br>*What's the word?* | touch the final letter and pronounce its sound, e.g., /n/<br>blend the sounds, e.g., /pla/ + /n/<br><br><br><br>say the word, e.g., *plan.* |

## Sample Lesson: Blending From the Medial Vowel

| Teacher | Students |
|---------|----------|
| 1. Point to the medial vowel in the word and ask student to touch it. Say: *What's the letter? What's the sound?*<br><br>bit | touch the medial vowel in the word and state the letter name and the sound it represents, e.g. /i/ |
| 2. Point to the first letter and say: *What's the letter? What's the sound?*<br>*Blend these sounds together.*<br><br>bit | touch the first letter in the word and pronounce its sound, e.g. /b/<br><br>blend the first letter and medial vowel together, e.g. /bi/ |
| 3. Point to the final letter and say: *What sound does this letter stand for? Now blend the sounds.*<br><br>bit<br><br>*What's the word?* | touch the final letter and pronounce its sound, e.g., /t/<br><br><br><br>blend the sounds, e.g., /bi/ + /t/ = bit. |

## Sample Lesson: Word Building With Medial Vowels

| Teacher | Students |
|---------|----------|
| 1. **Demonstrate** Say:<br>*I'll show you how to build a word.*<br>Build a simple CVC word with the tiles, thinking aloud as you do and saying the word.   c  a  t | build the word using the teacher's model as a guide |
| 2. **Guide** Prompt students to build new words by substituting the medial vowel. Say:<br>*Now, let's build a word together.*<br>*Put the letter c in the beginning*<br>*Put o in the middle. Put t at the end.*<br>*What word did you make?*<br>*Change the o to u.*<br>*What word is it now?*<br>*Where did you hear the change? At the beginning, middle, or end of the word? Thumbs to the left if it's the first sound, straight up if it's the middle sound, or to the right if it's the last sound.*<br>Continue to create 4–6 new words and substitute medial vowels. | • pronounce the word<br>• substitute the medial vowel<br>• identify where the change occurred<br>• substitute the initial or final letter to build new word |
| 3. **Provide Corrective Feedback**<br>Make the correct word directly under their word, and say:<br>*Let me show you the word.*<br>*Check it with your eyes, finger, and mouth. What's the word?* | run their finger under the word the teacher has made and pronounce the word. Next they build the word from their letters. |

## Sample Lesson: Word Sorting for Medial Vowels

| Teacher | Students |
|---|---|
| **1. Word Walk**<br><br>Show each word card to students as you read them and then ask them to read the word with you.<br><br>My turn: *sat*. Your turn: [students] *sat*<br><br>When you have read all the words, review by reading through them together.<br><br>*Let's read these words together.*<br><br>• Ask students to explain the meaning if a word is unfamiliar.<br><br>• Invite students to share where they have heard or read the word before and/or use in a sentence.<br><br>**Predict Possible Categories**<br><br>Prompt students to identify possible categories for these words:<br><br>*What did you notice about the words? How are some alike? How are they different? Make a prediction about our sort today. Tell your partner what you think the categories will be (sounds and/or letter sequences)* | look at the word cards and listen to the words as they are read<br><br>read the words<br><br>explain the meaning of the words<br><br>share where they have heard or read the word before<br><br>use the word in an oral sentence<br><br>notice how some words are alike or different in sound and spelling<br><br>make a prediction on how these words could be grouped together<br><br>share what they have in common with a partner |
| **2. Notice and Name**<br><br>Introduce the key words:<br><br>*Today we are working on reading and spelling words with two different vowels. Let's look at our key words. Can you see what is different? Look inside the word to tell them apart* [sat—sit].<br><br>*Stretch the word sat with me so we can hear the vowel sounds:* sat, s-a-t, sat; *The vowel we hear in sat is /a/. Now let's stretch the word sit, s-i-t, sit. The vowel we hear in sit is /i/.*<br><br>Model the sort:<br><br>Sort the first few word cards as you think aloud where they belong. Read and compare the spelling and sound of each word to the key word. Segment and blend the words to scaffold discrimination of the medial vowel as necessary. Say:<br><br>*I will look at the spelling and listen for the sound of each of these words.*<br>[hold up word card for win]<br><br>*Where does this word belong? I will compare it to the key words to find out:* win-sat; win-sit. Win *belongs with* sit [place the word card under sit] *because I see the letter* i *and hear the short vowel /i/ sound in both words.*<br><br>[Repeat with two more words for each vowel.]<br><br>Pass out the rest of the word cards so that each student has two or three, or turn them facedown for students to pick up and place under the key word headings. Prompt students to identify possible categories for their words before sorting them.<br><br>*What do you notice about the spelling and sound of your words? How might you sort your words? Think about what group they belong to and why. Turn and tell your partner what you notice.* | scan the word for the vowel<br><br>compare words with different medial vowels and discriminate the vowel sound<br><br>state what they notice about the spellings of key words and how this affects the vowel sound<br><br>segment and blend to read the words<br><br>observe the sorting process<br><br>compare and contrast words to determine which key word has the same pattern<br><br>group words by a common medial vowel<br><br>read their word cards and examine them for the medial vowel.<br><br>identify possible categories<br><br>tell their partner what they noticed about their words. |

| Teacher | Students |
|---|---|
| **3. Sort, Check and Correct**<br><br>Prompt students to take turns reading and placing their word cards under the category headings.<br><br>*Show me where the rest of the words go. Remember to compare your words with our key words to see where they belong.*<br><br>If a word card is misplaced by the student:<br><br>1) Read and point to the column, saying *One of these does not fit. See if you can identify which one it is, or Do all these words [sound alike in the middle]?*<br><br>2) Indicate the name of the key word and its position to give the student the opportunity to self-correct, e.g. *map*—word number three.<br><br>If more support is needed, provide additional modeling as you place the word in the correct category:<br><br>*Where does this word go? Let's check:* map-sat, ran-sit. Map *belongs with* sat<br><br>sit    sat<br>pig    bag<br>map    can | take turns reading their word cards and then the key word headings, compare what is the same and different about them<br><br>place the word cards under the key headings in columns on the table<br><br>self-correct |
| **4. Compare and Share**<br><br>When all the cards have been sorted, read the words in each column together and ask:<br><br>*What did you discover about the words in this column? What is the same about them? How are they different from the words in this column? What might you call this group of words? Turn and tell your partner what you discovered about this group of words.* | turn and talk—describe how words in each column are similar to each other and different from words in the other columns |
| **5. Two New: Read and Write New Words**<br><br>Present new words for students to read that require discriminating the medial vowel.<br><br>*I will show you a new word to read. Look for the vowel and use the sound [it stands for] to say the word.*<br><br>Give students a five-finger countdown, and cue them to say the word in unison.<br><br>*What's the word?*<br><br>Dictate words where the medial vowel changes each time.<br><br>*I will say a word for you to spell on your whiteboard. Listen for the vowel sound. Remember to use the vowel you hear to spell the word.*<br><br>*Check it. Touch and say each letter.* | generalize recognition of the medial vowels to decode and spell new words |

## Sample Lesson: Hearing and Recording Sounds in Sequence: Initial and Final Sounds; Medial Sounds

| Teacher | Students |
|---|---|
| 1. Distribute copies of the Sounds in Sequence form (Forms 4.12–4.14 on the CD) with two (initial and final sounds), three (medial vowels), or four (consonant blends and digraphs) sound boxes, depending on your teaching points | |
| 2. Model the steps:<br>  1. Say the sound. (/a/)<br>  2. Say the word. (sat)<br>  3. Tell students to listen for the sound at the beginning/middle/end of the word and indicate the position of the sound in the word with their thumb:<br>    first position: turn to left<br>    final position: turn to right<br>    middle position: straight up<br>  4. Record the letter that represents this sound on the form in the first/last/middle box<br><br>      s  a  t<br><br>      j  a  m<br><br>      p  a  n<br><br>/s/, sat /m/, jam /a/, pan<br>Have students repeat each process with you using the *same* words. | observe and practice the process<br><br>say the sound<br><br>say the word<br><br>discriminate the position of the sound in the word and the letter that represents this sound |
| 3. Present new words with familiar letter-sound correspondences. Repeat each step you have modeled and cue students to say the sound and the word, and indicate the position with their thumb before they record the letter. Say:<br>*I'm going to say a sound and a word with that sound. Tell me if you hear the sound at the beginning, middle, or end of the word.* | show the position of the sound/letter with their thumb |
| 4. Check and correct.<br>Review each exercise and provide corrective feedback. If a student records the letter in the incorrect position, repeat the steps with him or her and have the student write the letter in the correct box in a new section of the form. | write the letter in the sound box corresponding to the position of the sound in the word. |

## Vowel Pairs, Rimes, and Other Spelling Patterns

In this section we continue to the next level of complexity in the progression of phonics knowledge, recognizing and using commonly occurring vowel pairs, rimes, and other spelling patterns to decode new words.

Word families, or rimes, are often taught alongside letter-sound relationships in phonics programs. But instruction does not stop at learning and comparing families of words that sound alike. Commonly occurring letter combinations or pairs (such as *-or*, *-ee*) comprise the majority of phonics elements taught throughout the primary grades. This is particularly important for low-progress readers at all grade levels who do not always transfer letter pairs from word families to new words that don't have the same ending sound or to multisyllabic words with the same pattern. For example, they don't use the *ar* in *car* to read the new word *farmer*. Beyond word families, we use words that contain high-use letter patterns within sets of non-rhyming words in our lessons.

Demonstrate how to solve words using familiar parts and challenge students to solve new words using what they know.

## Overview of the Lessons

The following lessons offer students opportunities to manipulate letters, segment words and blend sounds, sort words based on vowel patterns, and explain their thinking. These activities consolidate and extend students' ability to do the following:

- Compare and contrast the features of words using concrete materials (e.g., short and long vowel patterns)
- Apply higher-level skills of comparing and contrasting in a scaffolded context
- Develop the strategic thinking required to solve new and complex words
- Verbalize word-solving processes
- Write to reinforce letter-sound relationships and pattern recognition
- Interact with peers in collaborative tasks for increased engagement

# Guided Word Sort Lessons

In order to develop the ability to recognize patterns that children must have to decode successfully, I have designed two guided word sort lesson sequences, one for grade-level readers and one for low-progress readers. Sorting words according to their vowel pair, rime, or other spelling pattern provides interactive learning in both of these lessons. The power of word sorting is that students are actively engaged in verbalizing what they notice about words and their features, and they use their observations to identify categories of words organized by a common feature. This stands in stark contrast to traditional, passive phonics instruction, with a predominance of teacher talk and minimal student interaction. With word sort lessons, students are the ones doing the thinking and learning.

For each lesson sequence, you will find a Summary of the Steps, followed by a two-column sample lesson that describes the interaction between the teacher and students. I have also provided an at-a-glance Lesson Guide with teacher prompts for each step that can be copied onto cardstock and kept on hand at the teacher station for easy reference (see Forms 4.23 and 4.25 on the CD).

Each guided word sort lesson guides students through the following processes:

- Analyzing the sequence of sound-spelling relationships in a key word that represents the target letter pattern
- Sounding and blending sequences of letter patterns
- Using familiar patterns to read new words, or decoding by analogy strategy

It is essential that word sorting go well beyond cutting out words and pasting them under key words with the same pattern. It must include a discussion of sound-spelling relationships, letter sequences, and most important, generalizations for the target pattern (e.g., silent *e* may indicate a long vowel sound; *ow* can spell different sounds, but the long *o* is the most common). Without this discussion, the activity reverts to merely training rote memory to decode and spell a finite set of words. While memorizing irregularly spelled high-frequency words is necessary, there are too many decodable words—80,000 by the end of third grade—for students to commit each to memory (Juel & Minden-Cupp, 2000).

## How Many Patterns Per Week?

Tier 1 students may learn two to four new patterns each week, depending on their grade level and complexity of the vowel patterns. Low-progress readers in Tier 2 may be introduced to two or three new patterns a week. Tier 3 students will require more practice and review, with one or two new patterns being compared to one previously taught. Using target patterns in reading and writing tasks further helps to consolidate recognition and transfer. The principle of ongoing monitoring and adjusting the pace of instruction applies to the rate new patterns are introduced and to the number of practice opportunities provided. Your informal assessments and observations during the lessons and student

"Sorting is an engaging activity that helps students look closely at features of letters or words and make connections between them ... making comparisons also helps them internalize patterns and features to form categories that give them ready access to examples rather than trying to apply principles as abstract and isolated as 'rules.'"

(Pinnell & Fountas, 2009, p. 243)

"Sorting words helps children attend more closely to different features in words and to generalize about letter-sound relationships."

(Taberski, 2000, p. 117)

practice will determine the number of vowel patterns. Remember, some are more complex than others and will take longer for students to master.

## PREPARING THE WORD SORTS

### Teacher Materials

You will need 3" x 5" cards of each word for the demonstration in the input lesson, as most commercially available sorts (see end of chapter) are too small for this purpose. Either enlarge them and copy onto cardstock, or print on index cards and store in labeled envelopes, bags, or plastic sleeves in a binder.

### Student Materials

- **Photocopies:** If you are using commercially available reproducible word sorts, photocopy words for students to cut apart and store in plastic bags stapled to their spiral notebooks, in 5" x 7" envelopes labeled with their names, or in a plastic bag along with their notebook in a two-pocket folder. Students paste their words on paper or in their notebooks at the end of the rotation. (For more on student notebooks, see page 141).

  You may wish to use a different colored paper for each group's words if students work alongside students from other groups, to avoid mixed sets. To avoid mix-ups among group members, have each student draw a different-colored squiggle mark across the back of their photocopy before they cut it apart. Some teachers give each child a number that they print on the back of each word or have them jot their initials or first name.

- **Cardstock:** If you want permanent copies of the word cards that are given out and then collected at the end of the rotation, copy words onto cardstock and have students or volunteers cut apart the word cards. Store these in labeled plastic bags ready to be distributed to the next group.

### Tips

- Keep a master copy of the sorts in a three-ring notebook if you are using photocopies to speed up the process.
- A quick way to create your own word sorts is to type the list of words, highlight the list in Microsoft Word, and go to the Table toolbar. Select Convert, and then Text to Table. You can even change the size and font so each student has space to write notes about the word during instruction, such as the meaning, part of speech, and a synonym or antonym.
- Follow these instructions if you wish to prepare your own word sorts with the Cut and Sort form (Form 4.21 on the CD): In the boxes at the top of the form, select key words for the category headings. Underline the key words, such as *game*, so they will be easily identifiable for students when they come to cut them apart.

## WORD SORT MATS

You may choose to provide file folders or sheets of cardstock ruled into two columns on one side and three on the other to be used as sorting mats. These can be stored

*Differentiating Reading Instruction for Success With RTI* © 2011 by Margo Southall • Scholastic Teaching Resources

in folders with students' notebooks or inside a plastic sleeve in a 3-ring binder.

## PROGRAMMING THE SORTS

You may add several picture cards so that students do not over-rely on visual cues by only attending to letter sequences. Picture cards require students to use auditory discrimination to identify the pattern, which is important in linking phonemic awareness to spelling.

## ADJUSTING THE LEVEL OF CHALLENGE

You can adjust the level of challenge by following these guidelines:

### Easier

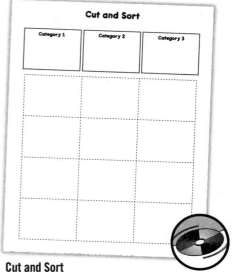

**Cut and Sort**
Form 4.21 on the CD

- Include familiar words and concepts; provide only one new category to compare to familiar pattern.

- Have students sort the known and easier words first, then the less familiar and more complex words.

- Provide words that contain obvious contrasts—for example, *pot* and *cat*.

### Harder

- Provide more categories; increase the number of words.

- Increase the complexity of the words, including words with digraphs, blends, and more than one syllable.

- Add an "oddballs" category—exceptions such as *said* in a sort for long-*a* patterns. Irregular sight words can often be used as the oddball or out-of-sorts words to check if students are truly attending to the sound-spelling relationship and not just the sequence of letters. A question mark is often used as the category heading

| back | cake | mail | ? |
|------|------|------|---|
| snack | flake | trail | said |
| backpack | rattlesnake | pigtail | what |

## HOME COMMUNICATION

To give a purpose for writing about their word-solving discoveries, have students do the following activities:

1. Write a note to parents that includes words from the current list. The Show What I Know independent practice task card on Form 4.39 is an example of this.

2. Explain the gist of the sort—the generalization—to parents. For example: "The words with *e* at the end had a long-vowel sound; the words ending in a consonant had a short-vowel sound."

3. Generate a list of words that fit the pattern.

# Teaching Letter Pairs, Rimes, and Spelling Patterns to On-Level Readers: **Five-Step Guided Word Sort**

The Five-Step Guided Word Sort lesson is designed for on-grade and above-grade students. If you are using a phonics program, the letter patterns will be introduced there, and the word sorting will supplement that work. Here's an overview of the Five-Step Guided Word Sort lesson.

## MATERIALS

- Word cards with key words: a set of word cards for each student with 2–4 key words and 10–20 words containing target letter patterns

- Two word cards with a "new" word for each pattern for students to decode after sorting

Step 1: Word Walk

Step 2: Notice and Name

## SUMMARY OF THE STEPS

### STEP ❶ Word Walk

- Show each word card to students as you read the word; then ask students to read the word with you.

- Reread all the word cards together.

- Discuss the meaning of any unfamiliar words or words that are useful for vocabulary building.

- Invite students to predict possible categories for the words based on what they notice about their features, similarities, and differences. Have them share their predictions with a partner. *What did you notice about the words? How are some alike? How are they different? Make a prediction about our sort today. Tell your partner what you think the pattern will be.*

### STEP ❷ Notice and Name

- Introduce each key word.

- Name the target pattern and show its pattern.

- Have students stretch the word with you so they can hear what the pattern sounds like.

- Compare and contrast the key words, discussing their sounds and spelling patterns.

- Model sorting the first two or three words for each pattern, thinking aloud about why you placed them under the particular key word.

- Distribute the rest of the word cards among the students.

- Invite students to identify possible categories before sorting them.

### STEP ❸ Sort, Check, and Correct

- Have students take turns reading and placing their word cards under the key word headings.

- If a card is placed in error, point to the column it is in and say: *One of these does not fit. Can you tell which one?* Alternatively, indicate the name of the key word and position of the word that does not belong to give the student the opportunity to self-correct—e.g., *lake* – word number 2.

- If the student cannot identify the error, think aloud as you put the word under the appropriate key word.

### STEP ❹ Compare and Share

- Ask students to discuss what they discovered about the words in each column, prompting them to consider how they are similar to each other and different from the words in the other column or columns.

- Encourage partners to talk to each other about their discoveries.

### STEP ❺ Two New: Read and Write New Words

- Present one new word with each pattern for students to read.

- Dictate one new word with each pattern for students to write.

**Independent Practice Task**
Give each student a set of the word cards with the target letter patterns. They will use this set of cards in their independent practice tasks.

Step 3: Sort, Check, and Correct

Step 4: Compare and Share

Step 5: Two New: Read and Write New Words

# FIVE-STEP GUIDED WORD SORT SAMPLE LESSON

**Focus:** Long-*a* Spelled Vowel-Consonant-*e*

**Review:** Short-*a* spelled Consonant-Vowel-Consonant (-*ag*, -*ack*, -*an*, -*and*, -*ap*, -*ast*)

**New Pattern:** Long-*a* spelled Vowel-Consonant-*e* (-*ame*, -*ake*, -*ade*, -*ave*)

**Key Words:** *cat*, *cake*

**Words to Sort:** *bag*, *back*, *ran*, *hand*, *map*, *fast*, *sad*; *same*, *game*, *lake*, *made*, *save*, *wave*

| Teacher | Students |
|---|---|
| **1. Word Walk**<br>Show each word card to students as you read them and then ask them to read the word with you.<br>*My turn:* cake. *Your turn:* [students] cake<br>When you have read all the words, review by reading through them together<br>*Let's read these words together.*<br>• Ask students to explain the meaning if a word is unfamiliar or is useful for vocabulary building<br>• Invite students to share where they have heard or read the word before and/or use in a sentence<br>**Predict Possible Categories**<br>Prompt students to identify possible categories for these words:<br>*What did you notice about the words? How are some alike? How are they different? Make a prediction about our sort today. Tell your partner what you think the patterns will be.* (e.g. sounds and/or letter sequences) | Read the words.<br>Explain the meaning of the words.<br>Share where they have heard or read the word before.<br>Use the word in an oral sentence.<br>Notice how some words are alike or different in sound and spelling.<br>Make a prediction on how these words could be grouped together. Share what they have in common with a partner. |
| **2. Notice and Name**<br>Introduce the key words:<br>*Today we are working on reading and spelling two vowel patterns. The a we hear in our key word* cat *has a short-a sound spelled a-t. The a we hear in our key word* cake *has a long-a sound /ake/ spelled –a-k-e. Stretch the words with me so we can hear the vowel sounds: c-a-t; c-a-k*<br>*What do you notice about the spelling of the words* cat *and* cake*?* [Wait time; help students generalize the pattern.] *When you see the final* e, *the vowel in the middle says its name.*<br>Model the sort:<br>Sort the first few word cards as you think aloud where they belong. Read and compare each word to the key word headings as you move it underneath them, comparing the sound and spelling to the key word:<br>*I will listen for the sound and look at the spelling of each of these words.* [hold up word card for *game*]<br>*Where does this word belong? I will compare it to both the key words to find out:* game-cat, game-cake. Game *belongs with* cake [place the word card under *lake*] *because I hear the long-a sound in both words.*<br>*I put the word card for* game *under* cake *because I hear the long vowel sound in both words and I see a spelling pattern with final* e.<br>[Repeat with two or three more words.]<br>Pass out the rest of the word cards so that each student has two or three, or turn them facedown for students to pick up and place under the key word headings. Prompt students to identify possible categories for their words before sorting them.<br>*What do you notice about the sound and spelling of your words? How might you sort your words? Think about what group they belong to and why. Turn and tell your partner what you notice.* | State what they notice about the spellings of the key words and how this affects the vowel sound.<br><br>Observe the sorting process.<br><br><br>Compare and contrast words to determine which key word has the same pattern.<br><br>Group words by a common vowel pattern.<br><br>Read their word cards and examine them for the pattern(s).<br><br>Identify possible categories.<br><br>Tell their partner what they noticed about their words. |

*Differentiating Reading Instruction for Success With RTI* © 2011 by Margo Southall • Scholastic Teaching Resources

| Teacher | Students |
|---|---|
| **3. Sort, Check, and Correct**<br>Prompt students to take turns reading and placing their word cards under the category headings.<br>*Show me where the rest of the words go. Remember to compare your words with our key words to see where they belong.*<br>If a word card is misplaced by the student:<br>1) Read and point to the column, saying *One of these does not fit. See if you can identify which one it is,* or *Do all these words [sound alike in the middle]?*<br>2) Indicate the name of the key word and its position to give the student the opportunity to self-correct, e.g., *lake—word number 2.*<br>If more support is needed, provide additional modeling as you place the word in the correct category:<br>*Where does this word go? Let's check:* ran-cat, ran-cake. *Ran belongs with* cat. | Take turns reading their word cards and then the key word headings, compare what is the same and different about them.<br><br>Place the word cards under the key headings in columns on the table.<br><br>Self-correct. |
| **4. Compare and Share**<br>When all the cards have been sorted, read the words in each column together and ask:<br>*What did you discover about the words in this column? What is the same about them? How are they different from the words in this column? What might you call this group of words? Turn and tell your partner what you discovered about this group of words.* | Turn and Talk – describe how words in each column are similar to each other and different from words in the other columns. |
| **5. Two New: Read and Write New Words**<br>Present a new word to read for each pattern.<br>*I will show you a new word to read. Remember to look for a final* e, *to see if the vowel says its name.*<br>Give students a five-finger countdown, and then cue them to say the word in unison:<br>*What's the word?*<br>Dictate a word with each pattern:<br>*I will say a word for you to spell on your whiteboard. Listen for the pattern that will help you. Remember to use a final* e *when you hear the vowel say its name.*<br><br>**Get Ready for Independent Practice/Next Lesson**<br>Provide each student with a set of word cards for their baggie to use for the practice tasks that follow<br><br>cat · bag · back · ran · hand · map<br>cake · save · gave · lake · make · wave | Generalize the pattern to decode and spell new words.<br><br><br><br>Put their word cards in their baggie ready for the Extending the Lesson Activities and Independent Practice tasks. |

# Teaching Letter Pairs, Rimes and Spelling Patterns to Low-Progress Readers: Six-Step Explicit Guided Word Sort

This lesson includes the steps that research has demonstrated make the difference in whether students are able to recall and use the letter pairs and patterns as they are taught (O'Connor, 2007; Gaskins 2005; Walpole & McKenna, 2009). When compared to the typical word sort lesson, here you will find an additional step at the beginning in which students analyze the sequence of sounds and letters (auditory-to-print connection) within a structured, metacognitive dialogue.

This step includes segmenting and blending the key words so students can store the pattern in their phonological and visual memory, an essential step if we want them to use the patterns to read and spell new words. It is especially powerful for low-progress readers who are not retaining recognition of letter sequences and patterns sufficiently to achieve an adequate rate of progress. This is evident when they hesitate and stumble over words containing the word patterns you have been teaching. They need to analyze one key word for each pattern thoroughly so they can recognize that same pattern in a new word.

Typically only one or two new patterns are introduced at a time in lessons for low-progress readers, especially with more challenging patterns or letter pairs that take longer to acquire, such as *r*-controlled vowels (e.g., *ar, ir*), vowel digraphs (e.g., *ee, ea*), and diphthongs (e.g., *ow, au, ou*).

Here's an overview of the Six-Step Explicit Guided Word Sort lesson.

## MATERIALS
- Whiteboard
- Sets of word cards for each student with two or three key words and 6–15 words containing target patterns
- Word cards with a new word for each pattern for students to decode after sorting

## SUMMARY OF STEPS

### STEP ❶ Sound and Spell

*Sound*
- Say the word; have students repeat it. (*game*)
- Stretch out the word; have students do the same. (*g-aaa-mmm*)
- Count the sounds in the word; students hold up a finger for each sound they hear. (3)

*Spell*
- Ask students what letter they think represents each sound.
- Stretch the word and record the related letter(s) for each sound on the whiteboard. (*g, a, m*)
- State that these letters represent the sounds we hear, but the word is spelled : *g-a-m-e*, pointing out the *e* at the end.

- Count the letters (4) and determine if they match the number of sounds (3); discuss. (silent *e*)
- Identify the vowel pattern and underline it. (underline -*ame*)
- Have students state the vowel pattern: *The vowel pattern is* -ame.
- Review the sound and spelling of the pattern.

   ✳ **Students segment and blend the key word in order to store the pattern in their phonological and visual memory.**

## STEP ❷ Word Walk
- Show students a word card with the target letter pattern on it.
- Read the word; then ask students to read the word to you.
- Repeat for all word cards with the first target pattern.
- Review all the word cards with the first target pattern by reading them together.
- Repeat for words with the second target pattern.

## STEP ❸ Notice and Name
- Place the two key word cards on the table.
- Mix the two sets of cards.
- Sort the first three or four cards, thinking aloud about why you are placing each one under its key word.
- Pass out the remaining word cards to students; each student should have two or three cards.

## STEP ❹ Sort, Check, and Correct
- Have students take turns reading and placing their word cards under the key word headings.
- If a card is placed in error, point to the column and say: *One of these does not fit. Can you tell which one?* or *Do all these words look and/or sound alike?* Alternatively, indicate the name of the key word and position of the word that does not belong to give the student the opportunity to self-correct—e.g., *cave*—word number 3.
- If student cannot identify the error, think aloud as you put the word under the appropriate key word.

## STEP ❺ Compare and Share
- Ask students to discuss what they discovered about the words in each column, prompting them to consider how they are similar to each other and different from words in the other column.
- Encourage partners to talk to each other about their discoveries.

## STEP ❻ Two New: Read and Write New Words
- Present one new word with each pattern for students to read.
- Dictate one new word with each pattern for students to write.

**Independent Practice Task**
Give each student a set of the word cards with the target letter patterns. They will use this set of cards in their independent practice tasks.

   ✳ *Note:* **Have low-progress readers sort words twice with the teacher before sorting independently or with partner.**

# SIX-STEP EXPLICIT GUIDED WORD SORT SAMPLE LESSON

**Focus:** Long-*a* Spelled Vowel-Consonant-*e*

**Review Pattern:** Long-*a* spelled Vowel-Consonant-*e*, rime -*ake*

**New Patterns:** Long-*a* (VCe), rimes -*ame*, -*ace*

**Key Words:** *make, game, race*

**Words to Sort:** *cake, lake, rake, shake, wake, same, came, name, tame, blame, face, lace, space, place, trace*

| Teacher | Students |
|---|---|
| **1. Sound and Spell**<br>**Introduce the Key Words**<br>**Sound**<br>*Let's learn two new patterns today that are in lots of words. First we will stretch our key words and listen for the sounds to help our reading brain remember the patterns when we spell.*<br>Say the first key word.<br>Ask students to repeat it: *My turn—*game. *Your turn—*game.<br>Model how to stretch the word: */g/ /a/ /m/*<br>Support students by stretching the word slowly together.<br>Ask students to count the sounds they hear and hold up one finger for each sound.<br>*I hear three sounds in* game.<br><br>**Spell**<br>Ask students to dictate the letters they would expect to see, stretching the word again for each sound and recording the letter(s) on the whiteboard.<br>*Let's hook the sounds to the letters that spell them. Then our reading brain will recognize the patterns when we read/see them in words we read.*<br>Count the letters with students to see whether the number of sounds matches the number of letters. In CVC words there will be a 1:1 correspondence. In words with final e and vowel digraphs, there will be a mismatch of the number of sounds and letters:<br>*We hear three sounds, but we see four letters. Why?*<br>*It's because the long-a is spelled with two vowels, a and e.*<br>*We call this a final e pattern. When you see the final* e, *the vowel says its name* (Vowel-Consonant-e pattern*)*<br>[CVC words]: *I hear three sounds and I see three letters because each sound is spelled with one letter.*<br>Identify the vowel pattern, underline it, and have students state it.<br>*The vowel pattern is -*ame. *What's the pattern? -*ame<br>Review the spelling and sound of the pattern:<br>*What letters stand for the /ame/ sound? –* a-m-e<br>*What sound do the letters* a-m-e *stand for? /ame/*<br><br>Repeat with the key word *race* for –*ace.* | Say the word.<br>Listen for the sounds in the word.<br>Stretch the word; say the sounds in sequence; show the number of sounds they hear by holding up that number of fingers.<br><br><br><br><br>Dictate the spelling of the word.<br><br><br><br><br>Count the number of letters in the word.<br>Check to see if the number of sounds matches the number of letters.<br>Say why the number of letters match or do not match and offer an explanation why.<br><br>State the pattern.<br><br>Say the letters that spell the vowel pattern.<br>Say the sound the letters in the pattern stand for.<br><br><br><br><br><br><br>Repeat for the next key word. |

 *Differentiating Reading Instruction for Success With RTI* © 2011 by Margo Southall • Scholastic Teaching Resources

# SIX-STEP EXPLICIT GUIDED WORD SORT SAMPLE LESSON (continued)

| Teacher | Students |
|---|---|
| **2. Word Walk**<br>Show each word card to students as you read them and then ask them to read the word with you.<br>*My turn:* shake. *Your turn:* [students] shake.<br>When you have read all the words, review by reading through them together.<br><br>*Let's read these words together*<br>Ask them to explain their meaning if the word is unfamiliar or is useful for vocabulary building.<br>Invite students to share where they have heard or read the word before and/or use it in a sentence. | Explain the meaning of the words.<br><br>Read the words.<br><br>Share where they have heard or read the word before.<br>Use the word in an oral sentence. |
| **3. Notice and Name**<br>**Model the Sort**<br>Sort the first few word cards as you think aloud where they belong.<br>Read and compare each word to the key word headings as you move it underneath them, comparing the sound and spelling to the key word:<br>*Our key words are* make, game *and* race. *In the word* make, *the long-a sound is spelled* a-k-e. *In the word* game, *the long-a sound is spelled* a-m-e. *In* race, *the long-a sound is spelled* a-c-e.<br>*I will sort these word cards under the key words. First I will say the word, listen for the sound, and look at the spelling. Where does this word belong? I will compare it to the key words to find out.*<br><br>Place-make, place -game, place -race. *I put the word* place *under our key word* race (*put the word card under* race) *because it has the same spelling pattern. The long-a sound is spelled* a-c-e.<br><br>*Listen for the sound and look at the spelling of each of these words.*<br>*Where does this word belong? Point to the key word*<br><br>Pass out the rest of the word cards so that each student has two or three, or set them facedown for students to pick up and place under the key word headings. Prompt students to identify possible categories for their words before sorting them.<br>*What do you notice about the sound and spelling of your words? Turn and tell your partner what you notice.* | Observe the sorting process.<br>Notice how some words are alike or different.<br><br>Compare and contrast words to determine which key word has the same pattern.<br>State what they notice about the spellings of words.<br><br><br><br>Point to the key word containing the same pattern.<br><br>Read their word cards and examine them for the pattern(s).<br><br>Identify possible categories. Tell their partner what they noticed about their words. |
| **4. Sort, Check, and Correct**<br>Prompt students to take turns reading and placing their word cards under the key word headings.<br>*Show me where the rest of the words go. Remember to compare your words with our key words to see where they belong.*<br>If a word card is misplaced by the student:<br>1) Read and point to the column, saying, *One of these does not fit. See if you can find which one it is, or Do all these words sound and/or look alike?*<br>2) Indicate the name of the key word and its position to give the student the opportunity to self-correct:<br>*game—word number 3*<br><br>If more support is needed, provide additional modeling as you place the word in the correct category:<br>*Where does this word go? Let's check:* tame-make, tame-game, tame-race. | Take turns reading their word cards and then the key word headings, compare what is the same and different about them.<br>Group words by a common pattern; place the word cards under the key headings in columns on the table.<br><br><br>Self-correct. |

| Teacher | Students |
|---|---|
| **5. Compare and Share**<br>When all the cards have been sorted, ask:<br>*What did you discover about the words in this column? What is the same about them? How are they different from the words in this column? What might you call this group of words? Turn and tell your thinking partner what you discovered about this group of words.*<br>Students will say something like, *The words under __ all end in __ . The words under __ have the __ sound/pattern.* | Turn and Talk - describe how words in each column are similar to each other and different from words in the other columns. |
| **6. Two New: Read and Write New Words**<br>Present a new word with each pattern for students to read:<br>*I will show you a new word to read. Remember to look for the long vowel a pattern that will help you.*<br>Give students a five-finger countdown, and then cue them to say the word in unison:<br>*What's the word?*<br><br>Dictate a word with each pattern:<br>*I will say a word for you to spell on your whiteboard. Listen for the pattern you know and use it to spell the word. Remember, two letters stand for the long vowel sound in our patterns today.*<br><br>**Get Ready for Independent Practice/Next Lesson**<br>Provide students with a set of word cards for their baggie to use for the practice tasks that follow. | Generalize the pattern to decode and spell new words.<br><br>Put their word cards in their baggie ready for the Extending the Lesson Activities or Independent Practice task. |

# Extending the Lesson Activities

After we have introduced the vowel pair, rime, or spelling pattern with a guided word sort lesson, additional small-group sessions are provided during the instructional cycle to reinforce and extend the learning. These reading and writing tasks offer further practice with the target letter patterns. Extension activities include:

- **Word-Sorting Games:** These train students for automaticity in pattern recognition.

- **Multimodal Guided Practice Activities:** These activities provide fun and engaging practice with the target skills.

- **Training-for-Transfer Lessons and Games:** These require students to use familiar patterns to read and spell new and more complex words.

- **Writing Activities:** These support long-lasting learning and transfer to both reading and writing.

At the end of the lesson cycle, you'll assess students to see if they've mastered the pattern and are ready to move on, or if they need more practice (see assessment tools on pages 150–152).

## WORD-SORTING GAMES

Following the teacher guided word sort lesson, students can practice sorting their words with these two games, which build automaticity and fluency.

### Partner Sorting Game

Each partner takes turns sorting and reading the words while the other checks for accuracy. Students can gain a total of two points, one for sorting and one for reading the words correctly.

#### Materials

- 1 set of word sort cards with key words for each pattern (given to each student after word-sorting lesson)
- Photocopy of the completed sort for self-checking ("cheat sheet")
- Optional: word sort mat

#### Procedure

- Partner A sorts the words under the key words for the patterns.
- Partner B checks the word sort on the cheat sheet. If words are placed under the correct key word, partner A receives one point. If partner B can find any words that are incorrectly sorted by partner A, he or she receives a point.
- Partner A reads the words for each pattern.
- Partner B listens and checks if the words are correct. If partner A reads them accurately, he or she receives a point.
- Partners switch roles and repeat the process.
- The player with the most points at the end of the sorting wins.

Concentration can also be played with the word cards (Ganske, 2003).

### Group Speed Sort

The purpose of this game is to increase the fluency with which students visually scan words, identify the pattern, and assign a pronunciation. Students are timed or given a set time to sort the words. This can be a small-group or whole-class task, where students all sort their own words from their word sort bags. Ensure students have sorted these words at least once before doing a speed sort. Cue students to begin sorting all at the same time. Repeat the speed sort three times and have students note their own progress with each sort. Be sure to have them shuffle their cards or mix them up on the table each time. There are two options for this speed sort. In option A, students compete to sort their words the fastest—holding up their hand as soon as they finish, and the rest of the group has to stop sorting. In option B, you provide a set amount of time for them to sort, such as 20–30 seconds. Students should be holding fewer words each time they sort them as they become quicker at identifying patterns.

#### Materials

- Word sort for each student (stored in a plastic bag)
- Optional: word sort mat

### Option A: Competitive Timed Sort

**Procedure**

- Students put key words for the patterns across the top of their desk.
- Students hold cards, as with playing cards.
- Teacher begins timing and students begin sorting: *Ready, set, sort*.
- The first student to finish raises his or her hand. The rest of group puts up both hands so they can't sort while you check whether this student has sorted them correctly. If he or she has not, the sort continues. If he or she is correct, state the time to beat. *Who can beat __'s time of _?* Repeat the timed sort two more times.

### Option B: Less Competitive Alternative

**Procedure**

- Students put key words for the patterns across the top of their desk.
- Students hold cards, as with playing cards.
- Provide a set amount of time for students to sort their words.
- Students count the words they have left in their hands when time is up.
- Repeat. Students will see they have fewer words left in their hands, which tangibly reinforces their increased fluency. In this way, students only compete with themselves.

#### Modification

Students with fine motor difficulties complete this activity with a partner using the No-Peeking Sort procedure (see page 142).

## MULTIMODAL GUIDED PRACTICE ACTIVITIES

Incorporating multimodal activities helps engage all students. Choose those that you think will appeal to your students, and strive for variety.

### Sound Boxes (Clay, 1997; McCarthy, 2008)

Sound boxes consist of a series of connecting boxes; the number of boxes corresponds to the number of sounds in the word. Use them as a graphic representation of the match or mismatch of sounds and letters in a word as you teach phoneme detection, segmentation, and blending. Students say and stretch the sounds in the word, use their fingers to indicate how many sounds they hear, and draw that many boxes. Next they stretch the word again as they record the letters that represent the sounds. (See Hearing and Recording Sounds in Sequence on page 117 for a sample lesson using sound boxes; you'll find templates for this activity on Forms 4.13–4.15 on the CD.)

### Strategy Chants

Have students practice strategy statements from the strategy charts (see Forms 4.4–4.6 on the CD) by chanting them. For example:

*When I see a new word,*
*I say the chunks I know.*
*I blend the chunks together*
*And my word bank will grow.*

### Letter Signs and Actions

Assign specific motions for each letter and have students pronounce the letter's sound as they do the action. Students can do the motions in combination for blends and digraphs (right and left hand are used to form each letter-sound action or sign), and individually in sequence for CVC words. See Resources on page 156.

### Hearing and Recording Sounds in Sequence

Students use physical cues to indicate the position of sounds in words by turning their thumb to the left for initial, pointing the thumb straight up for medial, or turning the thumb to the right for final position. See sample lesson on page 117.

### Role-Play Strategy Puppets

Demonstrate the word-solving strategies of Sound and Say (Form 4.4 on the CD) with fish and snake puppets or stuffed toys; for instance, Lips the Fish gets his mouth ready for the sound, while Stretchy Snake segments and blends words. Model the chunking strategy with a monkey puppet, Chunky Monkey (Bunyi, 2010).

A Chunky Monkey puppet demonstrates the strategy.

### Letter Formation Sorts

Have students sort letter manipulatives by attribute on a T-chart. For example, students could sort letters into these categories: with tails and without tails; with circles and without circles; humps and no humps.

### Sound Sorts With Manipulatives

Have students sort picture cards or objects by their initial sounds.

### Sound Boxes (Clay, 1997; McCarthy, 2008)

Have students push a marker into the appropriate box as they articulate each of the phonemes in a word. (See Hearing and Recording Sounds in Sequence on page 117.)

### Build and Blend Dominoes

Students match cards with the initial consonant and vowel to the final consonant to form words (see page 109).

### Word Building

Guide students to manipulate tactile letters to form new words (see Word Building for Medial Vowels lesson on page 114).

### Picture and Word Sorting

Have students compare and contrast picture and word cards by sound, spelling, and meaning to determine the feature they have in common.

### Guided Practice During Reading

**Bookmarks** for the Think-Pinch-Share Routine (page 76) provide the language for each of the word-solving strategies: Sound and Say, Chunk the Word, Use What I Know, and Switch the Vowel (see Forms 4.4–4.6 on the CD).

**Sticky Flags:** Students mark the edge of the page where they applied a word-solving strategy, such as chunking, to a new word. This is shared with their partner in a turn-and-talk format, and/or with the rest of the group. Sticky flags are stored on a bookmark made of cardstock.

**Math manipulatives:** The transparent counters (commonly found in math resource catalogs) are used to locate and highlight parts of words, scan the word effectively, and blend sounds in sequence.

### Games

- **ABC Pick-Up:** Letters are printed on popsicle sticks. Students take a handful and scatter them on the table. Next they take turns picking up a stick, saying the beginning letter, the sound it represents, and a word that begins with that sound (see Southall, 2007).

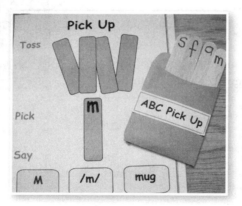

ABC Pick-Up Game

- Partner word sort activities such as the No-Peeking Buddy Sort on page 142.
- **Group Speed Sort Formats:** Students try to beat their own time or increase the number of words they can sort within a set amount of time (see page 131–132)
- **1-2-3—Show the Key!:** Students listen for the familiar chunk inside a single or multisyllabic word and hold up the appropriate key word card containing that chunk (see pages 138–139).
- **Onset-Rime Match-Ups:** Students find the matching onset rime cards and hold up the two cards to form the word (see page 139).

*Differentiating Reading Instruction for Success With RTI* © 2011 by Margo Southall • Scholastic Teaching Resources

## TRAINING-FOR-TRANSFER LESSONS AND GAMES

We want to train students to transfer their knowledge of the patterns they've studied to new words. The teaching point is to model and guide student practice in using familiar key words from the word-sorting lesson to read new words—what's known as the analogy strategy. The effectiveness of this approach to teaching the analogy strategy has been demonstrated by Clay (2005), Gaskins (2005), Pinnell and Fountas (2009) and many other researchers. With these training-for-transfer lessons and activities, students have the opportunity to practice the strategic actions of using what they know to read new words in connected text, and teachers have the opportunity to observe the level of student understanding and strategy use.

I meet with groups later in the week, after the guided word sort lesson, and, using a text containing words with our target patterns, I model the analogy strategy to decode a few words before inviting students to do the same. (You'll find a full description of this type of lesson in *Differentiated Small-Group Reading Lessons*; I call it the I Can Use Words I Know Lesson. An abbreviated version is on page 136.) Alternatively, I do the I Can Read and Write New Words Lesson (see page 138), in which students use analogy to read and write new words containing our target patterns, based upon the work of Irene Gaskins (2005) and Walpole and McKenna (2009). I've included student forms for both lessons—Forms 4.26 and 4.27 on the CD. Following these two lesson templates you will find writing tasks in which students apply the spellings of the vowel patterns, and games in which students are required to demonstrate their strategy use during interaction with their peers.

### Lesson Templates

- I Can Use Words I Know (Form 4.26 on the CD)
- I Can Read and Write New Words (Form 4.27 on the CD)

### Game Formats

- Rime Time Chart Practice (page 138)
- 1-2-3 – Show the Key! (page 138)
- Onset-Rime Match Ups (page 139)

### I Can Use Words I Know

Students practice the analogy strategy by using key words taught in the word-sorting lesson to decode a set of new words containing the same patterns.

### Materials

- Form 4.26 from the CD, with key words written in the boxes across the top

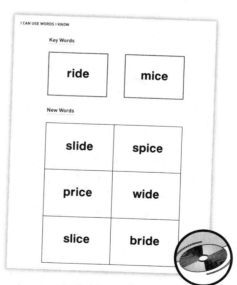

**I Can Use Words I Know**
Form 4.26 on the CD

**Procedure**

Students follow these steps:

- Read the key words and scan each for patterns they know.
- Touch and scan each of the new words for one of the patterns in the key words. They look for the vowel and the letters that follow.
- Use the analogy phrase to solve the new word:
  *I know [key word]; the pattern is __, so this word is ___.*

## Sample Lesson: I Can Use Words I Know

| Teacher | Students |
|---|---|
| **1. Demonstrate the Strategy With a Think-Aloud** <br><br> Display two key word cards with familiar patterns. Read them and ask students to read them together: <br><br> *We are going to use two of our key words for the patterns -et and -ot. Our words are* pet *and* pot. *We will use these words to read other words with the same patterns.* <br><br> **pet**      **pot** <br><br> Hold up a new word that contains one of these patterns. Do not say the word. <br><br> **trot** <br><br> Demonstrate how to use this pattern to decode by thinking aloud. Move the new word underneath both key words to check for a visual match and then place it under the key word containing the same pattern as you say: <br><br> *If I don't know a word, I look for the first spelling pattern (the vowel and what comes after it). I think about my key words. This word looks like our key word [pot]. I will use it to help me. I am thinking, what is the same about our key word and the new word? They both have the same pattern. The pattern is [-ot]. I will look at the rest of the word and blend the parts together.* <br><br> *I know [pot]. The pattern is -ot, so this word is [trot].* <br><br> **pet**      **pot** <br> **trot** <br><br> Have students repeat the last statement with you so they practice this metacognitive dialogue. | Read the key word cards. <br><br><br><br> Visually discriminate which word contains the same pattern. Or use auditory discrimination if it is a sound-based pattern—where same spelling represents two sounds as in _ow. <br><br><br><br><br> Listen for the dialogue structure. <br><br><br><br><br> Repeat the analogy phrase with the teacher. |

*Differentiating Reading Instruction for Success With RTI* © 2011 by Margo Southall • Scholastic Teaching Resources

## Sample Lesson: I Can Use Words I Know (continued)

| Teacher | Students |
|---|---|
| **2. Scaffold Student Strategy Use**<br>Present a new word with the same pattern as one of the known words.<br><br>`yet`<br><br>Ask students to indicate which of the two key words will help them to solve this new word by turning their thumb up or down as you move the new word card under each key word.<br><br>*I am going to show you a new word. I want you to look for the key word with the same pattern. Which one of our two key words will help us solve this tricky word? [move the card under each one]. What's our key word?*<br><br>*What's the same about these two words? What's the pattern? [cue students to say it together]*<br><br>*We know ___. The pattern is _, so this word is ___.*<br><br>Ask students to verbalize their use of the strategy | Show which key word has the same pattern by holding their thumb up (yes it matches) or down (no match). |
| **3. Repeat With New Words**<br>Repeat step 2 with further word cards, each containing one of the key word patterns | Say the key word.<br>Say the pattern.<br>Say the new word. |
| **4. Guide Student Practice:**<br>Distribute the I Can Use What I Know activity (Form 4.26) that you have prepared with the key words and new words containing the same patterns.<br><br>Review the Strategy:<br><br>*When I see a word I don't know, I will think about my key words with the same pattern. I tell myself that if I know this key word, the new word must sound like it.*<br><br>Introduce the Activity:<br><br>*I will show you a new word. We will solve the new word using one of our key words in the boxes on your sheet.*<br><br>Show one of the new words on a card or point to it on the sheet. Guide students through each of the steps to solve the new word:<br><br>*Find this word on your sheet. Point to our key word with the same pattern.*<br><br>*Say the key word with me. [Provide a cue: The word is _.]*<br><br>*Now, we will use it to read the new word.*<br><br>*Let's solve it together:*<br><br>*I know [key word]. The pattern is ___, so this word is ____.* | Identify which key word will help them solve the new words.<br><br>Use the analogy phrase to verbalize how they used a familiar pattern to decode a new word.<br><br><br><br>Find the new word.<br>Point to the key word with the same pattern.<br>Say the key word.<br>Use the key word to pronounce the new word.<br>Verbalize their strategy use. |

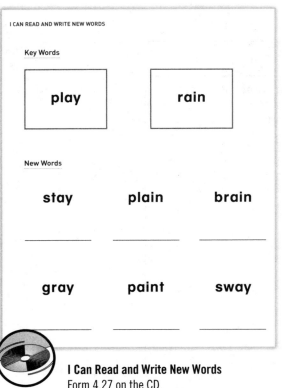

**I Can Read and Write New Words**
Form 4.27 on the CD

Students practice looking inside words to find the pattern that will help them.

## I Can Read and Write New Words

Students use the analogy strategy to read and write new words with the same pattern as their key words.

### Materials

- Form 4.27 from the CD, with key words written in the boxes across the top

### Procedure

Students follow these steps:

- Read the key words and scan each for patterns they know.
- Scan each new word for one of the key word patterns; they look for the vowel and the letters that follow.
- Underline the pattern in the new word using the key word as a visual reference.
- Write the key word on the line under the new word.
- Use the analogy phrase to solve the new word: Point to the key word, and then the new word as they verbalize their strategy use:
  *I know [key word]. The pattern is ___, so this word is ___.*

## Game: Rime Time Charts

Use the charts you have generated containing words with the same rime or pattern for this review activity. The focus here is to reinforce the analogy dialogue from the lessons, so that students will internalize the process and use it in their independent reading whenever they confront unfamiliar words. Take a few minutes each day to have students practice the analogy phrasing and review how to use the pattern.

### Procedure

- Construct a chart with the key words at the top and several words containing those patterns underneath (words you sorted and/or generated together).

| mice | ride |
|------|------|
| slice | wide |
| price | bride |

- Point to the key word and then one of the words in each column as you say: *I know* [point to key word]. *The pattern is ___, so this word is ___.* [point to new word in column]
- Extend this by pointing to the words in the columns in *random order* and asking students to identify which key word will help them and to verbalize how they used it, as modeled and practiced in the lessons (Gaskins, 2005; Gaskins et al., 1997).

## 1-2-3 - Show the Key!

In this all-student response game, students do the following:

- Discriminate the target letter-sound or pattern in a word that is presented orally (auditory discrimination).
- Identify the key word card containing the same feature (visual correspondence in print), and hold it up on a cue from the teacher.

**Materials**

- Lists of words for this activity are included on Form 4.28 on the CD. These include multisyllabic words containing consonant clusters (blends and digraphs) and vowel patterns.
- Two index cards or pieces of paper for each student

**Procedure**

- Ask students to write a key word you have used to teach the pattern on each one of the cards. To assist them, spell the key words on your whiteboard or hold up cards for them to copy.
- Say a word that contains the same pattern. You might choose a multisyllabic word to challenge students to apply the pattern to words with more than one syllable.
- Give students a moment to think and then say "1, 2, 3, show me the key!" This is the cue for students to hold up the card with the matching pattern.

Vowel Pattern Example:                    Multisyllabic Challenge Word Example:

 **rest**    **nest**               **forest**    **nest**

- When all students have responded and held up their cards, say: *Cards down*.
- To add additional challenge, present a word that contains both patterns. For example the word *estimate* contains the patterns –*est* and –*ate*, a "two-hander" (Gaskins, 2005; Gaskins, Ehri, Cress, O'Hara & Donnelly, 1997).

 **estimate**    **nest**    **gate**

## Onset-Rime Match Ups

Another variation of 1-2-3– Show the Key! is to have students hold up the onset and rime cards for words you present to them orally. In this way, they have to identify the parts of words, breaking them apart and blending them together in the process.

**Materials**

- Onset and rime cards for a set of no more than six words, four for low-progress readers. As an example, for the word *trail*, you'd supply cards with *tr* and *ail*. Store these in plastic zip-top bags.

### Procedure

- Have students place the onset and rime cards face up in two separate groups or columns in front of them.
- Say a word and give a timed cue, such as a three-second countdown.
- Students find the matching onset and rime cards and hold up the two cards that form the word.

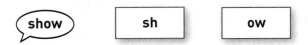

### Writing Activities

Interactive or shared writing can be as simple as a dictated sentence or as involved as a language-experience story—the key is that whatever text you write must incorporate the words with the target letter-sounds or vowel patterns. First, generate a chart of words sharing the same feature with the students. Then ask the group to generate a topic; this might be a problem from a story you have read together or a nonfiction topic that is relevant to class experiences and student interests. I try to use children's names in the chart stories we compose. As you write, refer to classroom resources such as the chunking word wall and high-frequency Words We Know Wall. With interactive writing, students take turns writing words on the chart, while the rest of the group remains engaged by providing positive feedback (thumbs-up), tracing the word on their hand, or turning and talking to a partner to share a rhyming word or to tell how they would spell the word.

When a language-experience approach is used in shared writing, the result may not be standard English, as it is based on the children's use of oral language. The strength of language experience lies in the oral rehearsal of student-generated content based on individual or collective experiences, such as a class event; this is then followed by the teacher transcribing the experience for students to read. For these chart stories or nonfiction topics, I translate student input into standard English to reflect the more formal language of the books we read. This provides a source of personally relevant reading material for students. If possible, make copies for each student to add to their "I Can Read" folder, which makes a great partner and independent reading time resource. I have students locate and underline words containing the target features.

### Independent Writing: Word-Solver's Notebook

Each student should have a word-solver's spiral or composition notebook (see page 141). In their notebooks, students record their sorts and also compose sentences, stories, or informational text containing words with the same spelling patterns, as a follow- up to the lesson. Poems are often the easiest for students to write when you are working on rimes. If it is a rhyming structure, I provide pairs of rhyming words for them to use to generate their poem.

## Part 3

# Activities for Independent Practice

Before you begin meeting with word-solving groups, train your students to complete each of the independent practice activities you have selected. Use familiar words taken from whole-class shared reading, such as poems and songs, to model the activities. See page pages 102–103 for suggestions on creating a rotation schedule for the word-solving independent practice activities; you'll find icons for the various tasks on Forms 4.29–4.32 on the CD.

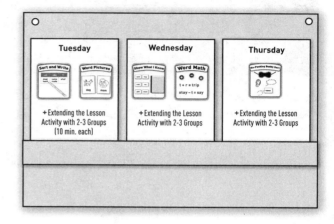

### PREPARE STUDENT WORD-SOLVER NOTEBOOKS OR JOURNALS

Make sure each student has a notebook to use during class and small-group lessons, as well as independent practice. For teachers, these provide an important record of student growth. For students, they provide a visual reminder of how to complete each task. I make copies of the practice task cards for students to paste into their word-solving notebooks as each task is taught and practiced. (Samples of task cards are shown next to each activity.) In that way, on the opposite page of each task card is a completed example for students to use as a reference when they are working independent-ly—showing what the page layout should look like. These pages are numbered so they can easily be retrieved during independent work.

### SORT AND WRITE

This is usually the first independent task completed after the input lesson on Day 1. Students now sort their words on their own and record them under the key words in their notebook. Younger students and low-progress readers may record two or three words for each pattern and illustrate one from each category with a pencil sketch. More advanced students can record more words, at least five for each category.

All students write a sentence about each group of words, describing what they have in common. Provide sentence starters for students to record in their notebook or on a poster and model completing this in small-group lessons. Sentence starters may include:

I sorted my words by …

**Sort and Write Task Card**
Form 4.33 on the CD

Students complete the Sort and Glue task at the end of their rotation.

Some of my words ... but the other words ...

These words go with __ because

I put the words in this group because they ...

I noticed that ...

All the words in this column...

This group of words ...

### Materials

- Set of word sort cards
- Notebook
- Optional: sorting mat

### Procedure

Ganske (2008) points out the importance of having students:

- Say the words—look at each word and say it.
- Spell the words—whisper the spelling in their head.
- Sort the words—write them in columns under the key words.
- Describe what each group of words has in common (vowel pair, rime, or spelling pattern).
- Ask themselves: *What did I learn that would help me to read and spell other words with the same pattern?*

Students may brainstorm and list more words with the same pattern and add these to the columns, as well as use one word from each category in sentences.

**No-Peeking Buddy Sort Task Card**
Form 4.34 on the CD

## NO-PEEKING BUDDY SORT (Bear et. al., 2008)

This sort is also called a blind sort; it helps students make the connection between the sound of a pattern and its spelling. Just like the Training-for-Transfer lessons, here students need to orally discriminate the pattern within a word and match it to print. This is especially important for students who over-rely on visual cues; they look at the letters and sort the words without even reading them. When you consider a sort of short vowel words and words with silent *e* pattern (e.g., *hop* and *hope*), you can see how this could easily happen. I always include this activity in my rotation for this reason.

### Materials

- Set of large word sort cards for group practice
- Pocket chart or sorting mat for the group practice
- Word sort cards for partners
- Optional: sorting mat
- Cheat sheet of completed sort or student notebook copy (if copied during a previous small-group lesson)

**Procedure**

First, practice in small-group lessons:

- Place the key words across the top of a pocket chart (or a sorting mat) so that all students can clearly see them.
- Call out the same words that you have already sorted together. Do not show them to the students.
- Ask students to indicate the column where the word should go in the pocket chart by pointing their thumb or holding up their arm and moving it to the left, right, or middle (rather than calling out).
- Show them the word.
- Check that it is placed in the correct category. Read the key word, then the new word.
- Allow one second "sneak peeks" at the word card when students struggle to identify the category.

Then students work on their own:

- You may wish to post a list of sorting buddies, and move a sticky note next to one who goes first. A cheat sheet or copy of the completed, correct Write and Sort is helpful for students to refer to in this activity.
- Have partners from the same group work together, using one of their bags of word cards.
- Key words are placed in front of them.
- The first child holds all the cards and calls them out one by one.
- The second child, without looking at the cards, points to the correct key word and reads it to his or her buddy. The first child places the word card under the key word. The second child tells the partner why it belongs there.
- Roles are then reversed.

## NO-PEEKING WRITING SORT

In this variation of the No-Peeking Buddy Sort, students write the words instead of pointing to the key word card.

### Materials

- Set of word sort cards
- Notebook or copy of the Dictated Writing form (Form 4.49 on the CD)

### Procedure

- Provide the key words for the sort; students write them as headings at the top of columns in their notebooks.
- As one child reads a word card, the other writes it under the key word containing the same pattern.
- Partners switch roles.

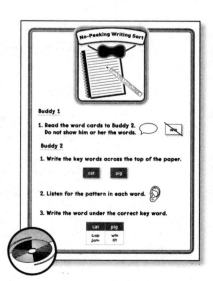

**No-Peeking Writing Sort Task Card**
Form 4.35 on the CD

## WORD DETECTIVE

This activity, also known as a word hunt, supports transfer to reading as students notice familiar parts in new words.

### Materials

- Set of word sort cards
- Reading materials, such as poems, charts, or student independent reading materials
- Notebooks

### Procedure

Students follow these steps:

- Write key words across the top of the page in their notebook.
- Scan (not read) through reading material to find words containing the target pattern.
- Write them under the key words.
- Tell where they found each word in a sentence (for a example, in the title of book).
- Partners and groups may contribute to a collective chart of words they have found and put their initials next to the words they find, for credit.

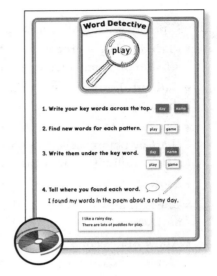

**Word Detective Task Card**
Form 4.43 on the CD

## SHOW WHAT I KNOW

After a shared or interactive writing activity, students write a message, story, poem, or factual account to share with their family members or friends.

### Materials

- Set of word sort cards
- Sheet of paper or notebook

### Procedure

Students follow these steps:

- Choose 4–6 of the word sort words to compose a message to their parents, caregiver, or friends.
- Circle the words from their sort.
- Draw a picture illustrating one of the sentences.

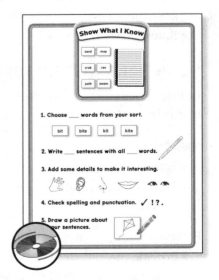

**Show What I Know Task Card**
Form 4.39 on the CD

Students compose a message using their word sort for the Show What I Know task.

## FAST SORT

This is similar to the Group Speed Sort (page 131), but here partners time each other, or students time themselves and set a goal for how quickly they can sort all their words. The time is graphed over three sorts in succession. Provide students with a sheet of the correct answers so buddies can check their partner's words. Only correctly sorted words are counted. If you have completed the Sort and Write activity (page 141) as a group, then they can refer to it in their notebook instead of using a cheat sheet.

### Materials
- Set of word sort cards
- Notebook
- Cheat sheet or student copy of Sort and Write
- Optional: sorting mat

### Procedure
- Have partners from the same word-solving group work together, using one of their sets of word cards.
- Place key words in front of them.
- The first child holds all the cards and sorts them as quickly as possible.
- The second child times the first child and records it.
- Repeat two more times.
- Switch roles.

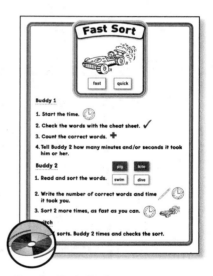

**Fast Sort Task Card**
Form 4.41 on the CD

**Word Pictures Task Card**
Form 4.37 on the CD

**Picture Sort Task Card**
Form 4.36 on the CD

## WORD PICTURES

This activity requires students to draw and label their word cards. You may designate a number of words they are to depict. In this way, you can see whether they have understood the meaning of the words they have read.

### Materials

- Set of word sort cards
- Notebooks

### Procedure

Students follow these steps:

- Choose 4–6 the words from their sort.
- Draw a simple sketch to show the meaning of each word.
- Write the word under the picture.

## PICTURE SORT

In this activity, discriminating the sound of the letter, consonant cluster, or vowel pattern is the focus. Students draw and label pictures of words that contain the same sound. This is a useful task for discriminating short vowels, comparing short and long vowels, discriminating consonant blends or digraphs, and many other features. Review the picture names with students to avoid ambiguity, such as puppy/dog, and so on.

### Materials

- Set of picture sort cards
- Notebooks
- Optional: sorting mat

### Procedure

Students follow these steps:

- Look at the key pictures.
- Say the name of each picture.
- Sort the picture cards under the key pictures.
- In their notebooks, create a two-column chart and draw the key pictures, then draw the other pictures in the appropriate column.
- Label each picture beside or underneath it.

## SORT AND GLUE

This activity is used at the end of an instructional cycle, when students paste word cards that they have sorted multiple times into their notebooks or onto paper.

**Materials**

- Set of word sort cards
- Notebooks or paper (construction or art paper)

**Procedure**

Students follow these steps:

- Paste the key words across the top of a sheet of paper.
- Read each word.
- Sort the words.
- Paste the words under the key words.

## WORD MATH

The goal of this activity is to add or subtract letters from a word to build new words. This encourages students to notice how changing one letter changes the meaning of the word, and to flexibly apply the patterns they have been learning to spell new words.

**Materials**

- Set of word sort cards
- Notebooks

**Procedure**

Students follow these steps:

- Add or subtract letter(s) from 4–6 words to make new words.
- Record these words in their notebook.

**Sort and Glue Task Card**
Form 4.38 on the CD

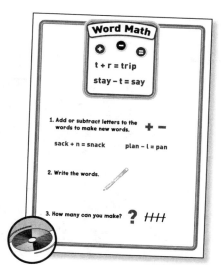

**Word Math Task Card**
Form 4.47 on the CD

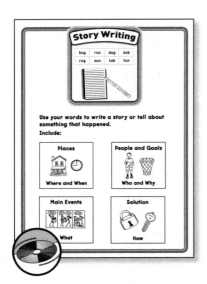

**Story Writing Task Card**
Form 4.46 on the CD

**S.A.W. Task Card**
Form 4.40 on the CD

## STORY WRITING

Using the words in meaningful ways, such as composing a story, facilitates long-lasting learning and transfer to new contexts.

### Materials
- Set of word sort cards
- Notebooks

### Procedure

Students follow these steps:
- Use the word cards to write a story or informational text, such as describing the life of an animal.
- Generate more rhyming words to use in their writing.

## S.A.W.—SORT, ALPHABETIZE, AND WRITE YOUR WORDS

Sorting and then alphabetizing the words under each key word provides a homework task or activity for the Word Study Center (Ganske, 2000).

### Materials
- Set of word sort cards
- Notebooks

### Procedure

Students follow these steps:
- Read the words.
- Place the words in alphabetical order.
- Copy the words in their notebooks.

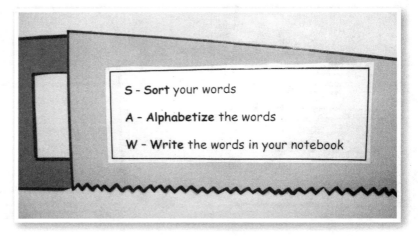

Sorting and then alphabetizing the words provides a homework task or activity for the center.

## WHAT'S MY SORT?

This is an open sort where you don't provide the categories. Students are free to sort the words by phonics or meaningful concepts, such as describing words, action words, words about insects, words about weather—whatever they see in the words they're presented with. You can include new words containing the same pattern that have been read with students but not sorted before. I use this activity to review previously introduced patterns, and I provide a plastic bag with a collection of words from those sorts for partners or individuals in the group to sort and then describe in writing the commonalities they see in these words.

I also use it for thematic words, and social studies and science vocabulary (see Chapter 6). The possibilities are endless. I always remind students that not all the words may fit into their categories—there may be some words that are "out of sorts," and that that's okay. You may stipulate a certain number of categories, such as two or three, and have students write their categories and the words that belong to each one. Form 4.49 on the CD can be used for this purpose, or students can write the category headings they decided upon and the related words in their notebooks.

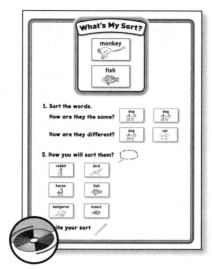

**What's My Sort Task Card**
Form 4.42 on the CD

### Materials

- Set of word sort cards
- Notebook
- Optional: sorting mat

### Procedure

Students follow these steps:

- Read the words.
- Decide how these words could be grouped by a common spelling pattern or meaning.
- Sort the words into groups and copy them in their notebook.
- Describe what each group of words has in common, why they grouped them together.

Classroom posters and task cards provide step-by-step directions for the core weekly tasks.

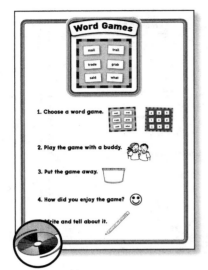

**Word Games Task Card**
Form 4.48 on the CD

## WORD GAMES

Games like concentration are an example of other ways to use the word cards.

### Materials

- Set of word sort cards
- Games like Concentration, Snap, and Go Fish or other commercial word-building and sorting games

### Procedure

Students follow these steps:

- Select a game.
- Play the game with a partner or group.

## Part 4
# Assessment

Assessment is an integral part of the word-solving cycle of instruction. See pages 105-106 for suggestions on how to schedule regular assessment sessions with your word-solving groups, and use the tools and tasks below to evaluate whether your students have mastered the skills they've been working on.

## Letter-Sound Relationships

To assess whether students have mastered discriminating the sounds in words and recording those sounds with the letters that represent them, I use the same Hearing and Recording Sounds in Sequence format (see page 117) and (Forms 4.13–4.15 on the CD) that we practiced during the lessons. For students who are just learning letter-sound correspondences I also assess students individually. Resources such as *An Observation Survey of Early Literacy Achievement* by Marie Clay (2008) and the Kindergarten Spelling Inventory in Bear et al. (2010) are two useful resources for this purpose. Some of the tasks include identifying the letter name and the sound it represents, generating a word beginning with that sound, and writing a dictated sentence or list of words. Observation and documentation of student progress during the lessons provides continual information on the level of student understanding.

## Vowel Pairs, Rimes, and Spelling Patterns

Once students have participated in the word sorting lessons, training-for-transfer lessons, and independent practice, we assess their ability to transfer what they have learned to reading and spelling (writing) new words. This completes the cycle of

*Differentiating Reading Instruction for Success With RTI* © 2011 by Margo Southall • Scholastic Teaching Resources

instruction, and the assessment allows me to know if students mastered the patterns or need further instruction and practice. Teaching word-solving is different from teaching irregular sight words, where we assess mastery of whole- word recognition. In word-solving assessment we do not dictate or present all the same words students have worked with that week. We provide some new words for them to spell and read.

You can use the "Two New" activity from the Five- or Six-Step Guided Word Sort lesson on pages 122 and 126, as well as observations during the I Can Use Words I Know and I Can Read and Write New Words training-for-transfer lessons (see pages 135–138) to assess students' understanding. Each week, I assess using a dictated word sort, described in the following section. Sentence dictations can also be used to assess pattern recognition.

The Assessment Record: Word Solving (Form 4.2 on the CD) provides a space to record student progress in the features being taught each week or the cycle of instruction. This form includes the following tasks:

- **Sort and Write:** A closed sort task in which students record the words under each category and describe in writing what they noticed about each group of words—the generalization (see page 141 for a description of this task). Students can gain a mark for recording the words in the correct columns.

- **Use Words I Know:** Note observations from the group lesson. What level of understanding does the student demonstrate? Was he or she able to verbalize the concept? (See the lesson plan on pages 136–137.)

- **Dictated Word Sort:** Dictate several words from each pattern that students have worked with, along with new words that contain the same feature to test the students' application of the concept. The description below explains how to allocate one mark for recording the word under the correct category and a second mark for spelling the entire word correctly (not just the feature).

## DICTATED WORD SORT

A Dictated Word Sort allows you to assess whether students can discriminate a letter pattern both by its sound and spelling (Bear et al., 2008; Ganske, 2000). Students are required to identify which key word contains the letter-sound relationship or vowel pattern that will help them spell it and write it under that word. The Dictated Word Sort Form can be used by students to record their responses to the teacher-dictated sort (see Form 4.49 on the CD).

### Preparation

- Write the key words on a chart or whiteboard for students to copy at the top of their page, spacing them apart to allow for writing words in columns underneath.

- Select four words used in the sorting lesson and six new words that contain the letter pattern. If you're working with more than one group of students, select words for each group.

**Materials**

- Dictated Word Sort Form 4.49 on the CD, or writing paper and pencils

**Procedure**

- Say the word, then say a sentence containing the word, then repeat the word. You can dictate to multiple groups: *Green Group, your word is … Yellow Group your next word is …*

- Students identify which key word on their page will help them to spell the dictated word and write it in the same column.

- Students receive one point for spelling the word correctly and one point for recording the word in the correct category. Record scores on the Assessment Record: Word Solving, Form 4.2 on the CD.

- Beware of words with more than one possible spelling. Students may make errors in such cases—for instance, *plain* and *plane*. Use the words in a sentence where the meaning is clear. The activity "Does it look right?" in which students try two ways to spell a word and cross out the wrong one, supports students to distinguish visual errors due to multiple possible spellings, e.g. ~~site~~ sight, (Cunningham, 2009).

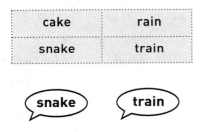

## Putting It All Together: Sample Cycles of Instruction

The two charts that follow represent examples of a weekly sequence of instruction for on-grade and low-progress students. The lessons and activities with an asterisk are essential and must be repeated for each new phonics skill. You may select additional lessons and guided practice activities from the Extending the Lessons ideas (page 130–140) and from the independent practice tasks (page 141–150) to give variety throughout the year.

In Part 1 of this chapter, under Scheduling the Group Rotations, we noted that more than one of the lessons and activities can be completed in the days following the introductory lesson on Day One. In a five-day cycle, Day One is the teaching of the pattern, and on Day Five, student assessment takes place in the form of a dictated word sort (see pages 105–106).

## Sample Word-Solving Cycle of Instruction

| Teacher Scaffolded Lessons | Independent Practice |
| --- | --- |
| *Five Step Word Sort | Sort & Write |
| Interactive or Shared Writing With Pattern Words | Show What I Know |
| I Can Use What I Know | No-Peeking Buddy Sort |
| *Dictated Word Sort (see Assessment) | |

* Essential lessons done for each instructional cycle

## Example of a Cycle of Instruction for Low-Progress Readers

Low-progress readers require more teacher scaffolding and more practice in acquiring and applying new knowledge, skills, and strategies. Tier 2 and 3 students sort a set of words at least twice within teacher-guided lessons, and you will need to closely monitor the sorting tasks so that any confusions or errors are identified and corrected before the remaining tasks are attempted. The Sort and Write and partner No-Peeking activity are often completed with teacher scaffolding so that you can provide corrective feedback and immediately address any confusions. Following the group lessons, students can engage in the Buddy Sort on their own. More time is also devoted to training in strategy use in small groups, using the I Can Use What I Know lessons, to support students as they learn to apply their knowledge during reading and writing. Independent Practice consists of writing applications as a follow-up to the interactive or shared writing of a sentence, poem, or story, such as the Show What I Know activity. Students also illustrate the meanings of their words and label them in the Word Pictures task.

## Sample Word-Solving Cycle of Instruction for Low Progress Readers

| Teacher Scaffolded Lessons | Independent Practice |
| --- | --- |
| *Six-Step Explicit Word Sort | Show What I Know |
| Interactive or Shared Writing With Pattern Words | Word Pictures |
| *No-Peeking Buddy Sort | |
| Speed Sort | |
| *I Can Use Words I Know | |
| I Can Read and Write New Words | |
| * 1-2-3 - Show the Key | |
| *Dictated Word Sort (see assessment) | |

* Essential lessons done for each instructional cycle

## Checklist for Effective Word-Solving Instruction

☑ Ongoing assessment guides teaching points, and the level of phonics knowledge, skills, and strategies.

☑ Students are grouped for instruction by the concepts, skills, and strategies they need to develop.

☑ Teachers verbalize word-solving strategies during daily think-alouds.

☑ Students regularly verbalize word-solving strategies during guided practice and peer work—for example, "Turn and talk with your neighbor about how you solved this tricky word" or "What do you know about this word?" or "What else helped your solve it?"

☑ Students compare and contrast spelling patterns through word-sorting activities.

☑ Demonstrations and guided practice help students recognize and use "what you know" to decode new words. Students get daily practice of this analogy strategy with new and complex words.

☑ Students read and spell the same sets of words to facilitate transfer.

☑ Reading materials (charts, books) for shared reading and small-group lessons contain the decodable elements.

☑ Decodable elements are used in writing activities.

☑ Students are coached for transfer of word-solving strategies during reading in small-group lessons.

*Differentiating Reading Instruction for Success With RTI* © 2011 by Margo Southall • Scholastic Teaching Resources

# Summary of Key Principles:
## Implementing Word-Solving Instruction

### Assessment

❯ Determine students' decoding knowledge, skills, and strategy use.

❯ Use developmental assessment to identify appropriate complexity of the phonics and structural elements.

❯ Monitor student progress with regular informal assessments.

### Instruction

❯ Model and demonstrate word-solving strategies in whole-class think-alouds.

❯ Form small groups based on assessment.

❯ Provide independent practice tasks in rotation during small-group instruction.

### Scheduling

❯ Devote one whole-class read-aloud/think-aloud lesson each week to modeling word-solving strategies.

❯ Select one of two options for small-group lessons:

1. Integrate word-solving lessons into current differentiated reading groups—one to three of the lessons each week, depending on student need, and taught in balance with comprehension (Grades K–1).

2. Teach word solving in small groups for 20 minutes 3–5 times a week *apart from* reading groups. Rotate students through the teacher station and independent practice tasks (Grades 1–6).

### Materials

❯ Word building and sorting materials (see list of resources)

❯ Decodable reading materials—books, poems, chart stories (see list of resources)

❯ Authentic leveled text (instructional level text at 90–94% accuracy rate)

❯ Word-solving strategy charts (Forms 4.4–4.6 on the CD)

❯ Independent Practice Task cards or pasted in student journals/inserted into plastic sleeves in 3-ring notebook

❯ Word-solving literacy centers (see Southall, 2007)

# Resources for Differentiated Word-Solving Instruction

### Resources With Motions and Story Associations for Letters and Word Patterns

Animated Literacy: www.animated-literacy.com (motion, visuals and story association)

Jolly Phonics: jollylearning.co.uk (motion and visuals)

The Secret Stories: www.thesecretstories.com (visuals and story association to explain patterns and rules)

Stylized Alphabet Cards: www.child-1st.com (motion and story association)

Zoo Phonics: www.zoophonics.com (motion and visual association)

### Manipulatives

Contact 1-800-ART-READ or peruse math resource catalogues for clear translucent counter chips for highlighting word parts.

### Picture and Word Sorting Resources

*Word Sorts and More: Sound, Pattern and Meaning Explorations Grades K-3* by Kathy Ganske

*Mindful of Words: Spelling and Vocabulary Explorations* Grades 4-8 by Kathy Ganske

*Letter and Picture Sorts for Emergent Spellers* by Marcia Invernizzi, Francine Johnston & Donald Bear

*Word Sorts for Letter-Name Alphabetic Spellers* by Marcia Invernizzi, Francine Johnston & Donald Bear

*Word Sorts for Within Word Pattern Spellers* by Marcia Invernizzi, Francine Johnston & Donald Bear

*Word Sorts for Syllables and Affixes Spellers* by Marcia Invernizzi, Francine Johnston & Donald Bear

### Word Building Resources

*Word Solvers* by Michelle Dufresne

*Word Building* by Thomas Gunning

*Easy Lessons for Teaching Word Families* by Judy Lynch

*Systematic, Sequential Phonics They Use* by Patricia Cunningham

### Phonics Poems

*Phonics Through Poetry and More Phonics Through Poetry* by Babs Bell Hajdusiewicz (grades K-1, 2-3)

*Phonics Poetry: Teaching Word Families* by Timothy Rasinski and Belinda Zimmerman

*70 Wonderful Word Family Poems* by Jennifer Wilen and Beth Handa

### Decodable Book Series

Books to Remember (Flyleaf Publishing)

Phonics Readers (Capstone Press)

Ready Readers; Best Practice Phonics (Pearson Education)

Rhyme World (Rigby)

Power Phonics/Phonics for the Real World (Rosen Publishing)

First Story Rhymes; Second Story Rhymes; Sound Stories (Oxford University Press)

Scholastic Phonics Readers (Scholastic)

### Professional Reading

*Making Sense of Phonics* by Isabel Beck

*Teaching Word Recognition to Students With Learning Difficulties* by Rollanda E. O'Connor

*Word Journeys: Assessment-Guided Phonics, Spelling and Vocabulary Instruction* by Kathy Ganske

*Words Their Way* by Donald Bear, Marcia Invernizzi, Shane Templeton, and Francine Johnston

# DIFFERENTIATING FLUENCY INSTRUCTION

The word-solving skills and strategies in Chapter 4 provide the foundational skills for accurately reading words with regular spellings. In Chapter 6, we'll discuss scaffolding comprehension strategy use, which includes vocabulary building. In this chapter, we examine the link between word solving and comprehension by addressing these aspects of fluency instruction:

1. Accuracy and rate when reading high-frequency words with irregular spellings—for example, *does* and *said*.

2. Appropriate phrasing—recognizing phrase boundaries and reading meaningful groups of words together.

3. Appropriate expression—attending to intonation cues in the text to maintain the meaning and grammatical integrity of the passage (prosody).

It is here that we address common questions regarding the differentiation process:

● What are the components of an effective fluency program?

● What are the common student profiles of need?

● How can we differentiate instruction to target the needs of low-progress readers?

● Where does fluency instruction fit in a differentiated reading program?

"Fluency has often been called the bridge from phonics to comprehension."
(RASINSKI, 2010, P. 33)

## Chapter Overview

In **Part 1** of this chapter (pages 159–165) we examine common student profiles of difficulty, assessment tools to monitor progress, and considerations for differentiating our program.

**Part 2** (pages 166–178) includes lessons and multimodal learning tools for teaching accuracy and rate with high-frequency words, especially those with irregular spellings.

In **Part 3** (pages 179–188) you will find lessons and multimodal activities for teaching phrasing and expression.

## Journey to Differentiation in Fluency—All Things in Balance

In the past decade, an enormous amount of time and attention has been devoted to reading rate in fluency instruction. The fact that the norms for reading rates (expectations for the number of correct words read per minute for each grade level) have

Frequent reading builds fluency.

continued to increase reflects an emphasis placed on training students to increase their reading speed so they will succeed on commonly available fluency-screening and progress-monitoring tools (Rasinski & Hamman, 2010). The rationale for this emphasis on reading speed stems from research indicating a reciprocal relationship between fluency and comprehension. In reality, this is not always the case, and you will no doubt have students who contradict this premise. Some students read slowly but they comprehend— and some students read quickly and still don't understand what they are reading.

My goal continues to be for students to meet grade-level and/or progress-monitoring goals for reading rate as I teach fluency skills in a way that positively impacts their comprehension. In order to do this we need to know which aspect(s) of fluency have the greatest causal relationship to comprehension. *Phrasing* is the key; students must be able to recognize the meaningful semantic and syntactic chunks at the sentence and passage level (Torgesen, 2005; Rasinski, 2010). When you listen to students read word by word at a very fast rate, it's clear they are not recognizing phrase boundaries—and probably not comprehending the text.

We model appropriate reading rate, phrasing, and expression during every read-aloud. We can talk about these concepts from kindergarten on, alongside discussions of decoding strategies and high-frequency words, during shared reading and small-group lessons. The predictable and syntactically regular nature of shared reading materials used in the primary grades is ideally suited for teaching phrasing.

*Differentiating Reading Instruction for Success With RTI* © 2011 by Margo Southall • Scholastic Teaching Resources

Teaching phrasing is not simply so students "sound good" as they read. We teach phrasing because this positively impacts both reading rate and comprehension. Fluency training is an essential part of reading instruction, and regular fluency lessons should be a part of every comprehensive literacy program.

## Part 1

# Preparing to Differentiate Fluency Instruction

Knowing which aspect of fluency is presenting an obstacle to student progress is the first step in planning differentiated instruction. Here we look at common profiles of student need and explore assessment options that can help us identify areas of need and teaching tools that can help us address them.

## Profiles of Student Need

Many adults with a reading-based learning disability read slowly but accurately. However, because of their disfluency, they are self-conscious about reading anything aloud in public (Shaywitz, 2003). We work with children who will face this reality without sufficient targeted fluency training, and it is within our grasp to help them.

Students who struggle with fluency skills struggle in different ways. You might recognize the following types:

Students use feedback phones to help them self-monitor their fluency skills during reading.

- **Word stumblers** or "bumper car drivers" (stop and go, stop and go) lack automaticity with irregular sight words (such as *eight*, *would*) due to difficulties in storing and retrieving the sequences of letters in words in their visual or orthographic memory.

- **Word-by-word readers** do not recognize how groups of words are read together to convey the meaning.

- **Robot readers** read in a monotone voice, without expression.

- **Impersonators** attend to punctuation cues and use appropriate expression but do not make inferences about the character's intent or use this to determine cause-and-effect relationships.

- **Stoplight runners** take no notice of signals, such as punctuation marks and text features (subheadings, lists, questions, and so on) or other signs in the text that tell them they need to adjust their reading speed.

- **Speed demons**, or stopwatch readers, read as if they're in a race to get to the end as soon as possible, to the detriment of their comprehension.

| WHEN the student profile of need is a: | THEN provide these lessons and tasks | Page Number |
|---|---|---|
| **Word Stumbler, work on:**<br>•Increasing accuracy in reading irregular high-frequency words<br>• Increasing the rate of reading of irregular high-frequency words | • Cumulative Blending With CVC Words<br>• High-Frequency Word Lesson #1<br>• High-Frequency Word Lesson #2<br>• 3-2-1 Pick Up | 113<br>169<br>169–170<br>170 |
| **Word-by-Word Reader, Impersonator, Stoplight Runner or Speed Demon, work on:**<br>• Reading with meaningful phrasing<br>• Attending to punctuation marks and text features | • Phrasing Mini-Lesson<br>• Construct Phrase Pyramids<br>• Label the Phrases<br>• Choral reading of high-frequency word phrases<br>• Step to the Beat—Phrase Walk<br>• Phrase Sort<br>• Be the Phrase | 179<br>182–183<br>184<br>184<br><br>186<br>187<br>187 |
| **Robot Reader, Stoplight Runner or Speed Demons, work on:**<br>• Reading with intonation and expression<br>• Adjusting reading rate based on text | • Fluency with Humor<br>• Inside/Outside Circle<br>• Readers Theater<br>• Music and Lyrics<br>• Technology Assisted Reading<br>• Emotion Cue Cards<br>• Poetry Four Corners | 181<br>182<br>184–185<br>185<br>185<br>188<br>188 |
| **All Profiles** | • Guided and Independent Practice Activities<br>• Fluency Five-Day Lesson Sequence | 171–178;<br>181–188<br>189 |

## Linking to Assessment

We can use a variety of assessment tools to determine student performance in the areas of reading accuracy and rate, phrasing, and expression. The following tools can help you collect the data you need to plan instruction.

- **Running Records:** We maximize this useful tool as a source of fluency data by timing student reading, marking phrase boundaries where the student used phrasing effectively or ineffectively (breaking the sentence apart where it did or did not maintain the syntax or sentence structure), circling any omitted punctuation, noting the use of appropriate expression, marking pauses and hesitations with a "W" ("wait"), and recording any omissions, miscues, or substitutions (for high-frequency words).

- **Informal Reading Inventories:** See Chapter 2.

*Differentiating Reading Instruction for Success With RTI* © 2011 by Margo Southall • Scholastic Teaching Resources

- **Rubrics:** Use rubrics such as the Adapted Version of the NAEP Oral Reading Fluency Scale and Multidimensional Fluency Scale in Timothy Rasinski's *The Fluent Reader* (2010).

- **Observation Rubrics:** The programmed Observation Rubrics on Form 2.5 on the CD includes a rubric for fluency.

- **High-Frequency Word Reading Tests:** Typical word list assessments include the most frequently occurring words in reading. In kindergarten and first grade, when students learn many new words through writing and spelling, high-frequency words are the ones students need to begin as readers *and* writers, using them in stories and journal writing daily. These include words such as: *the, is, a, I, we, my, have, can, go, going, to, the, it, went, he, she, mom, dad, was, want, were.*

- **One-Minute Reading Probes:** These are (typically) graded passages used to assess accuracy and rate. To gain a more complete picture of students' reading rate and skills, increase the time to three minutes. This provides a picture of their ability to sustain a reading rate over stretches of independent reading, and whether they adjust their reading speed in response to the text.

- **Profile as a Reader:** Form 2.1 on the CD provides a summary of the fluency assessments that have been administered, including informal observations.

- **Student Reading Goals, Observations, and Instruction:** Form 2.3 on the CD is used for recording student progress during a one-to-one reading conference and focuses on the student's current reading goal.

- **How Was My Reading?** Provide students with an opportunity for self-assessment with a picture-cued form, Form 5.1 on the CD, on which students monitor their fluency for rate and expression.

- **Prompting for Self-Monitoring/ Assessment During Reading Conferences:** Encourage students to monitor their own reading for each aspect of fluency.
  *Do you think you read too fast, too slow or just right?*
  *How do you know when you need to read a bit slower? Faster?*

### How Was My Reading?

Name: _____  Date: _____

Partner's name: _____

I listened to my partner read: _____.

**Reading # 1: Here's how my partner's reading got better:**

**Circle the face that best fits the reading**

**Reading # 2: Here's how my partner's reading got better:**

**Circle the face that best fits the reading**

**How Was My Reading?**
Form 5.1 on the CD

# Differentiating Fluency Instruction

In Chapter 3 we examined the Wide Reading Approach model for fluency instruction (see pages 73–74), which includes structures for choral, partner, and independent reading to scaffold access to instructional-level texts. This model demonstrates how to teach fluency across whole-class, small-group and independent learning contexts. Within each of these contexts, we can incorporate the lessons, multimodal learning activities, and resources in this chapter to further differentiate our instruction.

## IDEAS FOR INTRODUCING AND DEMONSTRATING FLUENCY

You model fluent reading during every read-aloud and shared reading experience. Here are some ideas for making fluency instruction more explicit as you model so students understand exactly what makes your reading fluent.

### Incorporate Think-Alouds

I suggest incorporating fluency think-alouds during read-alouds and shared reading lessons so that students can hear the thinking processes of a fluent reader. You can conduct a detailed fluency think-aloud on one or more of the three aspects of fluency each week, based upon assessment data.

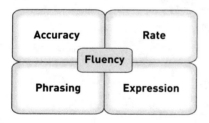

During a fluency think-aloud, be sure to verbalize the internal processes and on-the-run decision making that occurs during fluent reading. As always, using consistent terminology is key; see the I Can Read Smoothly chart on page 164 for the language I use. I expect students to use the same language and thinking processes in their turn-and-talk partner discussions. Model think-alouds and guiding prompts are included in the following sections (see pages 166–167, 170, and 180–181).

### Bulletin Boards

Introduce and display the strategy statements from Chapter 3 with graphic cues (Forms 3.7 and 3.8 on the CD) as you teach each aspect of fluent reading, so that students will become familiar with the terminology you're using to talk about fluency. I label this section of my strategy bulletin board "I Can Read Smoothly" and post the following statements on sentence strips, which I refer to during think-alouds and demonstrations:

- I see words I know. [accuracy and rate in reading high-frequency words]
- I read groups of words together. [phrasing]
- I look at my marks. [attending to punctuation as a cue for use of expression]
- I use my voice. [expression]
- I can read at the right rate. [rate]

### Strategy Charts and Strategy Bookmarks

To introduce and reinforce aspects of fluency in small-group lessons, use the I Can Read Smoothly strategy chart on page 164 (Form 5.2 on the CD), pointing to the cue for the skill you are focusing on.

*Differentiating Reading Instruction for Success With RTI* © 2011 by Margo Southall • Scholastic Teaching Resources

To help students use fluency strategies during reading, prepare individual copies of fluency bookmarks on Form 5.6 on the CD. I model how to use these tools during small-group lessons and guided practice; naturally, these tools incorporate the same visuals and language as my bulletin board.

### Fluency Help Walls and High-Frequency Word Walls

Lines from literature can be lifted from class read-alouds and displayed on a bulletin board using sentence strips, or on a wall chart, as an example of how punctuation, emphasis, and/or the use of expression can convey meaning. Discuss how readers use the information authors provide to understand the point they are making. These lines from literature provide examples during whole- and small-group lessons, and support self-monitoring for meaning during independent reading.

Example: (*Charlotte's Web* by E.B. White, p. 1)

> **"Where's Papa going with that axe?" said Fern to her mother as they were setting the table for breakfast.**

High-frequency word walls are common in primary classrooms, and I recommend giving irregularly spelled high-frequency words priority in this space. Words such as *was, because, what,* and *people* need to be up there. They take longer for students to learn because they can't be completely decoded using sound-spelling relationships or analogy. These words will require repeated multimodal practice, and having them on a word wall facilitates those activities.

## GROUPING STUDENTS FOR INSTRUCTION

As we assess students within classroom and intervention programs to determine their current reading goals, there will be some students for whom fluency is a priority at this time in their development as a reader. In response to their assessed needs, we form groups of students with a common need in one or two aspects of fluency (e.g., accuracy and rate, phrasing, and expression) as part of our small-group reading rotation, where there will be some groups working on comprehension while others work on word solving or fluency (for more on group rotation see Chapter 3). The When/Then Chart on page 160 lists lessons and activities that will enable you to provide guided practice for fluency groups.

## READING LEVELS AND FLUENCY INSTRUCTION

Text level is important for fluency training. Students should work with independent-level texts to practice fluent reading. You can use instructional-level text when you're working with a small group and scaffolding their reading, or in repeated reading formats, but avoid frustration-level texts (Minskoff, 2005). If members of a group are at different reading levels, simply choose a text at the level of the least-developed reader; it doesn't hurt other students in the group to work with easy text for fluency development.

# I Can Read Smoothly

I can...

### see words I know.

I see a word I know.                              said

I see 2 little words I know.              some thing

I see words I know inside big words.  re read ing

### read groups of words.

I can look for groups of words.

I can read the words in one breath.

### look at the marks.  ? ; !

I can use the signs on the way.

### use my voice.

I can make it sound like talking.

### read at the right rate.

*Differentiating Reading Instruction for Success With RTI* © 2011 by Margo Southall • Scholastic Teaching Resources

# I CAN READ SMOOTHLY
## Bookmark

I can...

see words I know.

> **I see a word I know.**
> said

> **I see 2 little words I know.** some thing

> **I see words I know inside big words.**
> re read ing

**read groups of words.**

> **I can look for groups of words.**

> **I can read the words in one breath.**

**look at the marks.** ? ; !

> **I can use the signs on the way.**

**use my voice.**

> **I can make it sound like talking.**

**read at the right rate.**

# I CAN READ SMOOTHLY
## Bookmark

I can...

see words I know.

> **I see a word I know.**
> said

> **I see 2 little words I know.** some thing

> **I see words I know inside big words.**
> re read ing

**read groups of words.**

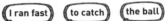

> **I can look for groups of words.**

> **I can read the words in one breath.**

**look at the marks.** ? ; !

> **I can use the signs on the way.**

**use my voice.**

> **I can make it sound like talking.**

**read at the right rate.**

## Part 2

# Teaching High-Frequency Words

In the following section, we look at teaching high-frequency words explicitly and scaffolding recognition during reading to increase students' reading accuracy and rate. Word learning lessons and multimodal activities require students to analyze the sequence of letters in these tricky words with irregular spellings, such as *was*, *said* and *through*. To support the transfer of learning to new contexts, you will also find examples of think-aloud demonstrations together with prompts for coaching students during small-group lessons and reading conferences.

## SELECTING THE TEXT TO SUPPORT THE TEACHING

Once we have established the high-frequency words students need to learn, we look for resources to provide practice in reading these words within connected text. There are series specifically designed to provide multiple exposures to specific high-frequency words (see list of Resources on page 190). Emergent-level texts with predictable structures typically focus on the first 100 sight words, and many publishers provide lists of words that accompany each title in their basals and guided reading sets. The sight words in high-frequency readers are introduced cumulatively to build automaticity. For example:

What do you like to do?          What do you like to do?

I like to paint.                          I like to draw.

(from *We Like to Play*! by Ellen Tarlow, 2000, Scholastic)

## IDEAS FOR INTRODUCING AND DEMONSTRATING HOW TO READ HIGH-FREQUENCY WORDS WITH ACCURACY AT AN APPROPRIATE RATE

### Think Aloud About Accuracy

Demonstrate how you use knowledge of a word during independent reading with a think-aloud. During whole-class and/or small-group lessons, simply select a sentence from a text that contains the target word. If students do not have their own copy, display the sentence or passage where it is found with an interactive whiteboard, document camera, big book, chart copy, or overhead projector. Then model how to scan a word to discriminate between commonly confused words, or demonstrate how to read at a rate that conveys the author's purpose, which varies according to genre and text structure. Following are some model think-alouds.

## Accuracy

Model how to attend to each letter in sequence to ensure students store a complete image of the word in their visual memory. This is especially important for silent letters and phonics "rule breakers," or exceptions, such as *does, could,* and *people.*

Fluency includes accuracy with irregularly spelled high-frequency words, such as said and people.

*To read smoothly we need to know the words. There are tricky words in every book that can trip up our reading brain. We need to train our brain to remember them as soon as we see them. To help our reading brain know these words the second we see them, we look carefully at each letter in the words so our brain remembers them.*

***I see a word I know.*** *It is the word __.*

## Scanning Words Effectively

Model the importance of scanning across the word to avoid confusions between words with similar spellings, such as *for/from; was/saw; their/there; were/where; went/want; them/then; his/him.*

*I looked closely at the word and saw that it was not the word* were, *as I first thought. It's actually the word* where. *I read the sentence again and checked that this made sense, and it did. We must look closely at words, as some words share letters, and this can trick us.*

## Think Aloud About Rate

Demonstrate how reading too fast, too slow, or at the same rate throughout a book can interfere with comprehension. Show students how you use your knowledge of the book content and text structure as a guide to reading speed, and how you carefully attend to the signals the author has placed in the text for readers to follow, such as punctuation and text formatting. Verbalize how you adjust your reading speed flexibly as you navigate the text to find the right rate, one that allows you to understand what you are reading.

*When I come to [a bulleted list, complex sentence, new information], I slow down or I will not be able to hold onto this information when I read the next part.*

*When I read the part where the character was feeling sad, I slowed down to show how he was feeling.*

*When I read the part with facts I already know, I speed up because there is no new information here to remember.*

*When I read the exciting part, when the character was running as fast as he could, I increase my reading rate to show this.*

## Strategy Charts

Use picture-cued strategy charts and bookmarks with statements summarizing the various strategies. Check out the "I Can See Words I Know" section on the strategy chart on page 164.

### Picture Cues and Drawing

Help students remember irregular sight words by giving them—or having them create—picture-cued word cards that impose picture cues on the shape of the letters (see sample on page 173) or tell a story that draws attention to the sequence of letters and can be used as a memory hook. For instance, students might draw two ice-cream cones on the *w* in *two* or make a face inside the letter *a* in *head*. (See list of resources on page 190.)

You can also have students illustrate their word cards and collect them in a word wallet. They can write a phrase or short sentence containing the word, either below the word or on the back of the card, and then store it with other words in an index card holder, library pocket pasted to the back of their notebook, plastic bag, folded construction paper pockets, or other "wallet."

| pizza **for** me | spaceship **from** Mars |

### Link New Words to Known Words With Wordplay and Stories

Help students learn a new, tricky word by presenting it in a story with a familiar word that has a similar spelling. The similar word becomes the clue word. For example, use the name *Joe* in a story to introduce *does*: *Joe does magic tricks*. Stories that use rhyming words are particularly memorable: *Why did the guy buy this?* Students can create their own stories—the sillier they are, the more likely students are to remember them.

Keep word learning fun and light by pointing out visual memory cues for letter sequences such as the two *o*'s in *look* and *good,* four letters in the word *four*, and so on.

### Letter Pairs and Chunks

To teach letter pairs and chunks, divide the target word into pairs of letters, such as *bl* and *ue* or *co* and *me* or into chunks, such as *be + ca + use*.

### Words as Acronyms

Create sentences in which the initial letter of each word is used to spell the target word. For instance, for the word *who*, use the sentence <u>W</u>ho <u>h</u>as <u>o</u>ranges? If students remember the sentence, they can spell the word.

## GUIDED PRACTICE LESSONS FOR ACCURACY AND RATE

Different groups of students can work with words of varying complexity. In the first lesson, we examine the regular parts of a target word first, typically initial consonants and vowels. Then we examine the tricky parts, such as silent consonants and complex vowel sequences. This lesson format is appropriate for either whole-class or small-group contexts. The second lesson, which is adapted from Schirmer (2010), is designed for small-group settings and integrates auditory, tactile, and visual memory cues to help students recall these words during reading. The lessons also appear as Forms 5.3 and 5.4 on the CD.

## HIGH-FREQUENCY WORD LESSON #1 (whole-class or small-group)

**STEP ❶ Analyze the letter sequence.**

Show the word card to students.

> said

Say the word and have students say it with you.

Model how to analyze the order of letters. Point out the regular parts that aid decoding, such as beginning or final letter sounds—for example, the /s/ and /d/ in *said*.

*There are parts of the word we can sound out and parts that we cannot. In the word* said, *we hear* s *at the beginning and* d *at the end.*

**STEP ❷ Examine the match/mismatch of sounds and letters.**

Have students listen for the sounds in the word.

Say the word slowly and listen for the number of sounds you hear.

*Let's say the sounds together. How many sounds did you hear? Show me with your fingers. We hear three sounds in the word* said.

*Now let's count the letters in* said *together.* [Point to each letter as you count them together.] *We see four letters, but we hear three sounds. Why? Let's look closely at the spelling.*

*The first sound we hear is /s/ and it is spelled with the letter* s. *The next sound we hear is /e/ and it is spelled with the letters* a *and* i *together. The last sound is /d/, spelled with the letter* d.

Point out the irregular part(s) of the word. Draw students' attention to tricky parts, such as where more than one letter represents a single sound, silent letters, and different spellings of the same sound

*The tricky part is in the middle, the /e/. When we see this word in our book today, we will need to remember that this sound is spelled with* a-i *in* said.

**STEP ❸ Review familiar words intermixed with the new word.**

Shuffle three to seven familiar word cards with the new word. Provide a timed cue before presenting each word, such as a three second countdown, and prompt students to read the word in unison, by asking: "What's the word?"

## HIGH-FREQUENCY WORD LESSON SEQUENCE #2 (small-group)

**STEP ❶ Say the word.**
- Present the word printed on a flash card.

> could

- Say the word.
- Ask students to look at the word and say it, pronouncing the word together.
- Provide positive feedback: *You are correct!*

**STEP ❷ Repeat the word.**

Ask students to say the word five times while looking at the word card, speaking louder each time. Provide positive feedback.

STEP ❸ Identify the word.

- Show and review three word cards students have already learned.
- Shuffle in the new word card.
- Tell students to say "no" each time they see a word that is not the target word. Instruct them to say the word in a whisper voice when they do see it. Provide positive feedback.

STEP ❹ Provide multimodal practice.

Guide students through the following steps:

*Close your eyes and picture the word in your mind's eye. Now say it in a whisper.*

*Let's spell the word aloud together, letter by letter.*

*Let's write the word as we spell it.* [Have students write on the table or whiteboard surface with their forefinger while saying each letter aloud.]

STEP ❺ Turn and talk.

- Ask the students to describe the word; what does it look like and sound like? You may ask students to tell a buddy, or allow each child a turn to describe the word.

STEP ❻ Practice with reading materials

- Have each student locate the word in a sentence or page from the reading material they will read in this lesson. Students can frame the word with their fingers or highlight with a transparent counter.
- Have each student read the word in context.

## Small-Group Review Game: 3-2-1 Pickup

This review may be used after Lesson #1 or #2 to provide additional guided practice and the opportunity to monitor student progress.

### Steps

1. Distribute a set of 3 or 4 cards to each student. Have students place the cards in a row in front of them.

2. Say one of the words and ask students to select the correct word card and hold it up on your cue: *3-2-1! Cards up.* Students hold up their word card at the same time.

3. Provide positive feedback and ask students to return the card to their desk. Repeat.

## GUIDING PROMPTS FOR ACCURACY AND RATE

As students read the text on their own during small-group lessons and reading conferences, we coach them to recognize their target words in context and read at an appropriate rate using prompts designed for this purpose.

### Accuracy

When students stumble over a previously taught high-frequency word during reading, it's important not to immediately provide the word. This interruption will only reinforce word-by-word reading and encourage students to overly focus on accuracy, which can cause them to hesitate at each word and constantly seek affirmation of correctness. Instead, our goal is for students to scan the text for high-frequency words they have learned and recall the letter sequence of these words from their visual memory. Prompt for miscues at the end of a sentence or after several unsuccessful attempts to self-correct. Begin with prompts that encourage searching and self-monitoring behaviors.

*Do you see a little word you know?*

*Do you spy words you know?* (Play "I spy with my little eye" on the page.)

*You know this word. Show me this word.* [present word card for student to locate in text]

*Can you see the word in your mind's eye?* [recall visual image]

## Rate

When the rate or pace of reading interferes with maintaining meaning, as happens when students read in run-on sentences or too fast/too slow for the demands of the text, use these prompts:

*Speed up at the exciting parts.*

*Slow down when there is lots of new information.*

*Try reading it without using your finger.*

*Stop at the periods.*

## GUIDED PRACTICE ACTIVITIES AND IDEAS

To help students read high-frequency words automatically and fluently, we need to offer multimodal practice activities, which activate multiple pathways to the brain and enhance learning. You will find activities that are appropriate for all teaching contexts—whole-class, small-group, and independent practice.

### Sight Word Sorts

Have students sort a set of eight to ten words with similar patterns. Students scan the words for the target letter sequences, which are written in the top row of a two- or three-column sorting mat, then place each word in the appropriate column. For instance, you might have students compare words that begin with *wh* and *w*, as in *where* and *were*; see sample mat below.

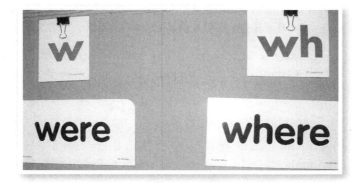

## Venn Diagrams

Use a Venn diagram as a graphic organizer to help students compare commonly confused words (*went, want; for, from*), including homonyms (*there, their*).

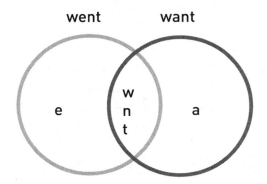

went        want

## Word Pyramids

Have students create word pyramids for target words by writing the first letter at the top of the pyramid. On each subsequent line, they add a letter, and the final line contains the whole word.

h

ha

hav

have

## X-Ray Eyes (Southall, 2009)

Train students' visual memory with this fun activity, perfect for a small group.

1. Print the word on the whiteboard. Say the word, then say the letters in sequence as you point to each one. Then say the word again.

2. Ask a student to choose a letter to delete from the word. Erase this letter wherever it occurs.

3. Repeat the process of saying the word, pointing to each letter, including the missing letter, and saying the word. Students will use their x-ray eyes to "see" (recall from memory) the missing letter.

4. Repeat the process so the letters are progressively removed. Students use their "x-ray eyes" to chant all the letters and then state the word each time— *t-h-e-r-e, there.*

*there*

*th r*

## Sentence Building: Connecting Word Cards

Print the target words on index cards as you teach them and display with picture cards of people, animals, objects, places, and actions. Provide 6–12 high frequency word cards for students to select from, depending on the students' developmental stage. Invite students to create sentences by combining the word and picture cards (see example below).

| Our |  | was | on | the |  |

## Picture-Story Words and Hand Motions

Word cards with accompanying picture stories (visual and auditory) imposed onto the letters in the word are available from teacher resource catalog and Web sites (see list of resources on page 190). Model and have students repeat the motions described with the picture stories (action). For example, move your fingers "through" the letters in the word *through*.

Incorporate meaningful associations to words with picture-based stories and hand motions.

## Sight-Word Poems

Rhyming sight word poems are fun to chant and can help students remember how to spell these all-important words. See the list of resources on page 190 for collections of sight-word poems.

## Songs

Set strategy statements (see Forms 4.4–4.6) to well-known tunes to help students remember them. For instance, use the tune of "If You're Happy and You Know It" to reinforce the "I see a word I know" strategy:

If I'm reading and **I see a word I know**

If I'm reading and **I see a word I know**

If **I see a word I know** and really want to show it

If I'm reading I see and say **a word I know**

Songs are also a great way to teach the spelling of high-frequency words. Just piggy-back the spelling to a familiar tune.

Examples:

**Three-Letter Spelling Song** (Tune: "Three Blind Mice")

*w-a-s, w-a-s*

*w-a-s, w-a-s*

I can spell *was*

I can spell *was*

*w-a-s, w-a-s*

**Six-Letter Spelling Song** (Tune: "Happy Birthday")

*F-r-i-e-n-d,*

*F-r-i-e-n-d,*

I just spelled the word *friend*

*F-r-i-e-n-d*

## List of Piggyback Tunes for Practicing High-Frequency Words

Use the spelling of the word as the lyrics to the entire song and add statements as in the previous examples, as necessary.

**Three-Letter Words**

"This Old Man"

"Jingle Bells"

"Three Blind Mice"

**Four-Letter Words**

"YMCA"

"Twinkle, Twinkle Little Star"

"Are You Sleeping?"

**Five-Letter Words**

"Row, Row, Row Your Boat"

"B-I-N-G-O"

"You Are My Sunshine"

**Six-Letter Words**

"Happy Birthday"

"The Farmer in the Dell"

"Skip to My Lou"

**Seven-Letter Words**

"She'll Be Coming Round the Mountain"

"Willoughby Wallaby Woo"

**Eight-Letters Words**

"For He's a Jolly Good Fellow"

**Nine-Letter Words**

"I'm A Little Teapot"

## Turn and Talk

Auditory learners benefit greatly from talking and listening to peers. Have pairs take turns spelling target words to each other.

## Nursery Rhyme Action Cloze

In this cloze task, students actively participate in repeated readings of a short text, often a nursery rhyme. After each reading, cover a non-high-frequency word with a sticky note; on subsequent readings, substitute an action (thumbs-up, swimming motion, and so on) for that word. Students end up with extensive practice reading the high-frequency words that are not covered.

### Steps

1. Copy the text of a nursery rhyme, song, or poem on chart paper.

2. Read the text together.

3. Cover one word that is not a high-frequency word with a sticky note and reread, substituting an action for the missing word.

4. Repeat this process until all but the high-frequency words are covered.

Example: (Traditional Rhyme)

I had a little turtle. His name was Tiny Tim.
I put him in the bathtub to see if he could swim.
He drank up all the water, and ate up all the soap
And now he's sick in bed with bubbles in his throat.

## Spelling Cheer

Larger muscle movements have a greater impact on memory that small muscle movements. So getting kids up and moving or using their whole arm as opposed to just their fingers can really help them learn. Integrate spelling cheers into your daily fitness routine.

### Steps

1. Print the high-frequency word on a line on the board or chart paper.

2. Point out the configuration of the word produced by the tall letters, letters that sit on the line, and letters with tails.

3. Practice reaching for the sky in a big stretch for the tall letters, such as *t* and *h*, placing hands on hips (the midline) for letters sitting on the line, such as *a* and *m*, and touching your toes (or as far as you can go!) for letters with tails, such as *g* and *y*.

4. When students know the movements, have them chant or cheer the spelling of the word as they do the movement for each letter. Begin by stating the word, and end with a rousing cheer as you call out the whole word again. For example:

*could—c-o-u-l-d—could!*

### Spell and Clap to a Rhythm

Auditory and kinesthetic learners in particular enjoy saying and clapping letters or syllables in words. You can use a rhythmic beat for this, saying the letters individually or in clusters. Begin by saying the letters with rhythm while students tap or clap along with you. I use a drum or tambourine to model the beat and add to the auditory experience. Next have students join in saying the letters with you to the rhythm. The beat you use will need to align with the number of letters. For example, a 2-3-2 beat for the word *because* would sound like this: b-e/c-a-u/s-e.

### Use Manipulatives

Tactile learners love manipulatives, and there are lots of fun ways to use manipulatives to learn high-frequency words These hands-on activities are ideal for small groups and independent practice. They provide an opportunity for students to construct a concrete representation of the word.

- **Word Ropes or Bracelets:** Students can string letter beads to spell high-frequency words on a plastic string, making a bracelet if desired. (See resources on page 190 for sources for letter beads.)

- **Building Words:** Students practice forming words with magnetic letters, letter links, or letter cubes.

### Games

The following games provide fun, interactive practice with high-frequency words.

### Word Relay

Partners or a small group of three or four students can play this game. Provide 8–12 previously taught high-frequency words printed on cards. Make a two-column sorting mat with a file folder and print Yes and No as the category headings.

**Steps**

1. Students place the high-frequency word cards facedown in a stack.

2. They take turns picking up and reading the cards.

3. If a student knows the word, he or she places it under the heading Yes.

4. If a student does not know the word, he or she passes it to another student.

5. If the second student can't read the word, it is placed under the heading No on the mat.

6. Students write the words under the two headings in their notebooks.

| Yes | No |
|-----|-----|
| *was* | *every* |

## I Spy

Ask students to find the target word(s) in a sentence or on a page. Display the target word(s) in a pocket chart, on the whiteboard, or on cards.

*I spy a word I know. The word is _____.*

## Sight Word Concentration

This game can be played with a group of students using a pocket chart or tabletop. After you have practiced it together, include it in your word study center.

- Print a set of 8–12 target words on index cards with numbers on the back.
- Turn over the sight word cards and mix them up. Ask a volunteer to turn over a card, say the word on the card, then try to find a match by turning over another card. If there is no match, go to the next player.

## What's Missing?

Make a familiar sight word out of lowercase magnetic letters. Ask students to examine the word, checking each letter in sequence. Next, have students close their eyes while you remove one of the letters. When they open their eyes, ask them to tell you what letter is missing. Repeat with other letters.

## INDEPENDENT PRACTICE IDEAS FOR ACCURACY AND RATE

Students benefit from lots of practice reading and rereading high-frequency words to build their automaticity. The following activities are fun and engaging and provide multiple exposures to high-frequency words.

### Use Manipulatives

### Flap Books

Students can create flap books, with a flap for each letter and the entire word written underneath.

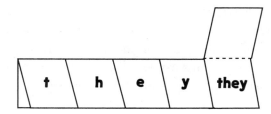

### Eye Pointers

Students use fun pointers to locate and read target words. Popsicle sticks with craft googly eyes glued on the end are perfect for pointing to words in books or charts.

### Key-Ring Word Collections

Write high-frequency words on index cards and punch a hole in the top left corner; then bind the collection with a book ring. Students enjoy flipping through words and reading them with a partner; you can add more words as you teach them.

### Word Collage

Have students cut up a large copy of the target word and paste it to a sheet of construction paper. Students can write, draw, or paste words and images around the target word that they associate with the word.

### Puzzle Words

Print target words or a short sentence containing them onto blank jigsaw puzzles available from teaching catalogs. Students put them together to read the "mystery" word(s).

### Make Textured Words

Mix powdered tempera paint and sand in baby food jars. Students use glue to write the target word on construction paper. Next they sprinkle the paint and sand mixture over it. When the word dries, they trace each letter with their finger, saying the letter name and then the word, for example, *t-h-e-y, they*.

Students make a word tree of words they are learning at the center.

Students build the word with magnetic letters, mix it up and rebuild it again three times.

### Squishy Words

Fill a resealable plastic bag about one-quarter to one-third full with hair gel, finger paint, or a mixture of tempera paint and Jell-O with a similar color. Secure the bag to cardboard with masking tape. Students choose a word from the word wall or a word card at the center and use their index finger to make each letter in the word by pressing into the gel or paint. Students can erase the word by gently rubbing the bag until the mixture is evenly spread again.

### Textured Placemat

Cover a student lapboard, clipboard, or vinyl table placemat using a fabric with a raised texture or a smooth surface, like velvet. Different students will prefer different textures (see Placemats on page 36). Students say the word, use their index finger to write the letters as they say them, and repeat the word.

*Differentiating Reading Instruction for Success With RTI* © 2011 by Margo Southall • Scholastic Teaching Resources

## Part 3

# Teaching Phrasing and Expression

Reading with phrasing and expression supports comprehension, but it doesn't come naturally to many children. We can demonstrate fluent reading in our read-alouds and offer students abundant guided and independent practice opportunities to practice reading with phrasing and expression.

## IDEAS FOR INTRODUCING AND DEMONSTRATING PHRASING AND EXPRESSION

Think aloud about reading in phrases and using expression during read-alouds, shared reading, and small-group lessons. Be sure to address the key ideas described in the model think-alouds in the next section.

### Phrasing Mini-Lesson: Introducing the Concept of Phrases

To introduce phrases, follow these steps.

1. Choose a sentence from a book you're reading with students, but don't show it to them. Read the sentence slowly, word by word, at a steady rate in a monotone voice. Then read it again, pausing at the phrases and using expression.

2. Ask students what they noticed about the two different readings. Which was easier to understand?

3. Now show them the sentence, and draw students' attention to the meaningful chunks, or phrases, within it.

4. Tell them that reading meaningful phrases together and pausing briefly between them makes for smooth reading. It also helps them locate and recognize important information within sentences.

5. Invite students to practice reading the sentence. You may also show them new sentences and ask them to read them, finding appropriate "pausing places" between phrases. Students may not always agree on pausing places, and that's okay as long as the meaning of the sentence is maintained.

6. To help students "see" the pausing places, you can mark phrases with slash marks in pencil or a sticky note strip. This is a new concept for young learners, and you can repeat this activity many times to help them understand it.

**Without Phrasing**

*Henry and Henry's big dog Mudge woke up one Saturday in February and looked outside.*

- - - - - - - - - - - - - - - - - - - - - - - - - - - - - - - - - - - - - - - →

**With Phrasing**

*Henry | and Henry's big dog Mudge | woke up | one Saturday in February | and looked outside.*

"Chunking phrases helps train readers to take in a number of related words each time their eyes stop and to read this chunk of words automatically, with accuracy and expression, picking up context and meaning. With practice, they are able to view more words at a time, increasing their eye span and decreasing the number of times their eyes stop per line."

(Weaver in Prescott-Griffith & Witherell, 2004, p. 156)

### Compare Reading With and Without Phrasing

Draw students' attention to the importance of phrasing by having them experience how it sounds and feels to read a long sentence without taking a breath. Have students read aloud a very familiar nursery rhyme, song, or poem without pausing—straight through to the end mark. Even those who have not grasped the concept of phrasing will notice what it feels like not to pause for breath.

### Modeling Expression

Think aloud often about how you decide what expression to use as you're reading. Point out how punctuation can help you, as does the meaning of the text. A quick think-aloud can make a big difference; it can be as simple as this:

*I see an exclamation point at the end of this sentence, and I know the characters are excited, so I'm going to use my voice to show excitement as I read.*

## GUIDED PRACTICE LESSON: PHRASING

When students are accustomed to pointing to each word as they read, they may find it difficult to switch to reading in meaningful phrases. To help with this transition, choose sentences from students' current reading, write them on sentence strips, and cut the phrases apart. Use noun and verb phrases at first; then add prepositional phrases.

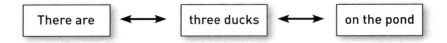

### Steps

1. Model reading each phrase.

2. Push the cards together and read the complete sentence. Invite students to do the same.

3. Progress to complete, uncut sentences, and model phrasing by scooping your hand under each phrase as you read it. Have students repeat the sentence after you.

## GUIDING PROMPTS

As students are learning to read in phrases with expression, it's important that you do not interrupt their reading for every decoding error. If meaning is maintained, let the error go. After a student has finished reading a selection, you may do one of the following to help them develop fluency:

- Prompt: *Try reading it with your finger. Now, take away your finger and read again. Which sounds smoother?*

- Frame two- or three-word phrases with index cards, and prompt students to read the phrase all together.

- Slide your finger or a card over the words the student has already read to push the student's eyes forward; this trains the eye to look beyond the word being read. Readers need to scan two or three words ahead to maintain fluency.

## Phrasing

As you listen to students read, use these prompts if they need support with phrasing:

*Look for words that belong together.*

*Where could you take a quick breath?*

*What does that phrase tell you?* [Isolate the phrase with masking cards.]

*Where would it make sense to break the sentence?*

## Expression

As you listen to students read, use these prompts if they need support with expression:

*Take a quick breath at the commas.*

*Watch for signs along the way.*

*How would the character say that?*

*How is the character feeling when she says this?*

*Can you read it like you're talking?*

## GUIDED PRACTICE ACTIVITIES AND IDEAS

### Repeated Reading to Support Fluency Development

Repeated reading is a classic technique for building fluency. As students become familiar with the text, they decode the words more quickly and can devote attention to phrasing and expression. The key is to make the repeated reading purposeful, and there are several ways to make the task fun for students.

### Repeated Reading: Fluency With Humor

Humor is another pathway to the brain that supports engagement and learning. It can certainly help overcome the reluctance some students have to reading the same text multiple times. Having an audience is essential, as is using a short, high-interest text such as comic strips, riddles, jokes, or a humorous excerpt from a book. In order for others to "get the joke," students must use appropriate expression—this might entail exaggerating a play on words, paying attention to punctuation, and of course, pausing before the punch line.

#### Steps

1. Locate comic strips, riddles, and jokes at an appropriate reading and interest level for your students.

2 Display an enlarged copy of the text on the overhead or make copies for students.

3. Read the text to the students, modeling fluent reading, and discuss the meaning of the joke. Focus attention on the vocabulary, connections, and inferences required to "get it."

4. Focus attention on the text features. Ask, *How do these affect the way we read the text? Does the use of phrasing and punctuation help convey the humor? Are the pauses important?*

5. Reread and ask students to listen for your use of intonation and inflection.

6. Choral-read the comic or joke based on the model of fluent reading you have just demonstrated.

7. Distribute jokes for students to discuss and read in pairs or groups.

Small groups of students may also select specific riddles from thematic riddle books that reflect a current topic you are studying. Groups practice reading these with expression before sharing them with the class. This can be a quick ten-minute-practice, or ten-minute-share activity.

### Whole-Class Repeated Reading: Inside/Outside Circle

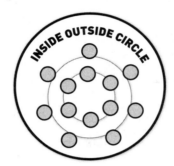

In this activity, students have multiple opportunities to practice oral reading fluency for an audience in a relatively short period of time. Consider having students practice their favorite character line quoted from a book, riddle, joke, or humorous story excerpt in readiness for this activity once a week for several weeks, then alternate this with Readers Theater (Prescott-Griffin & Witherell, 2004). On the day of the activity, have students form two circles with an equal number of students in each, one inside the other. Students on the inside circle turn and face their partner from the outside circle and read their text. Then the student in the outside circle reads his or her text. When pairs have finished reading, students in the inside circle rotate to the right and repeat the process with a new partner. Students can rotate all around the circle.

### Mark the Text

Mark off phrases in a text with slashes. Read the text aloud, modeling appropriate phrasing and expression. Then have students read it chorally several times. After they've practiced, give each student an unmarked copy of the text and ask them to read it aloud; this enables you to monitor for transfer to independent reading (Blevins, 2001).

*Will power// is trying hard// not to do something// you really want to do//," said Frog.*

(from *Frog and Toad Together* by Arnold Lobel)

### Construct Phrase Pyramids

Write a sentence on a sentence strip and cut it into phrases. You will be constructing a phrase pyramid, so you'll also need to create additional sentence strips with one phrase added each time. So, for the four-phrase sentence shown below, you'd create four phrase sentence strips for the first part of the activity (see Figure 1), then four more sentence strips, each with an additional phrase; the last strip will have the entire sentence (see Figure 2). Place the phrases vertically on the table. Read the sentence to and with students, pointing to each phrase as you read. Use the phrases to generate predictions and connections on the story or topic.

*Here is a sentence from our book today. In your book, the words are written across the page, but I am showing them to you like this so you can see how the author put important information in phrases. What have we already found out about this book from reading the phrases?*

> When evening came

> and Henry finally had to crawl into bed,

> he could hardly wait

> to finish the castle.

Figure 1

Next, display and read the phrases in the form of a pyramid sentence. Discuss the phrase breaks. Read each phrase strip and then the sentence together, attending to the phrases. You can mark the boundaries with a sticky dot or slash mark.

*What do you notice about the way these strips look?* [They get longer as you progress to the bottom.] *That is because I have added one more phrase to each line until we have the whole sentence at the bottom.*

*Now I'll read it to you. Listen for groups of words—the phrases—that belong together. You will need to know where the phrases are, so you pause briefly after each one, taking a breath if you need to. Where is the first phrase? Now look at the next strip. Can you spot the phrases? It's getting tougher. Now look at the third strip. Now the fourth. Take a breath, now let's read the entire sentence together.*

> When evening came

> When evening came and Henry finally had to crawl into bed,

> When evening came and Henry finally had to crawl into bed, he could hardly wait

> When evening came and Henry finally had to crawl into bed, he could hardly wait to finish the castle.

Figure 2

### Label the Phrases

In this activity, students write above the text (use a photocopy, or provide sticky notes if students are working with the original), marking and labeling phrases by the type of information they provide: who, what, where, or when. The text needs to be at students' independent reading level if they're working in a center; it can be instructional if they're working with you in a small group. Partners or table groups can work together to mark an enlarged or triple-spaced copy of the sentence.

Henry's mother stayed in the kitchen to read the morning paper.

### Choral Reading of Common High-Frequency Word Phrases

Combine previously taught high-frequency words with the new ones you are currently teaching to create phrases of two to four words to use for practice. Model identifying high-frequency phrases in familiar text using a pointer or highlighter tape in a big book or chart story. Frog and Toad books by Arnold Lobel are excellent resources, but you can use excerpts from any familiar text.

**Steps**

1. Create phrases using familiar words or select high-frequency phrases from reading material.
2. Print the phrases in a list on a whiteboard or overhead transparency.
3. Model fluent reading of the phrases.
4. Have students choral-read the phrases.

High-frequency words vary in their complexity or level of irregularity, just as regular words do, and the phrases we use reflect this. In the chart below we see three levels of complexity to meet the developmental stages of our students.

| Beginner | Intermediate | Advanced |
|---|---|---|
| **Regular spellings**<br>e.g., it can | **Irregular spellings**<br>e.g., are they coming | **Most common misspellings**<br>e.g., around the people |

### Readers Theater

Readers Theater has become very popular over the past decade, and there are differentiated resources available where each part in the script is at a different reading level. This allows low-progress students to participate in a class or group performance. Many leveled books can easily be adapted for this purpose. Fictional texts with dialogue are an obvious option. A narrator role can be created for the remaining text. Informational text can be organized into parts where animals, historical figures, continents, or countries tell all about themselves. This is an effective way to integrate reading (fluency and comprehension), writing, and content learning. Have students first summarize and write the information as a script in a shared writing activity or in small groups. In this way, Readers Theater offers a scaffold for learning new information within a highly interactive, repeated reading activity.

Readers Theater in action

## Music and Lyrics

Lyrics to popular songs downloaded from the Internet provide an authentic purpose for reading (see List of Resources on page 190). They also serve to model fluency and comprehension, especially when the lyrics convey a universal message students connect with, and they often require students to make inferences. Read lyrics aloud to students before singing them together, and display for independent reading.

Playing background music that varies in tempo and pace, from rap to polka, supports expressive reading of different types of poetry. Students will gain insight into how rhythm and mood impacts the listener's experience, including the interpretation of the poem's meaning. Music can be used as an accompaniment to a whole-class choral-reading activity. Load songs onto individual iPods or provide CDs that can be played on the computer and listened to with headphones as students independently practice reading their poem. Having music playing in the background during reading helps remove some of the anxiety they may feel when required to read aloud.

## Technology-Assisted Reading

Most books available on CD are not appropriate for fluency training due to the rate of the professional reader. Students simply cannot keep pace; they may be reading 70 words per minute while the reader on the CD reads 140. Students need to be able to keep pace, which means you have to select materials that are constructed specifically for fluency training practice. A number of these can be found in the List of Resources at the end of the chapter. For more on using the latest technology to make text accessible, see Using Technology Tools: Do You Have the Apps That Make Text Accessible? on page 33.

### Steps

1. Select books at or just above the student's instructional reading level. Choose both fiction and nonfiction on topics of interest and books rich in language and detail to develop vocabulary.

2. Explain to students that they will listen to how a fluent reader reads aloud and use the model to improve their own fluency.

3. Have students listen to the recording as they follow along in their books.

4. Tell students to stop at the end of each page (or at the end of the story) and reread using the same rate, phrasing, and expression as the narrator. Students repeat this process until they feel confident reading the passage in a fluent manner.

### Step to the Beat: Phrase Walk

Print phrases from familiar nursery rhymes, poems, or songs on cardstock or sentence strips. You can use picture cards for developing readers. Laminate for durability. Have students read the complete text, chorally if desired. Then have them read each phrase card together. Next, place the cards in sequence on the floor, spacing them apart so students can step from one to the next. Invite students to step from phrase to phrase, reading with rhythm and expression as they do. For a challenge, mix up the phrase steps and have students reorder them.

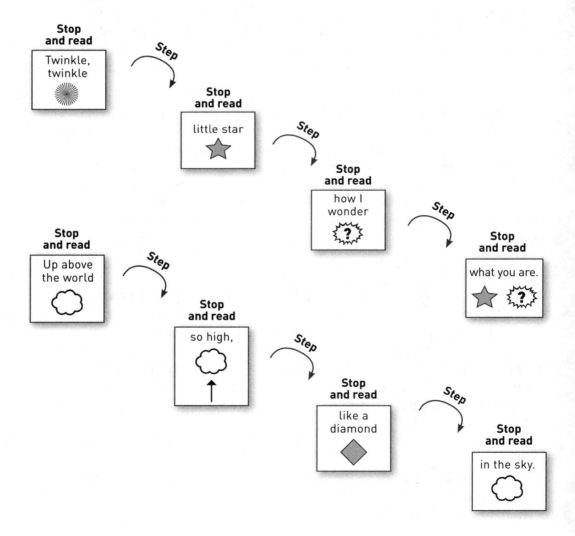

## Be the Phrase

On separate index cards, print each word in a phrase taken from familiar reading material. Read the phrase aloud, showing each word card as you say the word. Then distribute the word cards to students and have them arrange themselves to form the phrase.

## Where's the Phrase?

Copy a sentence from a familiar text onto cards, one word per card. Read the sentence aloud, showing each word card as you say the word. Distribute the cards to students and have the rest of the group decide how the students should arrange themselves to form a phrase. Those students move close to each other, leaving space between their "group" and the students forming the next phrase within the sentence.

## Phrase Sort

This activity addresses students' difficulty with the flow of reading by helping them examine how phrases tell us important information about characters, places, events, actions, or facts.

To begin, have students sort the phrases under header cards for Who, What, Where, When, Why, and How. Once they get the hang of the activity, try other possible categories, such as the following:

- Phrases that refer to actions
- Phrases that describe how something happened
- Phrases that tell us the amount—how many of something
- Phrases students make personal connections to
- Phrases that contain certain words, or a specific number of words

### Steps

1. Select phrases from the reading material that students will be able to sort in a number of different ways. Stories and poetry are both appropriate.

2 Print the phrases on cards so they may be read as a single unit.

3. Sort the phrases in a number of ways before reading and then again after reading. For example, you could sort by character, setting, and problem (who, where, and what).

4. Students may work with a partner and share their sort with the rest of the class. Any justifiable categorization is acceptable.

5. Ask students to use these sorts to make predictions about the text.

6. Locate the information embedded within the phrases. Ask students what is interesting and what is important information to use in the retelling or summary.

Here are two ways some phrases from the book *My Rotten Red-Headed Brother* by Patricia Polacco could be sorted.

| When | Where |
|------|-------|
| then she laughed | next to the rhubarb bushes |
| most of the afternoon | almost down to the leaf |
| as I went into the house | |

**Happy**

**Sad**

**Excited**

## Emotion Cue Cards

Draw simple faces showing different expressions—excited, angry, happy, scared, and so on—on cards and use them to prompt students to read with expression.

### Steps

1. Print a sentence from the story on a sentence strip or on the whiteboard.

2. Place an expression card alongside the sentence and have students read the sentence using intonation that matches the facial expression on the card.

3. Switch cards and repeat the process, having students use a different intonation this time to match the new emotion cue.

## INDEPENDENT PRACTICE ACTIVITIES

### Sentence Stems

Write high-frequency phrases or phrases taken from students' current reading material on index cards. Have students generate sentences containing the phrases, either orally or in writing. Introduce and model with the class and place at the fluency center.

### Poetry Four Corners

Students practice reading aloud a poem of their choice to perform for their classmates. At the end of the week, groups are formed in each corner of the room and students performance-read the poem to their peers, in turn. They read from a printed copy and may make an illustrated title on construction paper to display as they read. Students are reorganized into different groups each week. This same format can be used for reading aloud comic strips, riddles, and jokes. If you have students make an illustrated copy of the whole poem, display it at the fluency center after the performance for the rest of the class to enjoy.

### Phrase Sort

The activity from 187 can be adapted as an independent activity.

# Putting It All Together

The Fluency Five-Day Lesson Sequence incorporates each of the aspects of fluency together with comprehension in a cumulative, step-by-step format. This sequence enables teachers to achieve balance while meeting the needs of a range of student profiles within their classroom. It is appropriate for both whole-class and small-groups contexts. For Days 2–4, select from the activities in this chapter (see page range for each skill area) to add variety throughout the year. The lesson sequence is also on the CD in Form 5.5

| Fluency Five-Day Lesson Sequence |
| --- |
| **Day 1:**<br>**Teaching Point:** Do a read-aloud for understanding and enjoyment. (vocabulary and comprehension)<br>• Preteach vocabulary—e.g., word web, multimodal activities (see Chapter 6).<br>• Turn-and-talk in partners using familiar comprehension strategies (bookmarks and prompts)—e.g., making connections, generating questions.<br>• Hold a group discussion about the reading. |
| **Day 2:**<br>**Teaching Point:** High-Frequency Words<br>Select activity from those on pages 166–178. |
| **Day 3:**<br>**Teaching Point:** Expression<br>Select activity from those on pages 179–188. |
| **Day 4:**<br>**Teaching Point:** Phrasing<br>Select activity from those on pages 179–188. |
| **Day 5:**<br>**Teaching Point:** Self-Evaluation and Comprehension<br>• Partner Reading with feedback<br>• Writing in response to reading—written retelling or summary with graphic organizer or prompts on Strategy Placemats for integrated strategy use (see Forms 6.85 and 6.86 on the CD)<br>• Self-Assessment—rate, accuracy, phrasing and comprehension. (see Form 5.1 on the CD). |

# Resources for Differentiated Fluency Instruction

## HIGH-FREQUENCY WORDS

### Word Cards and Manipulatives

Picture-cued stylized sight word cards with actions: www.Child-1st.com

Fry's sight word cards can be downloaded from: www.flashcardexchange.com

Letter beads for high-frequency word strings or bracelets are available at: www.reallygoodstuff.com

### Videos

*Meet the Sight Words 1 & 2*, Preschool Prep Company, 2009 (available from online bookstores) presents kindergarten sight words in an animated format.

### High-Frequency Word Phrases

Download lists of Fry's 600 sight words ranked in order of use in reading and writing, as well as phrases at this website of Utah Education Network:

http://www.uen.org/k-2educator/word_lists.html#fryphrases

*Sight Word Phrases* by Connie Hiebert and *Sight Word Phrases* Grades 1-4: These books provide sets of cards and are available at www.crystalsprings.com

### Sight-Word Sentences and Reading Materials

*Sight Word Strip Book*: These strip books (five in all) contain sight words in increasing levels of challenge; available from www.Child-1st.com

*Language Tutor Sight Words*: This book contains high-frequency words in context, available at www.reallygoodstuff.com

*High Frequency Words*: This book by Ken Marland contains stories and memory cues; available at Sopriswest.com

*Sight Words That Stick*: This book by Janet Martin teaches sight words with drawing activities and other memory aids, with take home stories; available from the National Reading Styles Institute. www.nrsi.com

High-Frequency Readers: This series by Scholastic features 18 early emergent-level books, lap books, and student books with take-home copies.

Multilevel Readers' Theater scripts are available at: www.benchmarkeducation.com and www.eplaybooks.com

*My Very Own Poetry Collection: 101 Sight Word Poems* by Betsy Franco, available at www.trcabc.com

*The First Hundred Sight Words*: Multisensory Worksheets by Margo Southall available at www.onthemarkpress.com

### Songs for Sight Words

*25 Super Sight Word Songs & Mini-books* by Joan Mancini (2009)

*Silly Songs for Sight Words* By Joan Mancini and sung by kindergarten students available on CD or download at http://www.cdbaby.com/cd/joanmancini

### Music and Lyrics

Lyrics for popular songs are available from www.lyrics.com

Different musical versions of the book *Don't Laugh at Me* by Steve Seskin and Allen Shamblin, including folk and rap, as well as music from Peter Yarrow's songbooks are available free of charge to educators from www.operationrespect.org

Poetry reading with music is supported by the resource titled *Concert Reading* (Primary) by Nancy Polette at www.piecesoflearning.com

### Fluency Reading on CD

National Reading Styles Institute at www.nrsi.com

New Heights available at pacificlearning.com

Scholastic Fluency Formula

Read Naturally: Tapes and CDs of 24 nonfiction stories for grades 1-7. Students time themselves and graph their fluency rate over 3-4 readings, www.readingnaturally.com.

### Professional Books

*Building Fluency: Lessons and Strategies for Reading Success* by Wiley Blevins (2001)

*Fluency in Focus* by Mary Lee Prescott-Griffin and Nancy Witherell (2004)

*Partnering for Fluency* by Mary Kay Moskal and Camille Blachowicz (2006)

*The Fluent Reader* by Timothy Rasinski (2010)

**CHAPTER**

# DIFFERENTIATING COMPREHENSION INSTRUCTION

I n this chapter we examine how to differentiate comprehension instruction with a variety of multimodal learning activities and interactive tools. We'll also address two aspects of comprehension instruction:

**1.** Developing an understanding of word meanings (vocabulary)

**2.** Using a set of strategies to understand a text (comprehension strategies)

It is here that we consider common questions regarding the differentiation process:

- How can we differentiate instruction for students at a range of developmental stages and target the needs of low-progress readers?
- What are the common student profiles of need and what are the tell-tale signs of difficulty?
- What are the components of an effective comprehension program?
- Which visuals, interactive tools, and materials make the difference for low-progress students?

## Chapter Overview

In **Part 1** of this chapter (pages 192–197) we examine common profiles of student need, assessments we can use to identify student needs, and strategies for differentiating our comprehension program (including vocabulary).

**Part 2** (pages 197–210) includes a lesson sequence and multimodal learning tools for teaching vocabulary.

**Part 3** (pages 211–295) includes a lesson sequence for teaching comprehension strategies along with sections that contain ideas and activities for introducing and demonstrating each strategy, providing guided practice, and facilitating independent practice.

# Journey to Differentiation

Sometimes it seems we ask a lot of young children, from decoding words accurately to phrasing appropriately to using comprehension strategies. Recently, some educators have expressed concern that asking students to internalize a set of word-solving strategies (an essential part of instruction and intervention for primary and low-progress readers) already places cognitive demands on young readers and that adding comprehension strategy instruction may overload them. For this reason, Donna Scanlon and her colleagues (2010) have suggested that instruction in comprehension strategies be taught within the context of conversations that revolve around read-alouds, shared reading experiences, and reading done in small groups.

In order to address concerns about placing excessive cognitive demands on young students and to align instruction with current brain research, I provide multimodal scaffolds within highly interactive lessons and activities when teaching comprehension. Using these tools, we can realize the goal of constructive, strategic conversations with any reading material. To foster higher-level thinking, we must be sure to provide time in lessons for students to ask questions, make connections to familiar experiences and other readings, and talk about their understanding with a partner or small group. As we model comprehension strategy use and engage students in thinking and talking about texts, we are building bridges of understanding for our students.

Keeping in mind Susan Neuman's research-based principles for supporting knowledge acquisition in children (2006), I've integrated the following considerations into my teaching:

- Active learning and engagement must be a part of every read-aloud, shared-reading experience, small-group lesson, and guided and independent practice activity.

- Lessons should be centered around instructional goals and supported by multimodal activities.

- Teachers should continually model and scaffold strategy use during whole-class, small-group, and one-on-one interactions.

## Part 1

# Profiles of Student Need

Too often, students can read the words in a text, but they fail to comprehend—they either do not understand the words, do not recall what they've read, or cannot identify the main idea. The lessons, activities, and multimodal tools in this chapter address these issues and the following categories of comprehension difficulties:

1. **Word-bound students:** They have not yet acquired a sufficiently rich receptive or expressive vocabulary to unlock the meaning.

*Differentiating Reading Instruction for Success With RTI* © 2011 by Margo Southall • Scholastic Teaching Resources

2. **Disconnected readers:** They lack the background knowledge necessary to build a bridge between known and new concepts.

3. **Off-track readers:** They become distracted by other ideas that come into their mind that are unrelated to the events or facts in the text.

4. **Storytellers:** They over-rely on background knowledge, making up their minds about what is going to happen before they read the text and failing to integrate new information.

5. **Under-predictive readers:** They read without anticipating events or information, do not revise predictions when they do not match the text, and fail to monitor for meaning during reading.

6. **Passive readers:** They do not process the information in the text and are unable to respond to questions or provide a retell that reflects understanding.

7. **Literalists:** They depend solely on what is written in the text and have difficulty responding to questions that require inferring or integrating multiple sources of information (synthesizing).

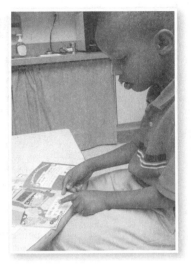

Young students learn to integrate multiple strategies as they read.

8. **Left fielders:** They are unable to answer questions, or they offer responses that are unrelated to the text.

9. **Unequipped readers:** They lack fix-up strategies to solve problems in comprehension, such as unfamiliar vocabulary and concepts that they find confusing.

10. **Solo-strategists:** They apply strategies in isolation rather than integrating them, resulting in a superficial level of comprehension.

The lesson formats and teaching resources in this chapter are designed to support each of these profiles of difficulty. In Part 3, you will find additional suggestions for ways to support students who have difficulty with a particular comprehension strategy. The chart below provides a guide to the sections that address each profile of need.

| WHEN the student profile of need is: | THEN provide these lessons and tasks | Page Number |
|---|---|---|
| • Word-Bound | • Vocabulary Lessons and Activities | 200–210 |
|  | • Making Connections | 212–225 |
| • Disconnected | • Making Predictions and Inferences | 238–253 |
| • Under-Predictive, Off-Track | • Generating and Answering Questions | 225–237 |
| • Literalists, Left Fielder |  |  |
| • Passive | • Making Predictions and Inferences | 238–253 |
| • Unequipped | • Clarifying and Self-Monitoring | 253–264 |
| • Passive, Left Fielder, Storyteller | • Retelling | 264–277 |
| • Literalist, Storyteller | • Summarizing | 278–287 |
| • Solo-Strategist | • Integrating Multiple Strategies | 288–295 |

# Linking to Assessment

To assess comprehension effectively, we must have students read text that requires them to apply integrated sources of information. Therefore, the following assessments are more time-consuming than one-minute fluency assessments.

- **Running Records:** The retelling portion is particularly helpful for evaluating comprehension (see Chapter 2).

- **Informal Reading Inventories:** Graded passages and a set of questions help you determine students' literal, inferential, evaluative, and summative thinking.

- **Rubrics:** Leveled descriptions of reading behaviors and strategy use provide a quick reference for teachers to ascertain students' level of strategy use and determine the next instructional steps. (See page 20 and Form 2.5 on the CD for a time-efficient way to record student strategy use.)

- **Profile as a Reader** The Profile as a Reader form (see page 16 and Form 2.1 on the CD) provides an at-a-glance summary of the assessments that have been administered, including informal observations.

- **Recording Student Talk:** Transcribe students' peer discussions to gain insight into their strategy use; for some students, their talk reveals much more about their comprehension than their written responses do. Recording Student Talk (see page 20 and Form 2.7 on the CD) is designed to enable you to record verbatim the language your students use.

- **Observation of Student Responses:** During group lessons, turn-and-talk partner discussions, and other interactive activities, note the depth and length of student responses using the Observing Student Responses form (see page 20 and Form 2.6 on the CD). For example, using a simple notation system, you can record the following symbols alongside student names as you listen to their discussion: a plus sign indicates adequate understanding; a minus sign indicates a lack of understanding; and an asterisk indicates that a student exceeds expectations. You can assess for specific strategies or integrated strategy use.

- **Reading Conference Summary Form:** The Student Reading Goals, Observations, and Instruction form (see page 19 and Form 2.3 on the CD) is useful for recording observations of student progress during a one-on-one reading conference that focuses on the student's reading current goal. Programmed labels (see the Observation Rubrics—Form 2.5 on the CD) can also be used for this purpose.

- **Conferring Notebook:** You can write notes about the progress students are making on their reading goals in a separate student notebook, which students can take home and share with parents as a form of ongoing communication for intervention students.

- **Self-Assessment**: Students may assess their own strategy use using My Reading Goals (Form 2.13 on the CD).

*Differentiating Reading Instruction for Success With RTI* © 2011 by Margo Southall • Scholastic Teaching Resources

- **Graphic Organizers:** Use the completed student tasks that accompany each strategy in this chapter for assessment purposes.

- **Reader's Notebook/Journal Rubric:** When students are regularly writing or sketching in response to whole-class read-alouds, shared reading, and/or small-group reading, then you may wish to select, or have students select, one entry each week from their journal for assessment. Journal entries can provide a window into the processes students are using to understand text. Use a rubric such as the one in Form 2.5 to assess the entries. Alternatively, you can have students complete a reflection sheet about their journal writing, answering a prompt such as: *Choose one entry from your reading notebook that helped you understand something better. Explain why you chose this entry. What kinds of writing and sketching did you do?* (Sibberson & Szymusiak, 2008).

- **Reading Log:** Students record the books they read during independent reading along with the date and pages read to ensure accountability and encourage diversity in their reading diet. Students should regularly review their log and complete a Reading Log Questionnaire (Sibberson & Szymusiak, 2008), answering a simple question, such as, "What did you learn about yourself as a reader this week?" or "What is a goal you have for your next book/next week of independent reading?" Monitor the logs to see if students are finishing books and selecting reading materials that are right for them in terms of complexity, genre, and interest.

Each of these forms enable teachers to gain insight into the strategic actions students are able to apply during reading.

## Implementing Differentiated Comprehension Instruction

The interactive tools, lessons, and activities in this chapter can be implemented during whole-class read-alouds, as well as in shared reading and small-group lessons.

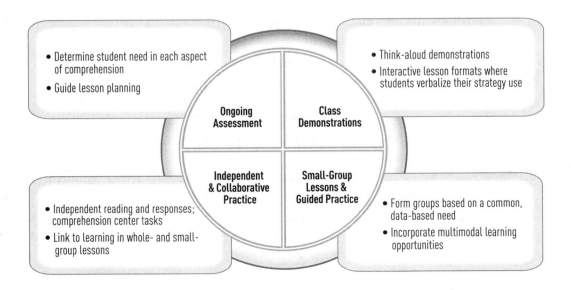

- Determine student need in each aspect of comprehension
- Guide lesson planning

**Ongoing Assessment**

- Think-aloud demonstrations
- Interactive lesson formats where students verbalize their strategy use

**Class Demonstrations**

- Independent reading and responses; comprehension center tasks
- Link to learning in whole- and small-group lessons

**Independent & Collaborative Practice**

**Small-Group Lessons & Guided Practice**

- Form groups based on a common, data-based need
- Incorporate multimodal learning opportunities

Scaffold students' access to strategies with engaging, multimodal tools.

In the Vocabulary and Comprehension strategy sections you will find teaching tools and learning activities correlated to the steps in a lesson sequence—demonstration, guided practice, and independent practice. In Part 2 on Vocabulary and for each Comprehension strategy in Part 3, these are organized into the following sequence:

- Selecting Materials to Model the Strategy

- Ideas for Introducing and Demonstrating the Strategy

- Guided Practice Ideas and Activities

- Guiding Prompts

- Independent Practice

Using multimodal, interactive tools engages all students and allows them to use their strengths to show what they know. By selecting a variety of multimodal activities and interactive tools over a week of whole-class and small-group reading lessons, our reading program becomes both inclusive and differentiated.

## Grouping Students for Instruction

In Chapter 3 the process of grouping students by common instructional goals was a central organizational principle. When it comes to comprehension instruction, I like to arrange students in groups that reflect a range of two to three reading levels but still focus on a common comprehension goal. This means that the text needs to be accessible to all students, so it will be easy for some and at instructional level for others. When working with early literacy groups, a shared reading or read-aloud format may be necessary so that you can use text with sufficient complexity to practice strategic thinking (Walpole & McKenna, 2009).

When we integrate the information from a variety of assessment tools (listed earlier in the chapter), in a typical classroom we find:

- One or more groups of students for whom it is appropriate to continue to teach small-group lessons on the same strategy you are teaching to the whole class and extend students' use of strategic actions to increasingly complex text from a variety of genres.

- One or more groups of students who need further scaffolding of a particular strategy with a range of multimodal tools and independent-level text or a shared reading/read-aloud format to focus them on the thinking process rather than being distracted by word-solving processes.

- One or more groups of low-progress readers for whom the whole-class strategy focus is not appropriate for small-group lessons. This often occurs when inferential and evaluative questions or summarizing is the instructional focus. If the foundation for these strategies is not in place, then we need to build it so that we can proceed

*Differentiating Reading Instruction for Success With RTI* © 2011 by Margo Southall • Scholastic Teaching Resources

to the next step in the continuum of reading processes. On pages 192–193 we examined the different Profiles of Student Need and the types of confusions and plateaus that occur in the acquisition of effective comprehension strategy use. These become our instructional focus with small groups. You may not have neat groups of 4–6 Under-Predictive Readers and Storytellers, but you will need to pull students by a common need in groups of varying sizes.

When only one student needs to work on a particular skill or strategy, then schedule more reading conferences with him or her. Five minutes of one-on-one time four or five times a week makes a difference for students who stumble or hit a plateau in comprehension.

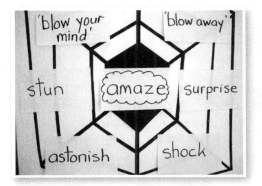

## Part 2

# Vocabulary Development
## Instruction That Impacts Student Comprehension

In Chapter 4 we examined the teaching of word-solving strategies to scaffold our students' use of letter and word patterns to decode new words within running text. In Chapter 5 our focus turned to word-learning strategies for recognizing the most basic words in our language: high-frequency words. Now we turn to expanding student vocabulary so that they can comprehend the increasingly rich language they will be exposed to in class throughout the year.

Students can understand a word after about six exposures to it; it becomes part of their receptive vocabulary. However, if we want students to use the words in their writing and speaking, we need to provide between 21 and 49 exposures before they add these words to their expressive vocabulary (Frey & Fisher, 2009). These exposures do not have to be lengthy encounters; students may simply hear the word in a repeated reading or another passage, and then turn and talk for 30 seconds about how it was used in the sentence. Making a personal connection to the word has the greatest impact on memory, which is why turn-and-talk and sketching a visual representation in vocabulary notebooks are effective vocabulary-building strategies. Keep in mind that in this context it is not the spelling we are focusing on, but the meaning.

Students collect interesting words as they read to share with the rest of the group.

It is not hard to see that much of the on-the-run, unplanned vocabulary-building opportunities that arise during classroom discussions and activities support the growth of students' receptive language. But it is when we intentionally plan and implement learning opportunities for students to interact with specific words in multimodal formats over a series of lessons and activities—and provide ongoing verbal and visual reminders—that we can achieve the instructional goal of moving words to students' expressive vocabulary.

## DIFFICULTIES STUDENTS EXPERIENCE WITH VOCABULARY

We know from research that low-progress readers have been exposed to thousands fewer words than their grade-level classmates, and it is imperative that we integrate vocabulary instruction into our classroom and intervention programs. It does not always have to be a separately scheduled lesson; it can simply be one additional step in our lesson sequence that benefits student comprehension. During the interactive discussions and activities, monitor students to determine if any confusion exists. When students do not demonstrate an understanding of the word during the discussion or in their sketches, provide more descriptions, explanations, or examples. Verbs are easiest. Nouns are harder to learn, and some are more abstract than others—for example, *government* is harder to comprehend than *bear*. Low-progress students require repeated oral exposures to words in order to store them in their phonological memory. It is the oral exposure, not the print, that matters for vocabulary learning, so students need to interact with the word in discussions and games where they have multiple opportunities to hear it and say it.

To support low-progress readers' vocabulary learning, be sure to do the following:

- Preteach key vocabulary words prior to reading the material for the lesson.

- Connect vocabulary to student reading of leveled text in small-group lessons wherever possible.

- Refrain from teaching new vocabulary and a new strategy in the same lesson. Students need time to learn the concepts and terminology before learning a new strategy and how to apply it to text.

- Have students keep a vocabulary notepad or notebook (see page 203).

- Model using context clues.

- Pause and give a cue to help students retrieve the word they are reading; for example, you can offer them a choice of two words, provide the first half of the word, say a rhyming word, give a category name, or state its function.

## Teach Word-Learning Strategies

Teach word-analysis skills to help students successfully store and retrieve new vocabulary:

- Segment words into syllables—e.g., *in-for-ma-tion.*

- Segment syllables into individual sounds [phonemes] e.g., *a-m-a-ze.*

- Segment word into their smallest meaningful units [morphemes] e.g., *photo-graph.*

Since words are stored in our memory by their sounds and meaningful associations, provide clues in a game-like activity to encourage word retrieval (Rubin, 2002):

- *This word sounds like* [provide a rhyme].

- *This word begins with* [name initial consonant and vowel].

- *The first half of the word is* [say first half of word].

- *This word is either* dog or wolf—*how can you tell?* [reveal initial letter only].

## SELECTING WORDS FOR INSTRUCTION

In deciding what words to teach, select words that will be useful across the curriculum, in multiple contexts. We often choose specific categories of words, such as descriptive terms or words that vividly depict action (adjectives and verbs) for explicit vocabulary building. Choose words that are not too difficult to explain, familiar ones that students can explain using their oral vocabulary. The new word should provide a more specific, precise way to express a known concept—for example, *amusing* is a more specific adjective than *funny*. Words with multiple meanings often present challenges to students and must be taught explicitly. If all the words in the text are familiar to students, bring in new words that fit the concepts in the story, even though they do not appear. For example, the word *tasty* can be extended with synonyms, such as *delicious* or *scrumptious*. These may appear to be sophisticated words for young children but research demonstrates that "earlier-acquired word meanings are more readily accessed in later life" (McKeown & Kucan, 2010).

Our goal is for these words to be part of students' personal word bank and quickly retrieved during reading and writing. To ensure this, we plan multiple interactions with the words, always including opportunities for students to learn new words by activities such as these:)

- Talking about the words' meaning

- Sketching what the word means to them

- Generating sentences

- Brainstorming synonyms and antonyms

- Building personal word banks, charts, and vocabulary walls

- Writing literal and actual meanings of words in idioms and expressions

(See the Guided Practice section on pages 206–209 for more ideas.)

## SELECTING MATERIALS TO TEACH VOCABULARY

I have used books such as *Thesaurus Rex* (Steinberg, 2003), which incorporates synonyms through the playful romps of a young dinosaur, to introduce this activity. *The Boy Who Cried Fabulous* by Leslea Newman, *The Boy Who Loved Words* by Roni Schotte, and the humorous wordplay of Marvin Terban's books provide the motivational springboards for seeking out new words and ways to use them.

## IDEAS FOR INTRODUCING VOCABULARY AND DEMONSTRATING THE MEANING: THE SIX-STEP VOCABULARY SEQUENCE

In Chapter 4 we examined the three ways we store and retrieve words, through sound (phonological memory), meaning (semantic memory), and spelling (visual or orthographic memory). We integrate all three sources of information into the vocabulary teaching sequence described on page 201 for read-alouds. The Six-Step Vocabulary Lesson explicitly teaches vocabulary words and provides opportunities for students to interact with the words. A summary of the lesson sequence appears below; descriptions of lesson components and follow-up activities follow the sample lesson.

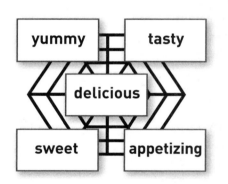

**Step 1:** Notice and name.

**Step 2:** Provide a student-friendly definition.

**Step 3:** Construct a Word Web.

**Step 4:** Provide additional examples and encourage personal connections.

**Step 5:** Add the word to Word Watcher Chart.

**Step 6:** Have students record the word in their Word Watcher Notepad.

Teachers introduce key vocabulary to support comprehension of a nonfiction passage.

## SIX-STEP VOCABULARY TEACHING SEQUENCE

**STEP ❶ Notice and name the word: Refer to the word within the context of the story.**

● Read a short story, poem, or article using the word.

● Reread a statement containing the word and/or rephrase the text being used, drawing attention to relevant context clues (if these provide support).

> *In the story ... was amazed when ...*

● Have students say the word with you.

● You may ask students to share with a partner where they have heard or read the word before.

● Ask students to generate possible meanings with a partner. Provide sentence starters where necessary.

> *I think it means*
>
> *It could mean*

**STEP ❷ Provide a student-friendly definition and present a visual cue.**

● Provide an explanation of the word using everyday language. Share a picture, photograph, or other graphic that represents the word and can serve as a visual cue.

> *Amazed means feeling really surprised and full of wonder about something*

**STEP ❸ Construct a Word Web.**

● Explore the meaning by constructing a Word Web. Brainstorm related words, including synonyms and antonyms, on a Word Web (see Form 6.3 on the CD).

> *It is like the word ...*

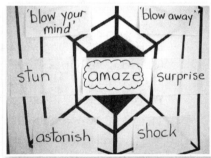

**STEP ❹ Provide additional examples and encourage personal connections with the word.**

You may choose to do several of the following activities:

● Explore other contexts.

> *Someone might be amazed when ...*
>
> *Tell me something you would be amazed about. Try to use amazed when you tell about it.*
>
> *You could start by saying something like: "I would be amazed if .."*
>
> *How is this word used and when do we use it? Why do we have such a word?*

- Offer questions, choices, and reasons.

    *If any of the things I say might be examples of something that would amaze you, say* amazed. *If not, don't say anything. [List situations.]*

    *Which of these things might amaze you? Give me a thumbs-up if you would be amazed. Thumbs down if you would not be amazed. [list situations.]*

    *Why? What could you do to amaze someone?*

    *What would you look like if you were amazed?*

- Use sentence stems.

    *I was amazed when _____.*

    *It would be amazing if _____.*

    *I thought that it was amazing because _____ .*

- Finally, review the word by having the students say it:

    *What's the word we've been talking about?*

    *Let's say our new word together.*

STEP ❺ **Add the word to the Word Watcher Chart.**

    *Let's write our new word on our Word Watcher Chart.*

    Invite a student to illustrate the word on the chart.

STEP ❻ **Record the word in Word Watcher Notepads.**

Have students copy and sketch the word in their personal Word Watcher Notepads (see page 203).

During the week, extend students understanding and usage of the word with interactive, multimodal activities (see Guided Practice Ideas and Activities).

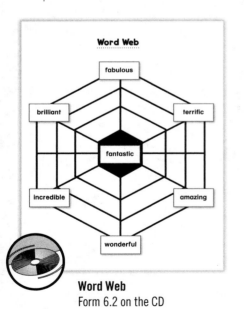

**Word Web**
Form 6.2 on the CD

During the Six-Step Vocabulary Lessons, students engage in the following activities.

### Word Web

The Word Web in Step 3 is an important visual tool. To show that we need to create associations with new words in order to store and retrieve them, we create Word Webs, surrounding the focus words with other words that have similar meanings. Make a chart of a web, laminate it, and use a wipe-off pen so you can reuse it. You can also record the words students generate on sticky notes. Write the focus word in the center of the web and prompt students to share words they know that are like it. What other words does this word make them think of? Discuss how these words help create a clearer picture of the word. You may have partners create their own webs or brainstorm a list of words that come to mind when they hear the focus word. Students construct their own Word Webs using the task card on Form 4.45 on the CD and the blank web template on Form 6.2.

## Word Watcher Chart: Collect Interesting Words

In Step 5 of the vocabulary sequence, students add the target word to a Word Watcher Chart. This is a simple sheet of chart paper that you will add to over time with the words you have selected for the lessons. The chart provides a visual reference for discussions, as well as a source of support for reading and writing tasks.

I also encourage students to look for interesting words in their own reading to share and record on the chart. Keep a marker and index cards nearby for this purpose. Students can also add words of interest to their personal vocabulary notepads. Model this by noting compelling words during whole-class and small-group sessions. Drawing students' attention to vivid imagery or humorous wordplay fosters an awareness of the power of words and encourages students to try new ones in their conversations and writing.

Giving credit to the student who contributed the word serves as a motivation to include interesting words in daily writing. Students can put their initials next to the words. You can also put tally marks next to words to show how often students are using them, as a visual reminder to you and your students to use these words throughout the day. Graph the words to see which ones the class uses the most.

## Word Watcher Notepads

In the last step of the vocabulary lesson teaching sequence, I have students copy and sketch the word in personal word watcher notepads (small spiral notebooks). It is important that each student also draw a sketch, pictograph, or symbolic representation of the word (Marzano & Pickering, 2005) and then describe their image to a peer. If students have trouble generating images, try playing Pictionary to help them grasp the concept and practice this skill. If students say they cannot draw, then teach the concept of speed drawing—making quick pencil sketches with stick figures. Share examples of other students' drawings or allow students to work in teams. (See Form 4.44 for a task card for this activity.)

In addition to the word and picture cue, students write an explanation of the word and image in their own words. They should not simply parrot the teacher's explanation. Ideally, students connect the word to their lives. They may also provide an example of the word used in context. Monitor student notebooks and correct misunderstandings.

Students may organize their notepads into categories such as the following:

*Words I Will Use in My Writing*

*Wow—Words I Really Like*

*Words That Are New*

In addition to the Six-Step Vocabulary sequence, there are other quick lessons and ideas you can use to introduce and demonstrate important vocabulary words.

### Think-Aloud Statements

Stop at planned points in the reading to discuss how the words are used in context. Discuss other possible uses of the word when it has multiple meanings. You can also use the Word Web for this purpose.

*We just read the word ___. What do you think it means? Have you ever heard or read this word before? Let's reread this sentence and think about what the author is saying.*

### Use the I Know Interesting Words Strategy Chart

Copy the I Know Interesting Words strategy chart on page 205 (Form 6.3 on the CD) onto cardstock. Introduce the chart and explain how the pictures and statements represent strategies we can use during reading to figure out the meaning of a word. As you demonstrate these during a think-aloud, point to the picture and statement you are using. You may also place a clothespin alongside the statement.

### Model Word-Learning Strategies

Examine any words that cause confusions during reading and model the use of word-learning strategies.

I think we can solve the meaning of this word together. Let's try [name strategy from the strategy chart, then model use].

### Build Vocabulary Words With Informational Text

When reading informational texts, use these strategies to explore new words:

- Introduce and explain two or three important vocabulary words students will need to understand the content.
- Brainstorm words related to the captions and/or subheadings.
- Examine words in context.
- Record new words on a thematic or topic vocabulary chart (temporary during this unit, unless it is on the list for essential academic vocabulary).

### Create Topic-Themed Vocabulary Word Walls

Record words related to a current topic or theme on a chart or word wall, and switch it out as you study new topics; these are temporary displays. You can also create a Wonderful Word Choice Chart to collect words students would like to use in their writing, or a Power Words Chart to remind students of alternatives to worn-out words.

As you collect words for your various charts, be sure to discuss their meanings and incorporate them into your daily classroom discussion. Try organizing vocabulary walls in any of these ways:

- Alphabetical order
- Topic or theme
- Part of speech

# I Know Interesting Words

**I can...**

look at pictures.

huge

use parts of the word I know.

undo    remake

look around the word.

new ← frisky → puppy

reread.

read on.

**I can think about...**

words like this.

yummy    tasty    delicious    sweet    appetizing

what the author is saying.

what I know. ✓

Form 6.3  on the CD

## GUIDED PRACTICE IDEAS AND ACTIVITIES

The following activities provide fun, engaging practice with vocabulary words.

### Sticky Flags

Students can use a set of two or three sticky flags stored on index cards to mark an interesting word they found during reading. Partners share these after reading, and students may record them in their notepads.

### Word Banks

An alternative to a notepad is an index card holder (smaller ones can be purchased at business supply stores) and cards. Students illustrate the word on one side and use it in a sentence on the other side.

### Question of the Day

Revisit the word on the word watcher chart by using it in a question related to class activities throughout the day:

*Was anyone amazed by something that happened during art today?*

### Word Cards

Write vocabulary words on index cards and encourage students to read and use them:

- Before lunch or dismissal, pick a card and ask for a meaning/sentence/example.
- Have magazines available and invite students to label pictures with vocabulary words.

**Vocabulary Role-Play Cards**
Form 6.5 on the CD

### Use the I Know Interesting Words Bookmark

The I Know Interesting Words bookmark on Form 6.4 on the CD can be copied onto cardstock for students to use during reading. The Think-Pinch-Share routine described on page 76 provides a format for focused partner turn-and-talk time, where students use the statements and picture cues to verbalize how they figured out the meaning of a word.

### Vocabulary Role-Play Cards

Give out vocabulary role-play cards (see Form 6.5 on the CD) to groups of four to six students. Each student has a role to play in the completion of a word chart:

**Word Connector:** This student leads the group in brainstorming what the word reminds group members of, including where they have heard or used the word or related experiences they have had. The Word Connection lists the brainstormed ideas in a notebook or on a sheet of paper.

**Word Illustrator:** This student draws a picture to represent the word.

*Differentiating Reading Instruction for Success With RTI* © 2011 by Margo Southall • Scholastic Teaching Resources

**Word Wildcat:** The student in this role describes how the word was used in the reading and how it could be used in other ways, such as idioms, similes, riddles, and jokes where the meaning may vary depending on its usage.

**Word Game-Show Host:** The student provides a student-friendly definition of the word and creates questions or statements that do and do not reflect the meaning of the word for their classmates to respond to in a yes/no format (thumbs up/down).

**Word Webber:** The student draws a web and lists synonyms and antonyms.

**Word Trainer:** The student makes actions that represent the word, helping to exercise our brain muscles.

## Word Finder Role in Small-Group Lessons and Book Clubs

The student assigned the Word Finder role in a small-group lesson or book club locates new and interesting words within the text and determines their meaning and importance to the story. He or she may select literary devices, such as metaphors, idioms, strong verbs and colorful language, or "golden lines." The role is to enrich the vocabulary of the group and identify how the language is important in conveying the writer's message.

### Words We Found Game

Ask students to listen and look for interesting words over the weekend, to share on Monday. Peers try to guess the meaning. They talk about what they know about the word and add it to the Word Watcher Chart (Ganske, 2003).

Students place the words in order of their intensity.

### Take the Temperature of Words: A Semantic Gradient

Select two words with meanings that differ markedly in intensity (e.g., *nice* and *fantastic*) that relate to a concept from a story you're reading or a topic you're studying. Choose words that are very common and overused, such as *good* and *bad*, *walk* and *run*. Write one of the words near the top of the chart and the other word near the bottom. You may create a visual of a thermometer and write the words on index cards or sticky notes.

As you reread the text, ask students to look for appropriate words in the story that fit on the continuum. Record these words on the chart, inviting student participation in deciding where they fit on the continuum. Generate more words if necessary, building on the words in the story. Encourage student discussion about the words and remember that disagreements are not a bad thing in this exercise; they require students to give evidence for their reasoning based on their understanding of the concepts the words represent.

Students can use Form 6.6 on the CD to record their gradient of words.

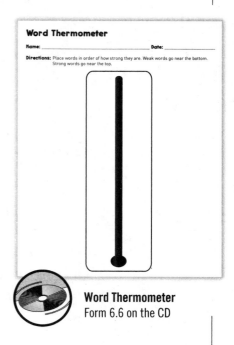

**Word Thermometer**
Form 6.6 on the CD

**What's My Sort?**
Form 6.7 on the CD

## Concept Sorts: What's My Sort?

For this open-ended sort, provide word cards that can be grouped together in several ways. To develop meaningful associations, include concepts from your class literature units as well as social studies and science topics. For example, living–nonliving, mammals–birds, healthy snacks–unhealthy snacks.

Model the procedure by presenting words from a shared text. Ask students, "How are some of these words alike?" Have pairs of students sort word cards and ask students to verbalize their categories: "Why did you put some words in this column and the others here?" (Ganske, 2000). An open sort is a motivating way to examine the meaning of words.

When students know the procedure, they can sort a set of words independently. They group the words into two or three categories and record the words in each category on the What's My Sort? graphic organizer (Form 6.7 on the CD; also see the task card for this activity on Form 4.42).

### Environmental Print

Write words from labels on index cards. Distribute cards and labels to partners or groups; have them find the label that contains the selected word. Possible words include: *unsaturated*, *crunchy*, *nutritious*, *healthy*, etc.

### Move and Match or Wear the Word

Print the words and definitions on separate index cards. Students attach either the word cards or definitions to headbands or simply hold the cards. The goal is to find your "partner" who has the definition/word card.

### Questions and Answers

Play this game like Jeopardy. Write vocabulary words on the board. Student groups make up a question to define each one. For a partner match-up version, write the words and questions that they answer on separate cards and distribute to students, who seek the word/question that matches their card. For example: Question card: How big is a whale? Answer card: Immense.

### Word Detectives Game

As in 20 Questions, provide clues for the word. This can be played with the whole class or in small groups.

*I'm thinking of a word ...*

- *It sounds like* [give rhyming word].

- *It begins with* /cl/.

- *It's one of these two words:* [offer choice of two words].

## Synonym Game

Start off by stating a simple sentence such as: *I am cold*. The next student repeats the sentence starter and substitutes a synonym (or antonym), e.g., *I am freezing* or *I am sweltering*. This can be played with the whole class or a small group.

## I Have…, Who Has…?

Write a homophone on one side of a card. On the other side, write a definition of another homophone. On the next card provide the answer to this and a new homophone. Students quiz each other to find who has the matching card. For example:

Player 1: *Who has "a word that means also?"*

Player 2: *I have* too, t-o-o.

## Word Charades

Students act out the meaning of the word for their group to figure out.

### GUIDING PROMPTS

Prompt students during reading to help them access the meaning of words that impact their comprehension. Use consistent language, such as the following:

- *Is there a word you don't understand?*
- *Do you know what that word means (point to the word)*
- *Have you heard that word before (use it in a sentence)*
- *Are there any clues about that word in the sentence or picture to help you?*
- *Do you know a word that is like this one? (e.g.,* part—depart)

### INDEPENDENT PRACTICE

#### Graphic Organizers

- **I Know Interesting Words:** Students select a line from a text being read in class, record it in the first column on Form 6.8 (on the CD), and in the second column describe what they know about the word—associations, where they have heard and read it before, etc.

- **Word Thermometer:** Students record the words from the guided practice lesson on sticky notes, order them by intensity of meaning, and then record on the thermometer (Form 6.6 on the CD).

- **I Remember Interesting Words:** The four-square chart on Form 6.9 (on the CD) provides students with an opportunity to use four ways to store the word in their reading brain—by sound, visual image, meaning, and context.

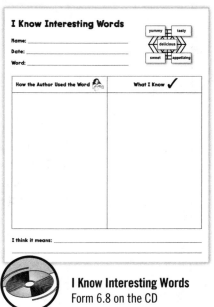

**I Know Interesting Words**
Form 6.8 on the CD

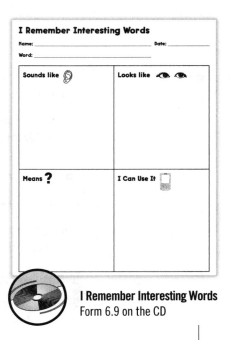

**I Remember Interesting Words**
Form 6.9 on the CD

### Flap Books

Provide flap books with two or three flaps (see templates on Forms 6.10 and 6.11). Students write the word on the flap and the definition in their own words on the inside, with a sketch of the word.

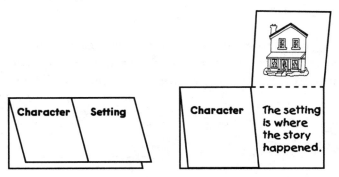

### Cube

Use a tissue box and cover with plain paper. On the six sides students draw and write an aspect/association of the word's meaning: print the word, draw an illustration, write a synonym, use in phrase or saying, describe what is means to them, and so on.

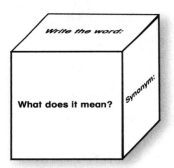

### Homophones

Generate sentences containing homophones, then write the sentences on colored paper, leaving a blank space where the homophone should go. Write the homophones that complete the sentences on cards. Students choose the correct homophone card and insert it in the sentence.

### Cloze Sentences

Students write a descriptive sentence, leaving a blank space where the target vocabulary word should go. Then they trade sentences with a peer to solve.

### Idioms and Expressions

Students illustrate the word's literal and figurative meaning in their vocabulary notebooks.

# Part 3

# Comprehension Strategies

Comprehension strategies are the in-the-head processes proficient readers use to make sense of text. To teach these processes to young readers, we must make them as explicit and concrete as possible, and provide plenty of opportunities for guided and independent practice. Here are the strategies addressed in the rest of this chapter:

- Making Connections
- Generating and Answering Questions
- Making Inferences and Predictions
- Clarifying and Self-Monitoring
- Retelling
- Summarizing
- Integrating Strategy Use

To teach each strategy, you can use the lesson template shown below. For each strategy, you'll find a definition along with a discussion of common difficulties students encounter while learning how to apply it on their own. Then I share ideas for explaining and modeling the strategy for students, guided practice activities for both the whole class and small group, and independent practice activities.

| Comprehension Lesson Teaching Sequence |
| --- |
| **Introduce**<br>• Make a connection to students' prior experience with this strategy, if appropriate. For example, if students made predictions or inferences regarding the outcome of a read-aloud, class event, or sports game, remind them of that experience.<br>• Explain the strategy and how it helps readers, why it is important and useful.<br>• Refer to strategy charts that you have constructed with students during class or group reading, together with examples of student work, such as completed graphic organizers and excerpts from reading journals. |
| **Demonstrate**<br>• Model how and when to apply the strategy using consistent teaching language. This often takes place within a read-aloud/think-aloud format.<br>• Continue to provide brief demonstrations in both whole-class and small-group contexts over a series of lessons or unit of study on this strategy. To scaffold transfer to independent reading, model how this strategic thinking is applied to different texts and genres. |
| **Guide Practice**<br>• Have students practice the strategy with your support during highly interactive sessions.<br>• Tell students when they are going to be applying this strategy during the instructional day, during independent reading, partner reading, literacy centers, writing, and so on. |
| **Provide Independent Practice**<br>Students apply the strategy to reading and writing tasks:<br>• graphic organizers        • partner reading<br>• reader's notebook        • literature circles or book clubs<br>• comprehension center tasks |

# Making Connections

**Strategy Statement:** *I can connect.*

Making connections is a foundational reading strategy in which readers integrate current knowledge with new information in a text in order to understand. When students are not able to make connections, it interferes with their ability to make inferences and compromises their understanding. It's easier to understand and remember something if we can relate it to something familiar—our prior knowledge and experiences. If we teach students to tap into their prior experiences from life and literature, they are more likely to remain on track and better able to monitor their understanding during reading.

Readers make three types of connections:

- **Text to self:** Students relate what happens in a text to their personal experiences, feelings, and opinions.

- **Text to text:** Students compare characters, events, facts, or themes across different texts.

- **Text to world:** Students relate issues in a text to community issues and global themes.

## DIFFICULTIES IN MAKING CONNECTIONS

Two common issues arise when helping students learn to make connections to texts.

- Students may not have the *background knowledge* or *experience* required to build a bridge from what they know to new information. Sometimes this is due to a very different life experience from the characters depicted in a fictional story or nonfiction text. Children living in poverty may find it difficult to connect to a problem of a character whose concerns center on experiences during a summer vacation or bountiful birthday party. The cultural background of the story also sets some children up for a disconnect. We can either select another book or attempt to build a bridge of background knowledge if it is likely to support understanding of the dominant culture's traditions that are common in children's fiction and will transfer to future reading.

- Students may make connections that are *not related to the text*. To address this, model the self-monitoring process—the internal dialogue you have with yourself when reading—during think-alouds. Make a connection, then say, *How is this helping me understand the story?* When the thinking is off track, show students how to get back on track by thinking about the purpose of the text or theme: *Why did the author write this? What message does the author have for us?*

## SELECTING MATERIALS TO MODEL THE STRATEGY

Select reading materials that students are likely to relate to, wherever possible. This means choosing books that contain experiences pertinent to this age group and their cultural context. In the resource list at the end of the chapter, I list books I have used to demonstrate the strategy and engage students in sharing

*Differentiating Reading Instruction for Success With RTI* © 2011 by Margo Southall • Scholastic Teaching Resources

their connections. For example, *City Dog, Country Frog* by Mo Willems (2010) speaks to the emotions associated with the loss of a friend, then addresses the renewal in making new friendships.

## IDEAS FOR INTRODUCING AND DEMONSTRATING THE STRATEGY

Use the following think-aloud statements, strategy charts and icons, and concrete demonstrations to help introduce and model the process of making connections. These teaching tools scaffold learning by providing a bridge from the abstract concept to something visual and concrete.

During your demonstrations with concrete materials and visuals, ask students to describe the analogy to a partner in their own words. Always provide a moment for students to verbalize what they see and hear to ensure adequate processing time and engagement.

### Think-Aloud Statements for Demonstrations

As you read aloud to the class or a small group, model the process of making connections between the known and new information. For example:

*When we are reading something new, we think about what we already know. This helps us understand new information. Looking at this book, I am thinking, What do I already know about this topic? What experiences have I had like this? What books have I read that are like this one? I know something about __ because I read a book/ saw on the Internet/a video about__. I know __ .*

As you model making connections during think-alouds, you can use some of the following sentence stems to frame your talk:

*This reminds me of …*

*This reminds me of … and now I see that …*

*I can relate to … because …*

*I already know …*

*I am thinking of …*

*I can remember …*

*This is like the time when …*

*When I saw the picture of …, it reminded me of …*

*When I read these words, it made me think about …*

### I Can Connect Strategy Chart

Introduce the I Can Connect Strategy Chart on page 214 (Form 6.13 on the CD) and explain the picture cues and statements. Point to the icon and statement that represent your thinking during think-aloud demonstrations.

# I Can Connect

I can connect...

I know...

This reminds me of...

me

a book or story

the world

Form 6.13 on the CD

## Picture Cards

The three I Can Connect picture cards on Form 6.22 on the CD represent the levels of making connections: text to self (me), text to another book or story, and text to the world (current events, global issues). As you demonstrate, display the thinking each one represents.

## I Can Connect Icons

Introduce the I Can Connect Icons of a spider's web, bridge, math links, or Lego blocks (see Form 6.14 on the CD) and explain how it represents the thinking that takes place in our reading brain when we make connections. Copy icons onto cardstock and display in a pocket chart or on the table in front of students as you demonstrate the strategy.

Making connections when we read is like:

- a sticky spiderweb that catches our thoughts and memories, linking them all together

- a bridge that connects what we know to new events and information

- a linking chain that joins our thoughts and the book together

- a building block that we add to each time we read something that reminds us of something else

I Can Connect Picture Cards
Form 6.22 on the CD

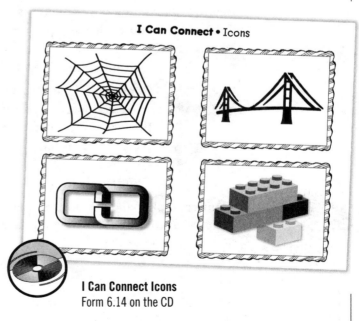

I Can Connect Icons
Form 6.14 on the CD

### Building Connections

Using the analogy of a sticky spiderweb (see icon on Form 6.14 on the CD), explain how our brain collects and stores ideas and facts (memories) in the same way and how we link these memories to new information to make sense of them. Write connections on sticky notes and then place them inside a head-shaped graphic. Cumulatively add to these observations as you read, to demonstrate how connections build upon one another. You might choose to color-code sticky notes by type of connection (self, text, world). You can refer to this as "the World Wide Web in your head," as described in the song on page 219, to represent how we integrate information from many sources.

### Magnetic Boards and Velcro

Use a magnetic whiteboard with a sketch of a head or draw a head on a sheet of posterboard. If you make a poster, laminate it so it won't tear. Before reading, think aloud about any knowledge and experiences that relate to this book or the section you are about to read and record them on laminated index cards. Then place these cards around the head. (You can use Velcro, magnetic tape, sticky notes or whatever is easy.) During reading, pause and record additional connections and/or place a completed connection card inside the head shape as you verbalize the connection to this part of the reading.

### Backpack

On index cards, record and share three or four things you already know about a topic or story, or gather objects, pictures, or other books that relate to the reading. Place the cards, objects, pictures, or books inside a backpack both before and during reading as you make connections to demonstrate how we store and retrieve background knowledge and prior experience and connect them to new learning.

### Building Blocks and Math Links

Connect toy building blocks, such as Legos or math links, as you make connections during think-alouds to demonstrate the strategy. Introduce the related graphic organizer, I Can Build Connections (Form 6.15 on the CD).

### Electrical Plug

Connect a plug and socket together as you explain how our brain connects what is familiar to what is new, using the circuits in our neural system (see Role-Play Cards, Form 6.16 on the CD).

### Lint Roller

Write your connections to the story or topic on slips of paper as you read a related part of the text. When you have several slips completed, roll over the slips with a lint roller, picking them up to demonstrate how we accumulate connections as we read (McGregor, 2007).

## Role-Play Cards

Use the analogy of an electrician who forms connections in our reading brain. Model the process by joining a plug and socket together as you hold up a puppet made from the role-play cards (Form 6.16 on the CD) attached to craft sticks with Velcro, or attach one to a visor to wear during demonstrations. You can also take on the role of a builder who builds bridges from the known to the new.

I Can Connect Role-Play Cards
Form 6.16 on the CD

> *My name is Cathy/Colin the Connector, and it is my job is to connect what is happening in the book to the network of information circuits in my brain, so I can make sense of what I read.*

> *My name is Bill/ Belinda the builder, and my job is to build a bridge from what I already know to the new information in the book. Using what I know helps me to understand.*

### GUIDED PRACTICE IDEAS AND ACTIVITIES

Since each individual's collection of experiences and prior knowledge differs, the connections students make to the same text will vary. Make the most of the range of knowledge and experience in your classroom by incorporating opportunities for peers to share with partners and small groups before sharing with the whole group. This process scaffolds students' ability to make connections by providing multiple peer examples. The following activities provide fun and engaging guide practice with making connections.

### Photos, Pictures, and Video Clips

Select a visual that students can relate to and that will engender a deeper rather than a superficial connection or comment. For example, you might choose a clip from a video based on a book you've read in which the character makes an important decision. Other ideas include book or magazine illustrations, or photos of an event or experience. Prompt for student connections and have them share their thoughts with a partner or in a group, then take up examples for the class to piggyback upon with their own connections.

### Songs on Familiar Themes

Select songs that deal with issues and themes students can relate to, such as friendship, pets, being teased, or struggling to learn something new. Take time to read the lyrics together and share connections. Groups can each record their connections on a chart and display these to the class to compare similarities and differences. There is an emotional aspect to learning, and by sharing songs about topics relevant to students' lives we can tap into a deeper understanding of what connecting is all about.

## Web It

Use the same process you demonstrated in Building Connections (see page 216), this time using student connections rather than your own. If you are working with the class, have pairs or groups record their connections inside the shape of a head they have drawn on paper, and then share with the class. When working with a small group, have each child write his or her own connection on a sticky note or card and place it inside the same head-shaped graphic you used in the demonstration, and read it to the rest of the group. Encourage students to piggyback off the connections of others, and indicate these connections by joining them with a strip of tape to show how we can expand upon our own thinking by listening to the connections of others.

## Graphic Organizers

Introduce the graphic organizers on Forms 6.18 to 6.20 on the CD in whole-class and small-group lessons. The What's New? Organizer (Form 6.18) helps students pay attention to new information and integrate this into their web of connections. The process of assimilating new information—confirming or disconfirming what we think we know and revising our thinking—is central to developing the synthesizing strategy. Display sentence stems like these to help them generate their connections:

> *Now I understand ...*
>
> *I used to think..., but now I know that ...*
>
> *This has changed my mind about ...*

In the I Can Connect organizer (Form 6.19 on the CD), students describe an event or fact and note their connection to it. For the Making Connections Graphic Organizer

**What's New**
Form 6.18 on the CD

**I Can Connect Graphic Organizer**
Form 6.19 on the CD

Puzzle (Form 6.20), students cut out the circles; then they write the event, fact, or topic in the larger circle and their connections in the smaller ones. Students arrange and paste them in a display that makes sense to them. Use these graphic organizers with small groups, then have students use them to respond to their independent reading.

### Hand Motions

Have students make one of the following motions when they have a connection to share at a stopping point in a read-aloud or during a small-group discussion:

- Form the letter C with their thumb and index finger; make the gesture for the letter C using American Sign Language.

- Make a circle with thumb and index finger, link with same fingers on other hand to form a chain.

- Snap their fingers to turn on the web of connections in their mind.

### Strategy Song and Rhyme

Reinforce the strategy here with song and rhyme. Copy onto a chart for shared reading. This one is sung to the tune of "He's Got the Whole World in His Hands":

*I've got the whole world in my head.*
*I've got the whole wide world in my head.*
*I've got the whole world in my head.*
*I've got the whole wide world in my head.*

*I've got all of my life in my head.*
*I've got books and stories that I've read.*
*I've got ideas that I've shared.*
*I've got the whole world in my head.*

This rhyme contains words from the Strategy Chart (page 214) in bold text.

*I can use what **I know***
*To understand something new,*
*Build connections as I go*
*To make ideas stick like glue.*

*I make connections to **me**, myself.*
*I make connections to **books** on the shelf.*
*I make connections to books I've read.*
*I make connections to the **world** in my head.*

## Turn-and-Talk

Plan pausing points in the reading for strategy-based discussions where students use the sentence stems you have incorporated in the demonstrations of the strategy. Display these on a chart to initiate and focus brief, one- to two-minute partner discussions.

> *This reminds me of...*
>
> *I already know...*
>
> *I am thinking of...*

### Strategy Bookmarks

Distribute the I Can Connect bookmark (Form 6.21 on the CD) to students. They can use it during turn-and-talk discussions or to help them write responses to their reading. See page 76 for more on using strategy bookmarks.

### Sticky Flags Mark Thinking Spots

Make a set of interactive flags for each student in the group. Use a permanent marker to label sticky flags with *R* (for *remind*) or a tick mark (for *I know*). You can also make flags with symbols for each type of connection: a happy face (text to self), a book (text to text), and a globe (text to world). Prepare strips of cardstock or index cards for each student with three to six sticky flags on the edge of each one. Students will place the sticky flags on the outside edge of a page where they make a connection to something they read. Then they can share the connections with a partner or the group. Once they share, the sticky flags can be put back on the cardstock and stored for future use.

**I Can Connect Bookmark**
Form 6.21 on the CD

Students place a sticky flag where they make a connection to a fact or event.

## Math Links

Provide students with two or three connected math links—the same ones you used in your demonstration. Students will use these to mark the place in the book where they make a connection, just like placing a bookmark on a page.

## Interactive Picture Cards

Copy the I Can Connect picture cards (Form 6.22 on the CD) onto cardstock and cut apart. You may provide individual students with one at a time, or allow them to select from two or three types of connection cards available in the center of the small-group teaching table. These support turn-and-talk discussions in a similar way as the bookmark routine: students hold up the card that represents their type of connection (self, text, world).

**I Can Connect Picture Cards**
Form 6.22 on the CD

Students enjoy taking turns with the puppet to act out the role of connector in their reading group (see Role-Play Puppets on the next page).

## Role-Play Puppets

Students can use the characters from the Role-Play cards (Form 6.16 on the CD) to think aloud about their own strategy use, just as you did in the demonstrations. Students take turns holding the puppets up as they describe their thinking during turn-and-talk discussions and group sharing.

**I Can Connect
Role-Play Cards**
Form 6.16 on the CD

## Connection Cube

Attach the picture cards (Form 6.22) to the sides of a cube. You will need two copies of each picture. Students can pass the cube around the small-group teaching table and use the cues to generate a connection.

## Connection Collection Game

Make several copies of the I Can Connect picture cards (Form 6.22 on the CD) and paste them onto index cards, or copy them onto cardstock. Place the cards in three piles by type. Students, in turn, take a card that represents the connection they made and place it in a collective pile or bowl in the center of the table labeled "Our Connections." As they place it on the pile they describe their connection to the event, fact, or page they have marked with their sticky or bookmark.

## GUIDING PROMPTS

As you coach students to make connections during guided practice sessions, use consistent terminology, such as the word *remind* so that students internalize the language of making connections. Below are some sample prompts:

*What do you already know about...?*

*What in the book/your life reminds you of..?*

*Turn on your schema.*

*Plug in to your thoughts.*

*Let me hear your thinking.*

*Does this remind you of a book you read, something you saw on the Internet or TV, or something that has happened in the real world?*

*How are you connecting this to your life? Did something like this happen to you or someone you know? What experiences have you had like ...?*

*Did you ever feel this way?*

*Piggybacking on what you said, I ...*

## INDEPENDENT PRACTICE

The following activities provide fun, engaging practice with making connections.

## Strategy-Based Reading Response Booklets

To make the booklet, copy the cover on Form 6.17 on the CD and the graphic organizers I Can Build Connections (Form 6.15) and What's New? (Form 6.18). Staple these pages together for students to complete in response to their independent reading, so they can hold onto their thinking. You can add pages to the booklet using prompts that you have used in guided practice, such as:

*What did you notice in the book that is like real life?*

*How did your connection help you to understand the book?*

**I Can Connect Strategy Booklet**
Form 6.17 on the CD

## Graphic Organizers

Students can complete the What's New? and I Can Connect graphic organizers (Forms 6.18-6.19 on the CD) in response to independent reading after practicing in whole-class and small-group contexts.

**What's New**
Form 6.18 on the CD

**I Can Connect Graphic Organizer**
Form 6.19 on the CD

## Sticky Flags

Provide the same ones from guided practice (page 220) for students to use during independent reading. After reading and marking the text with sticky flags, they write about the connections they made at each "sticky stop."

## Strategy Bookmarks

Distribute the bookmarks from guided practice (Form 6.21 on the CD) for students to keep with their reading journal. These support partner discussions and writing in response to reading.

## Paper Chain

Students cut out six to eight strips of paper, about 2" x 8" inches each. They write an event or fact from their reading on the first strip and then record a connection to this on the next strip and paste them in sequence. Students repeat the process to form a chain of three or four connections.

## Connection Cube

The cube used in guided practice (see page 222) can also support independent reading responses at the comprehension center.

## Character Roles and Puppets

These props can be used by partner book clubs, literature circles, and students working independently. Students use the props they worked with in guided practice (pages 220-222) to act out a strategic role as a way to focus and support collaborative discussion.

## Flip-Flap Booklet

Provide flap books with two or three flaps (see Forms 6.10 and 6.11 on the CD for templates). Students write the event from their reading on the flap, and their connection to that event inside.

# Generating and Answering Questions

**Strategy Statement:** *I can wonder.*

Questioning requires students to set a purpose for reading and then search for answers to questions of their own or those of the teacher. By pausing to ask questions and invite student questions, we provide opportunities for students to process the event or information and notice what is familiar and what they need to question in order to understand. We begin by modeling open-ended "I wonder" questions that have no right or wrong answer, as a form of self-monitoring to keep readers on track and engaged. Next we progress to types of questions that require different searching behaviors. Answers to literal questions can be located in the book, whereas inferential and evaluative questions are more dependent on the reader's interpretation (see the discussion of the making inferences strategy starting on page 238). This section includes three types of questions:

1. **Literal questions** include those we typically ask students to answer in a retelling, such as who, what, where, and when. These questions have an answer in the book that the student can cite as evidence. Examples: *What did Lily's cousin say about Julius at the party? Find the part that supports your answer.*

2. **Inferential questions** require the reader integrate multiple clues from the text with prior knowledge to arrive at a reasonable conclusion. Examples: *How do you think Lily was feeling when she heard her cousin describe Julius this way? How do you know? What are the clues?*

3. **Evaluative questions** elicit the reader's opinions and feelings about the motives and actions of characters or the perspective and/or opinions of the writer. These need to be supported with examples from the book and the reader's background knowledge. Evaluative questions require students to reflect upon parts in the reading that impacted them personally in some way, and describe their response to the reading—how the event or information made them feel. Examples: *What is your opinion about the way Lily behaved?* or *How do you feel about the way Lily treated her baby brother? Do you think she was right to behave this way? Why or why not?*

## DIFFICULTIES STUDENTS EXPERIENCE GENERATING AND ANSWERING QUESTIONS

Many low-progress students are understandably hesitant to answer questions in front of others. When possible, pose questions in terms of *possible* answers—where more than one answer may be correct. Below are ways to scaffold students during questioning tasks:

- Allow students some thinking time before cueing an all-student choral response/answer to your question.

- Provide visuals and tactile aids for partner questioning/answering before sharing with the group, so students have time to process and rehearse their responses.

- Make questioning tasks a safe activity for low-progress students by asking for possible answers to the questions you pose and asking students to suggest questions or answers that someone else might offer. Emphasize that there is more than one possible answer for inferential and evaluative questions. *What might be some possible answers to this question? What would someone you know give as an answer? What do you think your partner would say?*

- Prompt when students say they don't know the answer to a question: *If you did know the answer, what would you say?* This encourages them to "have a go" with less pressure to always be correct.

- Create a relaxing and game-like atmosphere where approximations and collaborative support are encouraged.

- Draw students' attention to visual information to support generating questions beyond the words in the text. Prompt them to notice the expression on a character's face, or "missing information" in a diagram or photograph in an informational text. Questioning should not be print-dependent; even early literacy groups can generate questions from illustrations.

- Use story structure picture prompts from retelling lessons (see page 267) as a reference for questioning the text or author. In nonfiction, use the table of contents, captions, and subheadings as categories for generating questions.

- Preteach critical vocabulary so students can express their questions using key words related to the topic or theme. Limit this to only a few words that they will be reading in this session.

## SELECTING MATERIALS TO MODEL THE STRATEGY

For literal questions, select informational books that stimulate students' natural curiosity so that lots of "I wonder" questions can provide a basis for discussion and learning. Not every book lends itself to generating inferential and evaluative questions. Examples of children's stories I have used that support inferential thinking and the process of questioning include: *The Three Questions* by John Muth (2002), about a boy who seeks answers to life's important questions; *The Heart and the Bottle* by Oliver Jeffers (2010), in which the death of a grandparent causes a young girl to guard her emotions, then regain her sense of wonder for the world; and *The Wise Woman and Her Secret* by Eve Merriam (1999), which also points to the importance of wonder as a means to discover the world around us for ourselves.

Fictional stories and nonfiction texts in which there is an issue to resolve will elicit evaluative thinking. As a teacher, you know which topics inspire the sharing of opinions (evaluative thinking) and which issues affect students' lives, such as friendship, bullying, sibling rivalry, and universal themes such as justice, honesty, and bravery. Books that allow for differences of opinion, such as *Should There Be Zoos?* by Tony Stead (2006) and nonfiction magazine articles describing issues surrounding new technology and current events are examples of materials to use for developing evaluative questions. Connect this questioning to students' persuasive writing in writer's workshop and at the writing center.

To support role-play in partner and group reading, select books that are written in an interview style, such as *An Interview with Harry the Tarantula* by Leigh Ann Tyson (2003). The list of Resources on page 296 includes additional texts for questioning.

## IDEAS FOR INTRODUCING AND DEMONSTRATING THE STRATEGY

Use the following think-aloud statements, strategy charts and icons, and activities to help introduce and model the process of asking questions. They are designed to support you in demonstrating how to do the following:

- generate literal, inferential, and evaluative questions before, during, and after reading
- search for answers to literal questions, locating evidence to support your answer
- use text clues and what you know to make an inference when the answer is not located in the text

Students use key words to generate questions about the passage.

### Think-Aloud Statements for Demonstrations

Integrate the same question stems that you will provide students, such as those listed on the Strategy Chart on page 229 (Form 6.23 on the CD). Focus on each type of question, then integrate them in successive readings, pausing in selected parts of the text to share how you generated a literal, inferential, and/or evaluative questions. Below are some examples.

#### Literal Questions

*Readers ask questions about what they are reading. We read to find out the answers to our questions. Often we ask something that we don't know yet. Sometimes we can find the answer right in the book.*

*Looking at the title and cover, I wonder _____. I am going to read the first part of the book and see if I can find the answer to _____. I will read to page __ . As I am reading, I think about the questions that come into my mind. I put a sticky flag where I have an "I wonder" question. Next I will put a sticky flag in places where I find the answer or even a clue to the answer. After reading the part about _____ I wonder, _____.*

#### Inferential Questions

*Using your head is part of being a reader. We ask questions in our reading brain that authors don't always answer, but thinking about these questions and wondering helps us understand what the author is really trying to say. We can figure out the answers for ourselves by using the clues in the words and pictures, and thinking about what we know.*

#### Evaluative Questions

*Using your heart is part of being a reader. Authors can make us laugh, cry, and even feel angry. They know that if we think about what they've written, we will understand their message even better. When we read about how a character behaves in a story or about a dramatic event in the text, we can't help having opinions about it. Remember, an opinion is how you feel about something; it does not have to be a fact.*

## Turning Statements into Questions

Read a statement from the book and model how to turn it into inferential and/or evaluative question.

*The author says here that Lily's nose twitched and her eyes narrowed. I wonder how Lily is feeling right now. I am also wondering why she seems angry when I thought she didn't like Julius anyway.*

## Strategy Chart

Include the language of questioning from the strategy chart to generate questions based upon a line lifted from the text, an illustration, photo, heading, or caption. Introduce the I Can Wonder Strategy Chart on page 229 (Form 6.23 on the CD). Place a clothespin next to the question starter you use in the think-aloud demonstration to model how to generate different types of questions.

*Differentiating Reading Instruction for Success With RTI* © 2011 by Margo Southall • Scholastic Teaching Resources

# I Can Wonder

**Who is...?**

**Why...?**

**Who did...?**

**How...?**

**What...?**

**How might...?**

**What if...?**

**Should...?**

**Where...?**

**I think...**

**When...?**

**I feel...**

Form 6.23  on the CD

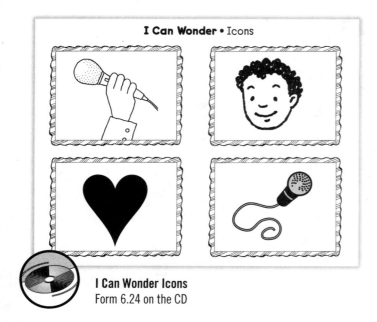

**I Can Wonder • Icons**

**I Can Wonder Icons**
Form 6.24 on the CD

## Icons

Display the I Can Question icons from Form 6.24 on the CD and explain how they represent the different types of questions we ask and answer as readers. Have students make the corresponding action along with you when you generate a question or locate an answer—point their finger (literal/quiz), touch their head (inferential/detective), or put their hand over their heart (evaluative/judge):

*Asking "I wonder" questions is like the microphone a quiz-show host might use when he or she asks all sorts of questions.*

*Sometimes we have questions that can be answered by walking our fingers through the book; we can touch the information we are looking for—it's right there.*

*Sometimes we ask questions that need our reading brain to work hard and use all the clues—what is in the book with what we already know—to figure it out.*

*Sometimes we have questions from the heart that show how we feel or our opinion about something we read.*

## Role-Play Cards

Three levels of questions are represented by the characters on the I Can Wonder Role-Play Cards (Form 6.25 on the CD) and the corresponding Role-Play Question Cards on Form 6.26. Each one reflects the type of thinking required at each level. Introduce each character and the type of question he or she represents, as you teach that level of questioning. As you proceed to teach the next level of questioning over a series of lessons, select between the characters to demonstrate the difference between the type of thinking and the answer required.

**I Can Wonder • Role-Play Cards**

**I Can Wonder Role-Play Cards**
Form 6.25 on the CD

- Quiz-show host represents literal questions. *My name is Quincy Questioner, and it is my job to ask questions and find answers right in the book.*

- Detective represents inferential questions. *My name is Detective Dana, and it is my job to ask and answer questions that can't be answered from the book only. I have to use clues in the words and pictures, and think about what I know to figure it out.*

- Judge represents evaluative questions, where the reader is asked to form an opinion about the actions or ideas in the text, drawing on background knowledge and experience

  *My name is Judge Jack and it is my job to form an, opinion and tell how I feel about what I read.*

*Differentiating Reading Instruction for Success With RTI* © 2011 by Margo Southall • Scholastic Teaching Resources

## Games

Display a board game, such as Trivial Pursuit, to show students how questioning plays an important role in many of our favorite games. Read and share one of the activities from the game to demonstrate how the reader is required to respond to the question.

## GUIDED PRACTICE IDEAS AND ACTIVITIES

The following activities provide fun and engaging guided practice in asking questions.

### Photos, Pictures, and Video Clips

Present pictures, book illustrations, or photographs that are likely to evoke "I wonder" questions from students. For example, the *Mysteries of Harris Burdick* by Chris Van Allsburg (1984) contains black-and-white drawings and statements that stimulate children's imagination and wonderings. Photos from children's magazines, such as *National Geographic for Kids,* are also useful for this purpose. Clips from book-based movies of pivotal scenes from the story can support evaluative thinking when students consider the actions and motives of the characters. Have students jot and share the questions that come to mind as they examine these visuals.

### Wacky, Weird, and Winsome Wonders

Share an object or picture of something that is out of the ordinary that will engender questions from your students, such as an artifact or food they may not be familiar with from another country. Startling facts or quotes can also encourage a variety of question types. Have students share their questions with a partner or group. You may have them record their questions on sticky notes and add them to a collaborative chart titled "Our Wonders." Use these questions for the Hand, Head, and Heart Question Sort on page 235.

### Wonder of the Day

Wonderopolis.com is a free site that presents a "wonder of the day" with information about the topic and a short video clip. Wonder #240, for example, is "How are dolphins and porpoises different?" The daily wonders are perfect for displaying on an interactive whiteboard or any projector, to stimulate all levels of questioning within an inquiry approach to learning.

### Songs on the Role of Questioning

The song "Where Have All the Flowers Gone?" by Pete Seeger is one of the first songs that comes to mind when considering unanswered questions, and it lends itself well to shared reading and sing-along. Take a look at the children's songs you have on your shelves that will also exemplify the important role of questioning in our everyday lives. Use them for shared reading and sing alongs.

### Strategy Song

Sing this song to the tune of "Twinkle, Twinkle, Little Star." Words from the I Can Wonder Strategy Chart are in bold print.

*I ask questions when I read:*
**Who**, **what**, **where**, *and* **when?**
*I seek the answers in the book.*
*I can find them if I look.*
*I ask questions when I read:*
**Why**, **what if**, **how might?**
*I* **think** *of questions so I know what's real.*
*I share my opinion and what I* **feel.**

### Hand Motions

When students need to show they have a question to ask the group or a partner, they can do the following:

- Wiggle their index finger to indicate they have an "I wonder" question during stopping points in a read-aloud.

- Make the gesture for the letter Q using American Sign Language.

To indicate a response for the different types of questions, students can touch the corresponding body part—hand, head, or heart—to identify the type of question being posed as part of a cued, all-student response.

For levels of questions represented by the three characters (I Can Wonder Icons Form 6.24), students can:

- Hold up a hand as if holding a microphone when asking literal quiz-show questions.

- Pretend to peer through a magnifying glass to ask inferential detective questions.

- Give a thumbs-up or thumbs-down in response to an evaluative question or show whether they agree or disagree with the character's actions.

State the type of question students have indicated with one of the above actions and invite them to share it with the group:

*I see you have a judge question. Let us hear your question.*

### Turn-and-Talk

Have students begin by asking questions to their partners or the rest of the group using open-ended starters, such as "I wonder." They can use the I Can Wonder bookmark on Form 6.77. Next, provide question stems for the different types of questions (see Quiz Questions on Form 6.27 and Role-Play Question Cards on Form 6.26) so that students have opportunities for scaffolded practice. Encourage students to build on the questions of others, to take them deeper into questioning the text or author:

*Do you agree with the decision of the character in this book? Why or why not? Turn to your thinking partner and share your opinion.*

*Piggybacking off [student's response], I think …*

## Turning New Learning Into Questions

List statements from literacy and content-area reading, and turn them into questions that students can ask each other, their friends, and families. Examples: *What is the difference between an alligator and a crocodile? What would you do if you… [were in same dilemma as a story character]? In your opinion, should we have zoos?*

### Quiz-Show Game

Pass the microphone around the table so each student can generate a question for the rest of the group. Display question starters or provide the question bookmarks to scaffold student participation.

## Quiz Questions

Use the Quiz Question cards on Form 6.27 on the CD or write question starters on index cards you've cut in half. Place them in a bag and pass around the table for student to pick a question and read it to the rest of the group. The rest of the students turn to a partner and tell what they think the answer is, then share it with the group.

## Question Cube

Attach question starters to the sides of a cube and incorporate the cube into your small-group lessons. Use the picture cards and icons or print question starters from the Strategy Chart onto index cards and attach with Velcro. Also include an open-ended "I wonder" card.

## Interactive Icons

Make simple response cards by copying the I Can Wonder icons (Form 6.24 on the CD) onto cardstock or pasting them onto index cards. Students hold their card up to show the type of question they have for the rest of the group—hand (literal), head (inferential), and heart (evaluative). These also support turn-and-talk partner discussions.

---

**Role-Play Question Cards**

**Quiz Show Questions:**
- Who, What, Where, When…?
- What happened in the beginning, middle and end?
- Tell me what happened so far.

**Detective Questions:**
- Why?
- What caused…?
- What do you predict will happen next? Why do you think so?
- What can you figure out about…?
- What does the author mean when…? What is the author trying to say on page…?
- What are the themes or big ideas?
- Tell me the main reason/biggest problem.

**Judge Questions:**
- What things did the character do that were…?
- Do you think…?
- Would you agree that…?
- What is your opinion of…? Which is better…?
- Do you agree with the author? Why or why not?
- How did you feel about the part where…?
- Would it be better if…?
- How do you know…?

**Role-Play Question Cards**
Form 6.26 on the CD

Students pass the Question Cube and use it to generate questions about the reading

### Sticky Flags Mark Thinking Spots

Prepare a set of two to four sticky flags for each student in the group by drawing question marks on the sticky flags to use for open-ended "I wonder" questions (with literal or inferential answers) and hearts for evaluative "I feel" questions or statements of opinion. Place these on the edge of index cards or strips of cardstock and distribute. Ask students to read to a specific place in the text and stick their flag(s) on the edge of a page where they have an "I wonder" or "I feel" question.

### Character Question Sort

During stopping points in read-alouds, record student questions on large stickies or have them record their own, individually, with partners, or as table groups. Collaboratively sort the student questions by their type under the picture cards of each role-playing character (Form 6.25).

**I Can Wonder Role-Play Cards**
Form 6.25 on the CD

## Hand, Head, and Heart Question Sort

Record students' questions on index cards. Shuffle and pass out to the group. Students take turns placing cards under the appropriate categories and justify why a particular question requires a particular type of answer. You can use the graphic organizer Hand, Head, and Heart Questions on Form 6.28 on the CD for this activity, with students using it as a sorting mat.

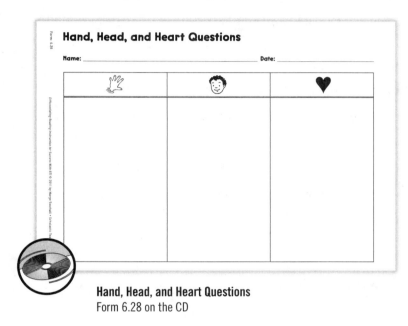

**Hand, Head, and Heart Questions**
Form 6.28 on the CD

## Role-Play Puppets

Make simple puppets by copying the Role-Play Cards on Form 6.25 on the onto cardstock and attaching to craft or paint sticks. Students act out their role by asking the rest of the group the level of questioning they represent. Provide the Role Play Question Cards on Form 6.26 on the CD to each of the "characters" in the group, so students can refer to the question starters as needed .

## Our Questions Game

Place copies of the Role-Play Cards for the three types of questions (Form 6.26 on the CD) in piles by type. Students, in turn, take a card that represents the type of questions they generated and place it in the collective pile, or bowl in the center of the table labeled "Our Questions." As they place the card on the pile they share their question related to the event, fact, or page they have marked with their sticky note or bookmark. (The I Can Wonder Icons on Form 6.24 can also be used for this activity—hand, head, heart.)

## GUIDING PROMPTS

Coach students to ask questions during reading using prompts such as these:

- Ask a question about what you just read. Use words like *who*, *what*, *where* and *why*.
- Why do you think the author wrote this book?
- What do you want to find out about _____?
- What are you wondering? Let's read and find out if any of our questions will be answered.
- Show me in the book where it says _____.
- Read to _____. What are you thinking and feeling as you read?
- Place a sticky note where you had a response with your head or heart.
- How do you feel about _____?
- What in the book [and your life] makes you think or feel that way?
- Do you agree with what the author has to day about _____?
- What would you do if _____?

## INDEPENDENT PRACTICE

Questioning continues during independent reading, partner reading, and book club meetings.

### Strategy Booklet

**I Can Wonder Strategy Booklet Cover**
Form 6.29 on the CD

Make booklets of strategy-based reading responses with the I Wonder Strategy Booklet Cover on Form 6.29 on the CD and blank sheets of paper. Have students complete the booklet for each section of the reading so they can hold onto their thinking. You can provide a sheet with questioning sentence stems or students can use the strategy chart to frame their responses.

### Reading Notebook

Students jot their questions about their independent reading. If they are reading the same title or topic with a partner or book club, they can exchange their journal to respond to each other's questions and piggyback on their queries.

### Character Roles and Puppets

Partners reading the same book and students working independently in literature circles/book clubs can use the props they practiced with you to act out a strategic role as a way to focus and support collaborative discussion.

*Differentiating Reading Instruction for Success With RTI* © 2011 by Margo Southall • Scholastic Teaching Resources

## Sketch Your Wonders

Students use a pencil to draw a visual representation of an important scene or fact. Next they generate a question or two that provides a literal, evaluative, or inferential response to the information depicted in the sketch. This could be in the form of a speech bubble added to their sketch—a way to question the author, content, or character and/or provide the basis for peer discussion.

## Flip-Flap Booklet

Provide flap books with two or three flaps (see templates on Forms 6.10 and 6.11 on the CD). Students write the event from the text on the flap and their question about it inside.

## Graphic Organizers

**Hand, Head, and Heart Questions** (Form 6.28 on the CD): Have students complete the three-column chart in response to their independent reading.

**I Can Wonder Graphic Organizer Puzzle** (Form 6.30): Students record their questions inside the question marks on the organizer and cut them out. On a separate sheet of paper, they write the title of the book or topic and paste the questions around it. You can also copy the organizer onto cardstock, laminate, and provide wipe-off pens with a file folder placemat for students to arrange the pieces on.

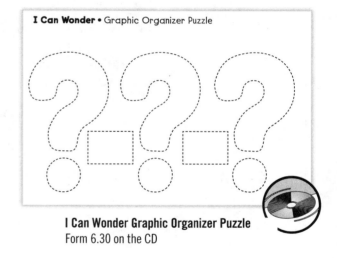

**I Can Wonder Graphic Organizer Puzzle**
Form 6.30 on the CD

## Sticky Flags

Provide students with the same sticky flags you practiced with in the guided practice tasks to use with their independent reading. They may write their questions and answers in their notebooks as a follow-up.

## Question Cube

Display the cube you used in the guided practice at the comprehension center for students to use when working with a partner, literature circle, or book club group. Students can also use the sentence starters for writing in response to their independent reading.

## Never-Ending Questions

Provide a roll of adding machine tape to represent never-ending questions. Give the lengthy rolls to groups of students. They can record their questions and compare to see which group has the longest list of questions.

# Making Predictions and Inferences

**Strategy Statements:** *I can predict; I can figure it out.*

Predicting outcomes and information is an important form of self-monitoring. By confirming or disconfirming predictions as they read, students are able to monitor if their thinking is on or off-track, and adjust their predictions as necessary. Teaching students to skim and scan the text to make a prediction about new information is part of the predicting strategy.

Predicting and inferring are both included in this section because they are related processes. Both involve making an informed guess about upcoming events or information based on clues from the text and prior knowledge. But predictions are confirmed or disconfirmed according to information found in the text, whereas inferences may never be confirmed. Inferring requires the reader go a step further to figure out what the author is saying between the lines, such as the reason characters act or feel a certain way. In both predicting and inferring, we prompt students to give a reason for their thinking in order to understand the thinking processes involved.

To make inferences, students must be aware of multiple sources of information in the text and identify causal relationships between events or facts. They must integrate information to draw a reasonable conclusion. The analogy of a reading detective relates to the process of gathering clues while reading. Authors leave a trail of clues and expect us to use these, together with our background experiences, to understand their message or intent.

## DIFFICULTIES STUDENTS EXPERIENCE MAKING PREDICTIONS AND INFERENCES

Many low-progress and on-grade students struggle to predict and infer. Here are some suggestions for them that I have found effective:

### Predicting

- Review and display key vocabulary. Have students reread and retell an important section of the text, then use the vocabulary to form a prediction. Refer to students' retellings and how they support a prediction:

Students discuss and record the inferences they made and then use these to draw a conclusion about the passage.

*Now that we know ___, what do you think will happen?*

- Prompt for predictions based on the story elements or facts learned so far:

  *What else might the author tell us about __?*

- Ask students to generate a question about the book, and then turn this into a prediction:

  *I wonder ___. I think ___.*

- To help students confirm or revise their predictions and keep their thinking on track, prompt them to examine if the information they just read supports the prediction:

  *You predicted____. What in the book makes you say that?*

- Use child-friendly terms, substituting the term *guessing* for *predicting*. Ask children to make a guess before they read the next part of the text.

## Making Inferences

- State the main idea and theme, as this can be very difficult for students to recognize without wide reading experience. Students who struggle with inferring may not be able to tell you the author's purpose.

- Have students share questions that the author left unanswered and infer several possible answers.

- Avoid a single answer/inference approach. Encourage risk taking by using language that suggests there's more than one right answer:

  *What are the possibilities? Let me hear your thinking?*

- Model how to cumulatively integrate multiple sources of information across the text by breaking it into short sections and analyzing the clues available to the reader:

  *What do we know so far? How does this help us figure it out?*

- Use tools such as the strategy bookmarks, icons, and game formats described in the Guided Practice Ideas and Activities to make applying the strategy visual, concrete, and a collaborative effort.

- Include role-play with props such as magnifying glasses to find clues across the text and the puppets described in the Guided Practice section. This helps alleviate the pressure low-progress students feel and deflects attention to the puppet and away from themselves.

- Use student-friendly language to represent the strategies from the Strategy Charts on pages 242–243:

  ○ *I bet...*

  ○ *I can figure it out.*

## SELECTING MATERIALS TO MODEL THE STRATEGY

Fiction books that support predicting have logical stopping points—at causal actions and just before the effect. They contain foreshadowing, have a problem that could be solved in different ways, and have an unexpected ending. Useful text features in non-fiction titles include a table of contents, headings, subheadings, and captions. During read-alouds, have students turn and talk to share their predictions before you turn the page. Two titles I use are *Quick! Turn the Page* by James Stevenson (1990) and Helen Lester's *Listen Buddy* (1995).

With inferencing, begin with print-free sources, such as illustrations and photographs, to scaffold inferential thinking. Select visual sources, such as wordless books, photos, and illustrations that present situations that are familiar to students, so they can use their connections as one source of information in the process of figuring the scene out. Focus student attention on the facial expressions of characters, their speech, actions, and body language, along with the use of color to establish mood and convey emotion with books such as *Peach and Blue* by Sarah Kilborne (1998); *Dear Mrs. LaRue* by Mark Teague (2002); and the Alexander series by Judith Viorst. Fables, such as the short, humorous ones found in *Squids Will Be Squids* by John Scieszka (2003), provide both word and picture cues to help the reader infer the message. Humor is another tool for increasing the processing of information in the brain and providing an additional memory hook.

Comic strips such as the Family Circus series and riddle books make motivating reading material to practice this strategy, because you need to make an inference to get the joke. Short mystery stories allow students to put themselves in the role of reading detective. For example, *The Case of the Missing Monkey* by Cynthia Rylant; *The Web Files* by Margie Palatini; *Detective LaRue* by Mark Teague; *Nate the Great* by Marjorie Weinman Sharmat; *Young Cam Jansen and the Pizza Shop Mystery* by David A. Adler; and *The Missing Mitten Mystery* by Steven Kellogg are perennial favorites. Texts with a cause-and-effect structure that support the teaching of predicting and making inferences by focusing on the action/reaction relationships in a series of events include *Why Do Mosquitoes Buzz in People's Ears?* by Verna Aardema (2008); *If You Give a Cat a Cupcake* by Laura Numeroff (2008); *Lilly's Purple Plastic Purse* by Kevin Henkes (1996); *The Lorax* by Dr. Seuss (1971); and *Why I Sneeze, Shiver, Hiccup, and Yawn* by Melvin Berger (2000).

## IDEAS FOR INTRODUCING AND DEMONSTRATING THE STRATEGY

Use the following think-aloud statements, strategy charts and icons, and concrete demonstrations to help introduce and model the process of making predictions and inferences. These teaching tools scaffold learning by providing a bridge from the abstract concept to something visual and concrete.

## Think-Aloud Statements for Demonstrations

Use the same language in your think-alouds as you use when coaching students during reading. (See the Guiding Prompts on page 251.)

### Predicting Think-Alouds

Demonstrate how to skim and scan before making a prediction:

*Let me show you how I make a prediction as I begin to read a new part of the book.*

Run your index fingers down each side of the page as you scan the text.

*Readers look for words that jump out at them and other clues. I am looking for any words or illustrations that can help me. I can see __, so I am predicting __. I notice the word __, so I predict that ___.*

Model confirming or disconfirming predictions:

*I will read on and check if that does happen. … Now I know that ___ didn't happen, so I need to use what I read to make a new prediction. I predict __.*

*Let's see if I can find any clues from the table of contents. Looking at it and thinking about what I know about the topic, I predict ___.*

### Making Inferences Think-Alouds

When thinking aloud about making inferences, include the sources of information or clues you use to make the inference, using language from the strategy chart on page 243. Here, we use the student-friendly term "I can figure it out" from the strategy chart when we are making inferences:

*When we read, we ask, how does this all fit together to make sense?*

*The author doesn't say _____, but I can figure it out using what I know and what is in the text.*

*I will search for clues in the pictures and in the words.*

### Icons

The I Can Figure It Out Icons on Form 6.33 on the CD represent the concepts of predicting and inferring. Copy onto cardstock or paste onto index cards and display in a pocket chart or on the table in front of students as you share your strategic thinking. You may also use objects for these instead of the pictures.

*Predicting is like guessing tomorrow's weather. We can't know for sure what it is until it comes, and sometimes our prediction changes when we learn more information*

*Figuring it out is like putting together a puzzle. We need most of the pieces to figure it out*

*Figuring it out is like using a magnifying glass to follow a trail of clues in a mystery*

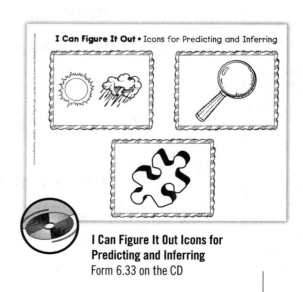

**I Can Figure It Out Icons for Predicting and Inferring**
Form 6.33 on the CD

# I Can Predict

## I can predict.

I bet...

I guess that...

I predict...

I think...

## I can check my prediction.

I can read and check.

I can think back.

Does it match? Yes? No?

Do I need to change it?

## I can predict again. ➡

Now I know...

I think...

# I Can Figure It Out

## I can look for clues...

in the picture.

    I see...

    This tells me that...

in the words.

    The author says ...

    This means that...

    I think...

    Maybe...

## I can think about what I know. ✔

The author doesn't say _____,

but I know that because _____.

## I can make a picture in my mind.

I can picture...

This helps me understand...

I Can Predict, I Can Figure It Out
Role-Play Cards
Form 6.34 on the CD

## Role-Play Puppets

The I Role-Play Cards on Form 6.34 on the CD can be made into craft stick puppets by attaching the cards with Velcro. You can also use generic hand puppets with the icons attached with Velcro as a badge. Using the puppets to verbalize the thinking behind the strategy will get students' attention. Demonstrate how the strategy character would operate on text using the language of the strategy charts (see pages 242–243) and Guiding Prompts on pages 251. Note that the Detective role is the same as the one for inferential questioning.

Weather Forecaster: *My name is Wally the Weather Forecaster, and it is my job to make a guess/a prediction about what I will find out or about what will happen next. I think I will find out how …*

Detective: *My name is Dana the Detective, and it is my job to find the trail of clues that will lead to an answer or important message from the author. Look, on this page I can see a clue in the word/picture that tells me …*

## I Can Figure It Out Picture Cards

Use the I Can Figure It Out picture cards on Form 6.35 on the CD. The first of these cards shows a detective, to represent the inferential thinking. The remaining two cards show the sources of information we use to make inferences—the book (or text) itself (Book Clues) and what we ourselves know (My Clues). Display the cards on the whiteboard with magnets or in a pocket chart. These are also helpful when categorizing the sources for your inferences during demonstrations. Use these cards as category headings, placing your inference on a sticky note under the I Figured It Out card, and the clues you used on sticky notes under the remaining two cards. Follow up your demonstration with the Detective Game (page 250) and the I Can Use the Clues graphic organizer (Form 6.43 on the CD).

I Figured It Out

Book Clues:
Words and Pictures

My Clues

I Can Figure It Out Picture Cards
Form 6.35 on the CD

## Strategy Charts

Refer to the strategy charts I Can Predict on page 242 (Form 6.31 on the CD) and I Can Figure It Out on page 243 (Form 6.32 on the CD) during demonstrations. Use a clothespin alongside any statements you use from the charts to highlight them.

## GUIDED PRACTICE IDEAS AND ACTIVITIES

The activities that follow apply to both making predictions and inferring.

### Hand Motions

At pausing points in the reading, prompt students to show you the hand signal that represents the strategy they are using:

*What are you thinking? Is it a prediction? Did you figure something out? Show me the signal for your thinking.*

Have students use these hand motions to signal their strategy use:

- Pretend to hold each side of a snow globe for predicting, or make a circle with their arms above their head to represent the sun and moon (weather analogy).
- Point to their brain when they make an "in the head" inference.

Students can share this with a partner in a brief turn-and-talk format.

### Role-Play Puppets

Use the Role-Play Cards (Form 6.34 on the CD) to create craft-stick puppets. Provide each student in the group with a puppet and invite them to role play making predictions and inferences. When students have had practice, allow them to choose a puppet that represents their thinking at that point in the reading. Students can hold their puppet as they share a prediction, a clue they found toward a possible inference, or an inference they made. Display the strategy charts to help students to verbalize their thinking as they role-play.

### Role-Play Cards

Students can also use the Role-Play Cards (Form 6.34 on the CD) without making them into puppets. Provide each student with one or both cards. Children simply hold up the corresponding card to show which strategy they are using. You can join the cards together with an O-ring so they are kept in sets for easy distribution, or store them in plastic bags.

### Turn and Talk

At regular pausing points in the reading, have students verbalize their thinking, using the strategy chart and bookmarks as visual aids for the language of predicting and inferring. These provide a focus for brief, one- or two-minute sharing session with partners in whole-class and small-group lessons.

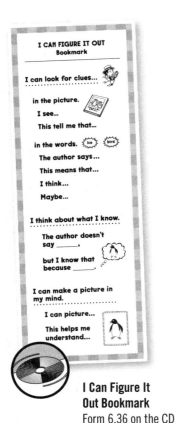

**I Can Figure It
Out Bookmark**
Form 6.36 on the CD

## Strategy Bookmarks

Prompt students to use the I Can Predict and I Can Figure It Out bookmarks (Form 6.36 on the CD) as a focus during reading and for sharing their thinking. Have them pinch the icon that represents their response:

*Hold up your bookmark to show me [your partner] if your prediction matched what you read.*

*Hold up your bookmark to show me [your partner] the type of clue you used to make your inference.*

## Sticky Flags Mark Thinking Spots

**For making inferences:** Draw a magnifying glass on a set of stickies with a permanent marker. Make two or three flags for each student and store them on the edge of index cards or bookmarks for students to use during reading. Distribute several sticky notes on index cards for students to place in the text where they made an inference and alongside any words or pictures they used as clues.

**For making predictions:** Have students place a sticky note where they made a prediction and another where they read events or information that confirmed or disconfirmed this prediction. For a more permanent set of predicting sticky flags, use a marker to print "yes" on one set of flags and "no" on another. Store these on the edge of a strip of cardstock or an index card and distribute to each student in the group.

Students jot their prediction on a sticky note and read on to check if it occurs or if they need to make a new prediction.

## GUIDED PRACTICE IDEAS FOR PREDICTING

The following activities apply to the strategy of predicting.

### Gadgets

Bring in unfamiliar kitchen gadgets, office supplies, or mechanical tools and distribute one to each group of students. Have students:

- draw a picture
- list their observations, questions, and connections
- label the item with what they predict it is used for

Conclude with a class presentation from each group.

### Vocabulary

Before asking students to make a prediction about a text, read an excerpt and/or introduce and display key vocabulary, so students have some information to base their predictions on. Do not rely on the title and cover of the book alone to support helpful predictions.

## Checking Our Predictions

Copy the Checking Our Predictions Game Cards (Form 6.37 on the CD) onto cardstock or paste them onto index cards. Invite children to share their predictions at stopping points in the reading and record the predictions on index cards (or sticky notes). Place predictions under the I Predict card displayed on the table or in a pocket chart. Prompt students for evidence; record the page and summarize the evidence on a sticky note. Then place the evidence under the Because card. At the end of the reading, take all the cards with predictions and collaboratively sort them under two category headings: Match and No Match. Discuss how some predictions were confirmed, citing the evidence, while others were contradicted by events or information or simply did not occur.

You can make a sorting placemat for this activity using a file folder. Then you can clip the cards to the top or paste them in place to form two columns on each side of the folder, I Predict/Because on one side; Match/No Match on the other. For whole class lessons, record the headings and student input on chart paper or the whiteboard.

## GUIDED PRACTICE ACTIVITIES FOR MAKING INFERENCES

The following activities apply to the strategy of making inferences.

### Mystery Person: Life in a Box

Fill a bag or shoebox with objects that represent a character, role, or job. For example, you might include tickets to sports games or shows, pet toys, empty food cartons, hobby items, and so on. Share the items with students and ask them to infer something about the life of the person they belong to. Explain how each object is a clue about the mystery person:

> By thinking like a detective, we can learn more about them and what they do, think, and feel about things.

### Reading Ring Game

Visit the website created by Jim Davis, creator of the Garfield comic strip, and go to the Reading Ring game at www.professorgarfield.org. To play the game, students will need to read the comic strip and then answer three questions about it, one of which always includes an inferential response.

### Solve-It Mysteries

The online mysteries, available at http://kids.mysterynet.com/ can be used as short read-alouds. Let your class or group select one of the possible solutions and give evidence for it.

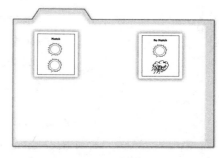

**Checking Our Predictions Game Card**
Form 6.37 on the CD

Sort student predictions under the Match and No Match Game Cards on Form 6.37.

### Reading Detective Props

Provide small magnifying glasses for each student in the group (purchased at party supply or toy stores) to use for locating words, pictures, and any clues to a question you posed that is not answered in the book.

### Strategy Music

Play music, such as the theme from *Scooby Doo* and *The Pink Panther*, before a read-aloud to engage students in detective-like thinking.

### Strategy Rhyme

Display the following rhyme near the I Can Figure It Out strategy chart (page 243) to help students internalize the strategy. Words from the strategy chart are in bold print in the rhyme below.

*When the author doesn't tell me*

*What's this all about*

***I can figure it out.***

*I put myself in a detective's shoes.*

*I use the **picture and word clues.***

***I think about what I know.***

*So the **picture in my mind** begins to grow.*

### Snap, Crackle, Pop

I have adapted the "Rice Crispie method" (Sprenger, 2008) described below to help students remember the steps involved in making an inference. You may not want your whole class snapping and popping at random intervals during assessments (but, hey, if it works...), but it is useful in a guided practice session. First, have students repeat the steps following your model. At the next stopping point in the reading, when students turn and talk, have them use the three-step process to share an unanswered question, how they figured it out, and the inference they made.

| Snap | Crackle | Pop |
|---|---|---|
| There is no answer right here in the book. | Turn the pages for evidence; turn on the lightbulb in your reading brain to figure it out. | Make an inference—Now I get it! My brain figured it out and the lightbulb is shining brightly. |
| My understanding is broken. | | |
| Snap your fingers together. | Wave fingers of both hands for the action or rub hands together to show your brain is "getting warmer." | Make a popping sound with your lips, like a cork popping out of a bottle. |

*Differentiating Reading Instruction for Success With RTI* © 2011 by Margo Southall • Scholastic Teaching Resources

## Strategy Poster

Following a read-aloud, have students share their unanswered question in partners or table groups. Identify a common question and complete the following chart format, discussing how to use the clues in the text and what we know to arrive at the most likely answer.

Our question: _____

Clues:

1. _____

2. _____

We think _____ because _____.

## Picture-Based Inferences

For a whole-class lesson, display around the room photocopies of illustrations or photos from a book or magazine and the book or magazine cover. Have students walk around the room and record something they infer about the message conveyed in each picture on a sheet of paper; clipboards are handy for this activity. Other options are to have students rotate to tables where the pictures are displayed, or to have groups pass the pictures on to the next group every few minutes. Be sure to number each picture so students can write this on their recording sheet along with their inference.

## I See, Know, and Figure Out

Ask students to examine visual information on specific pages in the book you are reading and use Form 6.38, individual whiteboards, or their reading notebooks to record the following :

**I See, Know, and Figure It Out**
Form 6.38 on the CD

- First Column: Describe the information they "see" in the visual, such as the expression on the character's face as an indicator of his or her feelings and motives, the mood established by the use of color and how this impacts the plot, details about the topic gleaned from the photo or diagram, and so on. Then they should add the connections they make from their own experience.

- Second Column: Record an inference they make based upon what they "see and know."

Have students share their thinking with a partner, and finally, share examples with the group for you to record on a chart or whiteboard.

| We see and know | We figured it out |
|---|---|
|  |  |

## Questions and Clues

Direct students to ask themselves a question as they read and to look for clues that will support a possible answer. Students can mark these with a sticky flag. Break up the reading into several sections, and take up examples of questions, answers, and the clues students used at each stopping point. Record these in a three-column format, like the one below, on a whiteboard or chart paper.

| Questions We Asked | Answers We Figured Out | Clues We Used |
|---|---|---|
|  |  |  |

## Turn-and-Talk: Stop and Think

Plan opportunities to stop and think during read-alouds and small-group reading so students can share their questions and/or inferences. They may record their questions and answers before sharing, as well as the sources for the clues or information they used, such as personal experience, other books, words the author used, illustrations, and so on. Display the strategy chart and provide bookmarks to support their efforts.

**Match Up Game: Events and Causes**
Form 6.39 on the CD

## Events and Causes Match-Up

Copy the cards on Form 6.39 (on the CD) and use them as category headings. At intervals in the reading, have students retell what they read and record the action or event on an index card. Place under the heading "What happened?" Read on to the next logical stopping point and have students identify the consequence or effect of the earlier action or event. Record their ideas on cards and place them under "Why did it happen?" Conclude by reading through the events and their effects and discuss how these relate to the main idea or theme. As a review, shuffle through the cards and display so that students can match each event with its cause. To further scaffold this activity and save time, record the actions or events before the lesson and have students identify the causes for each one. You can make a placemat for this activity by clipping or posting the cards to the top of a file folder

## Detective Game: What Clues Did You Use?

After reading the text in a small-group lesson, discuss and record student inferences and the clues that supported them on individual index cards. Read each inference ("I figured out") aloud to the group as you place the card on the table in front of the students. Read the clue(s) that supported the inference. Invite students to decide if the clues the student used were based on information the author provided (words and pictures), or what the student already knew (my clues) (see Form 6.35 on the CD).

### Mission—Possibilities

Print clues for an unanswered question in the book (events, facts, background information) on index cards and place them in an envelope. You may have separate envelopes for the beginning, middle, and end of the text and play after reading each of these sections or after reading the entire text. Students select a card and make an inference about the story using the clue.

## GUIDING PROMPTS

By using consistent terminology and prompts, students come to assume them as their own, internalizing the process. The Strategy Charts on pages 242–243 further support coaching for strategy application during reading.

### Guiding Prompts: Predicting

- *Skim and scan. Run your fingers down the sides of the page and look for clues—words that jump out at you.*
- *What do you think might happen/you will find out?*
- *What makes you say that?*
- *Now you know_____. Does that match your predictions? Do you need to make a new prediction?*

### Guiding Prompts: Making Inferences

- *On this page, the author says _. What does that tell you? How does the author help you figure it out?*
- *Use the clues the author has given you and what you know to figure it out.*
- *How do you know?*
- *What did you notice that helped you figure it out?*

## INDEPENDENT PRACTICE

Students now adopt the role of reading detective and predictor as they solve their own unanswered questions during independent reading.

### Strategy Booklet

Make a booklet using the cover on Form 6.40 on the CD and predicting and making inferences graphic organizers on Forms 6.41–6.43 on the CD. Staple these together for students to complete for each section of the reading so they can hold onto their thinking. You can also provide a sheet of statements from the strategy chart for them to use with blank sheets of paper.

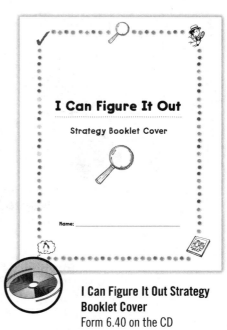

**I Can Figure It Out**

Strategy Booklet Cover

Name: _____

**I Can Figure It Out Strategy Booklet Cover**
Form 6.40 on the CD

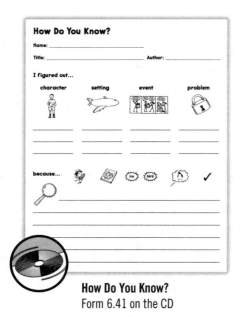

How Do You Know?
Form 6.41 on the CD

## How Do You Know? Graphic Organizer

Students record their inference under "I figured out" and explain their reasoning (clues) inside the magnifying glass (see Form 6.41 on the CD).

## I Can Figure It Out Graphic Organizer Puzzle

With this graphic organizer (Form 6.42 on the CD), students record an unanswered question inside one rectangle, inferences they made inside the thinking bubbles, and the clues they used from the book and from their own thinking inside the remaining two rectangles on the form. They cut these out and paste them on a sheet of paper in a way that makes sense to them.

## I Can Use the Clues Graphic Organizer

Students use this organizer (Form 6.43 on the CD) to record an unanswered question they had, their inference, and the clues they used from the book and from their own thinking under the remaining two columns on the form.

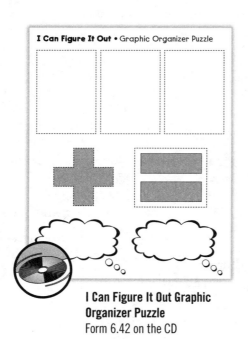

I Can Figure It Out Graphic
Organizer Puzzle
Form 6.42 on the CD

I Can Use the Clues
Form 6.43 on the CD

## Storyboards: Cause-and-Effect Sequence of Events

Provide a sheet of paper divided into four to eight sections in which students can sketch and label events in sequence. This activity supports both retelling and making inferences based upon these sequential events (cause and effect and relational inferences).

### Flip-Flap Book

Prepare flip books with two or three flaps; see templates on Forms 6.10 and 6.11 on the CD. Students write the unanswered question on the flap and their inference underneath.

### Character Traits and Object Attribute Strip Booklets

Students will make a strip booklet of 8" x 2" strips of paper that are stapled together: They write the character's name or object on the first strip. On the next three strips they draw a picture that represents an inferred character trait or attribute; this may be a facial expression, an object or representation, such as a heart for a character, or analogies to the object (straight as a __; green as a __) as well as other descriptive phrases. Students label their pictures with the attribute (object) or trait (character)—for example, *Charlotte ....clever ...loyal ...caring.*

# Clarifying and Self-Monitoring

**Strategy Statement:** *I can stop and fix.*

Breakdowns in comprehension can occur for any number of reasons. What is important is that we continuously model "fix-up" or clarifying strategies, and have anchor charts in the classroom that illustrate examples of how we applied them to shared texts—how we "fixed up" our understanding—for example, by reading on or thinking about what we already know (see Strategy Chart on page 256). Beyond a list of ways to clarify and self-monitor, students need access to an example of how to use these strategic actions so they will be able to transfer this understanding to their own independent reading. Clarifying is supported by visualization, which requires students to form a mental image. If students can create such an image, it means they're understanding the text; if not, it's a signal they need to apply a clarifying strategy.

## DIFFICULTIES WITH CLARIFYING

When reading, low-progress and other students are often reluctant to call attention to a point of confusion because they see it as a sign of weakness as a reader. Make the strategy of clarifying a safe activity by asking students to share something that would be puzzling or confusing for a younger student or sibling.

The analogy of driving a car is useful in teaching clarifying. The strategy chart and bookmark both depict a traffic light signal that supports this analogy. Provide the picture-cued visors, bookmarks, or puppets described in the demonstration and guided practice sections to initiate reflective, constructive thinking processes. Further suggestions include these:

- Remind students to use the "traffic signals" along the way that help a reader stay on course: punctuation and text features such as chapter titles, headings, subheadings, illustrations, diagrams, and captions.

- Provide orange and red stickies or colored dots for students to place next to parts of the text that were confusing or tricky. As you observe students reading, look for these as an indicator of difficulty and prompt accordingly (see Guiding Prompts on page 262). This will also provide a useful indicator of whether the topic and/or text is appropriate for this group of students. Alternatively, provide color wheels from a paint store or strips with gradients of a color, and ask students to touch the intensity that represents the level of ease or difficulty they are experiencing with this section/text as you rotate to each student in the group, with lighter colors indicating greater ease and darker colors indicating difficulty.

- Prompt students to adjust their reading speed when they are reading too quickly. For example, suggest that they go slower in parts containing lots of new information and important events or facts. Mark these places with an orange sticky, if necessary, to guide their reading speed.

- Review new vocabulary, especially words with multiple meanings, idioms, and unfamiliar expressions—especially if these have an impact on the story line or are instrumental in understanding a nonfiction topic.

- Guide students to create a picture in their mind by displaying the picture cue for the senses on the I Can Picture It strategy chart on page 258.

- Have students sketch a visual representation of what they have heard in a read-aloud; do not display the illustrations in the book as you read. Stop a few times during the reading and ask students to add to their sketches each time, updating the image based on the new information they heard. Without the support of illustrations, they will need to integrate multiple sources of information as they create their sketch.

## SELECTING MATERIALS TO MODEL THE STRATEGY

Select reading materials with a few vocabulary challenges—words that will be useful in both reading and writing that may not yet be familiar to students, as well as multiple-meaning words. Pause and examine the meaning of the words in context. Expository texts with summary charts and other helpful text features illustrate to students how to use multiple features in a book to support their understanding. For example, the Magic School Bus series by Joanna Cole and the National Geographic Readers series have sidebars, captions, diagrams, and photos to clarify important information in the running text. Stories with flashbacks and other literary devices that are likely to cause students to stumble provide a medium for teaching/learning clarifying strategies students will need when confronting these challenges in independent reading.

Much of the poetry we have at our fingertips in the classroom uses descriptive language to support visualizing and clarifying. *Come On, Rain* by Karen Hesse (1999), *Seven Blind Mice* by Ed Young (2002), *Toad* by Ruth Brown (1999), and *All the Places to Love* by Patricia McLachlan are just a few examples.

## IDEAS FOR INTRODUCING AND DEMONSTRATING THE STRATEGY

Use the following think-aloud statements, strategy charts and icons, and concrete demonstrations to help introduce and model clarifying strategies. These teaching tools scaffold learning by providing a bridge from the abstract concept to something visual and concrete.

### Think-Aloud Statements for Demonstrations

Read up to a challenging spot in the text, and model the thinking processes that help you repair your understanding. Include the language from the strategy chart in your think-aloud demonstrations. Have students describe what they saw you say and do.

*As I read I ask myself: Does this make sense to me? How does this part fit with what I just read?*

*Am I following what is happening? Am I getting the main idea?*

*Do I know what this word means? How can I fix this problem so I understand what I am reading? I can ... look at the pictures ... reread ... read on ... think about what I know ... use parts of words I know ... create a picture in my mind.*

*This part I read on page __ doesn't make sense to me. I don't understand __. Which fix-up tool will help me? First, I will reread/read on. No, that still doesn't make sense to me. I will try another fix-up tool, I will look for picture clues.*

*Authors choose words carefully to help us make a picture or movie in our minds. When I read the story today I will share what I see in my mind movie. Listen and think about what the author is sharing with us.*

### Clarifying Icons

The I Can Stop and Fix icons on Form 6.46 link the clarifying strategy to something familiar and concrete. Copy the icons onto cardstock and cut them apart. Display them as you think aloud and demonstrate the strategy.

*Using your fix-up tools as a reader when we read is like having ...*

*... a tow truck that comes to your aid when you hit a bump and have a breakdown in your understanding that needs to be repaired.*

*... a special set of tools that will help you repair your own understanding.*

*... a TV remote control: to fast-forward (read on) and rewind (reread), pause (stop to self-monitor and self-correct); access the menu of choices (our fix-up tools).*

*...a picture in your mind that you create as you read.*

Ask students to turn to a partner and state how one of the icons represents the strategy in their own words.

**I Can Stop and Fix Icons**
Form 6.46 on the CD

# Stop and Fix

I can stop and fix.

 I can stop and...

reread.

read on.

ask, what do I know? ✓

use parts of words I know.

 I can check that it makes sense.

 I can keep reading.

Form 6.44 on the CD

## Role-Play Puppets

You can use the role of a mechanic, doctor, or artist to personify the clarifying strategy. Copy the cards from Form 6.47 on the CD onto cardstock or paste onto index cards. You can make them into puppets by attaching them to a craft stick or paint stick with Velcro (see Role-Play Puppets for previous strategies). I use hand puppets and attach the icon of the tow truck on Form 4.46 to them to identify them. Hold up the character as you demonstrate the thinking role it represents.

**Stop and Fix** • Role-Play Cards

> *My name is Mandy the Mechanic, and it is my job to fix any breakdowns in my understanding. If what I am reading doesn't make sense to me, I stop reading, pull in for a pit stop, reach into my toolkit, and use one of my tools to repair it.*

**Stop and Fix Role-Play Cards**
Form 6.47 on the CD

> *My name is Doctor Dave, and it is my job to diagnose any problems and use just the right medicine so my reading brain understands the story again.*

> *My name is Vivian the Visualizer, and I will paint a picture of what has happened or what I learned in my mind.*

## Strategy Charts

Each of the picture cues on the Stop and Fix strategy chart (see page 256) represents a strategic action: reread, read on, think about what you know, use familiar parts of words, make a picture in your mind, check that it makes sense. There is also a separate chart for visualizing, I Can Picture It, on page 258 (Form 6.48 on the CD and a chart for self-monitoring strategies, I Watch My Driving, on page 261 (Form 6.50 on the CD). Clip a clothespin alongside or point to the picture of the fix-up tool you are using in your demonstration. The strategy chart is designed like a traffic light to represent the steps in clarifying:

**Stop:** When you notice that you have lost understanding or are confused as a reader, you use one of the fix-up tools.

**Wait:** Review the section that was puzzling and check that it makes sense to you now.

**Go:** If it makes sense, keep reading. If not , select another fix-up tool to use and re-peat the process.

## GUIDED PRACTICE IDEAS AND ACTIVITIES

The following interactive activities are designed to engage students in developing a set of clarifying strategies.

# I Can Picture It

I can see.

I can touch.

I can hear.

I can smell.

I can taste.

I'm picturing...

In my mind I see...

Form 6.48 on the CD

## Strategy Rhyme

To reinforce the language and strategic actions for clarifying, the words from the strategy chart and bookmark are in bold print below. Record on a chart and read together with the strategy chart (page 256) also on display.

*When I am reading along*

*And my understanding goes clunk,*

**I can stop and fix** *the part that sounds wrong*

*With the tools in my reading trunk.*

**Reread, read on,** *think about the purpose of this task,*

**Use parts of words,** *make a picture in my head,*

**Check that it makes sense,** *or I need to ask*

*Is this what the author really said?*

### Hand Motions

- **Cross-Check:** Students cross their arms to signal the process of cross-checking multiple sources of information.
- **Visualize:** Students form a "V" with the index and middle finger when they paint a picture in their mind.
- **Hit Pause:** Students can hold up their hands in the pause button signal when they find an event, fact, or word puzzling or confusing (Oczkus, 2009).
- **Snap, Crackle, Pop:** Use the activity described on page 248 for the strategic actions that clarifying requires. For this strategy, the snap represents a breakdown in understanding. Crackle means the use of a fix-up tool, and pop refers to the moment when comprehension is regained.

## Bookmarks

The I Can Picture It bookmark on Form 6.49 on the CD with picture cues of the five senses can be copied onto cardstock. You may also use the Stop and Fix bookmark on Form 6.45. During small-group lessons, the strategy bookmarks can be used as all-student responses; students show which fix-up tool they used to understand a tricky part and verbalize how they clarified.

## Sticky Flags

Provide students with Stop (red) and Fix (green) sticky flags stored on the edge of an index card. Students can place the Stop sticky flags to mark places in the text where they lost the gist of what they are reading. They can place the green flags to mark the spot where they regained understanding. They may have had to back up or read on, think about what they know, and so on. For visualizing, draw an eye on the sticky flag for students to mark the page where they saw a picture in their mind that put it all together for them.

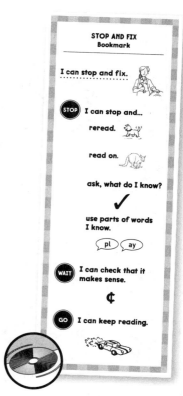

**Stop and Fix Bookmark**
Form 6.45 on the CD

### Role-Play

Students hold up craft-stick puppets like the one you used in the role-play demonstrations (Form 6.47 on the CD) as they share a part of the reading that was confusing and tell how they used a fix-up tool to repair their understanding.

### Pit Stop Game

Copy the Stop and Fix strategy chart (page 256 or Form 6.44 on the CD) onto cardstock. Cut out the fix-up tools and attach each one to a toy car with double-sided tape or Velcro. Place cars in the center of the table. Label a tray or bowl "Pit Stop" and place it next to the cars. Students, in turn, take a car that represents the fix-up tool they used and place it in the "Pit Stop" as they describe how they applied the strategy.

Alternatively, make a race track game board from a large file folder or posterboard. Label the sections of the race track with the fix-up tools. Give each student a toy car and have them drive their car to the fix-up tool they used during reading. Have them state how they used it with an example from the text.

### I Watch My Driving Strategy Chart and Bookmark

Building on the analogy of driving a car for clarifying and self-monitoring, the I Watch My Driving strategy chart (page 261 and Form 6.50 on the CD) and bookmark (Form 6.51 on the CD) describe the thinking processes essential to monitoring for meaning. These include using text features, adjusting the rate of reading, questioning the author's purpose, and always seeking the meaning or message the author is trying to convey. Display the chart as you demonstrate each of these components of clarifying. Copy the bookmark onto cardstock and have students touch the icon that represents how they monitored their reading for a short section of text, and share it with the group or a partner.

# I Watch My Driving

I ask where I am going.  Table of Contents

I use my reading map.

 ¢

I check my speed.

I slow down on the curves and bumps.

I look for the signs the author gives.

 caption

Whales are mammals.

I ask why the author wrote this.  **?**

I think about the big idea. 1 + 1 = 2

Form 6.50 on the CD

### Oops! Now I Get It

Sometimes there is an "oops" moment when our prior knowledge is contradicted by new information (Stead, 2005). Paste the icon of the tow truck or toolkit (Form 6.46 on the CD) onto one side of an index card and print "Oops!" on the other side. Distribute one to each student. Students hold up the "Oops!" card when they become confused, puzzled, and don't get what they are reading. When they are asked to share how they used a fix-up tool to gain understanding again, they hold up the card with the picture of the tow truck or toolkit. During small-group sessions, students can hold up the tow truck card during the independent reading part of the lesson to request your help (see prompts). Alternatively, wait until everyone has finished reading and have students share both their "Oops" and the fix-up tool they used with a partner. During whole-class shared reading or a read-aloud, have students share in the same way with a partner.

### Cube

Use the same cards from the Oops! Now I Get It activity. Attach the cards with Velcro to the sides of a cube. Students roll the cube and share with the group either an "Oops!" they had or a fix-up tool they used during reading.

### Picture It

Ask students draw a picture of the image they created in their mind as they read. When a student shares his or her mental picture with the group, ask the rest of the students what they see in the picture, encouraging them to make connections before the artist shares what the picture represents to him or her.

### What Do You See?

Glue googly eyes or toy eyeballs (like the ones you can purchase for Halloween) on a craft stick. Pass it around the small-group teaching table, inviting students to share what they "see" happening in this story.

### Through Their Eyes

Using the Through Their Eyes graphic organizer (Form 6.52 on the CD), students place themselves in the shoes of the character or narrator, describing what they experience through each of the senses. You may ask students to select an important scene or fact to focus upon for this activity.

**Through Their Eyes**
Form 6.52 on the CD

## GUIDING PROMPTS

As students attempt to apply the clarifying strategy during reading, support them with coaching language that directs their attention to a useful way to get unstuck:

*Differentiating Reading Instruction for Success With RTI* © 2011 by Margo Southall • Scholastic Teaching Resources

*Remember, keep a picture in your head.*

*Which fix-up tool could you use?*

*Which fix-up tool did you use? How did you use it?*

*Were there any clues that helped you?*

*Tell me what you see in your mind movie?*

## INDEPENDENT PRACTICE

Students use their fix-up tools to self-monitor during independent reading and record how they "stopped and fixed" a breakdown in their understanding.

### Strategy Booklet

Make a booklet with a cover (Form 6.53 on the CD) and copies of the graphic organizers Oops! and How Was My Driving? (Forms 6.54 and 6.55 on the CD). Staple these together for students to complete after their independent reading.

### Graphic Organizers

### Oops!

Use this graphic organizer (Form 6.54 on the CD) as a follow-up to the Oops! Now I Get It activity on page 262. Students record what confused or tripped them up during their independent reading in the first column, and in the second column they describe the fix-up tool(s) they used to clarify their understanding.

### How Was My Driving?

This graphic organizer (Form 6.55 on the CD) is a useful follow-up to the Pit Stop Game. Students place themselves in the role of a driver. Next to the tow truck, students

**I Can Stop and Fix Strategy Booklet Cover**
Form 6.53 on the CD

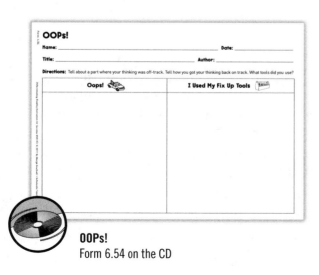

**OOPs!**
Form 6.54 on the CD

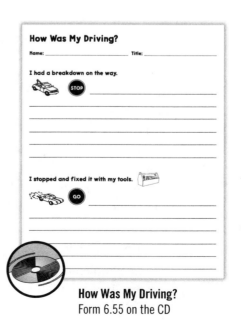

**How Was My Driving?**
Form 6.55 on the CD

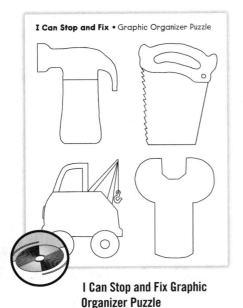

**I Can Stop and Fix** • Graphic Organizer Puzzle

**I Can Stop and Fix Graphic Organizer Puzzle**
Form 6.56 on the CD

describe the breakdowns they experienced while reading, and how they clarified their thinking.

### I Can Fix Graphic Organizer Puzzle

Inside the tow truck shape (see Form 6.56 on the CD) students describe the challenge or confusion they experienced during reading. Inside the tool shapes they write the clarifying strategies they used. Students cut out and paste these into a display. For a permanent center activity, the shapes may be laminated for use with a wipe-off pen and a file folder placemat to arrange them on. Optional: attach Velcro to the shapes and placemat.

### Flip-Flap Book

Provide flip books with two or three flaps; see templates on Forms 6.10 and 6.11. On the top flap, students record where they had a breakdown in their reading. Underneath, they describe how they used a fix-up tool to restore understanding.

### Words on the Page... Pictures in My Mind

Build upon the guided practice Picture It activity on page 262 with this independent task. On a sheet of paper or in their notebook, students read and record two or three words or phrases that elicited strong visual from their reading as they read. They can mark these with sticky notes as they read. Next to these words, they draw a picture of the mental image this word/phrase evoked in their reading brain.

| Words on the Page | Picture in My Mind |
|---|---|
|  |  |

## Retelling

**Strategy Statement: *I can retell.***

Primary students may not yet have grasped how characters drive the plot in a narrative text. What may appear to be a series of random actions are actually out-comes of the character's motivations and how he or she responds to situations and other characters. Key points for students to recognize are:

- The main character or characters are introduced early in the book, and we learn more about them throughout the book.

- Main characters are usually involved in some sort of conflict. This conflict often causes a change to occur. Conflict, struggles, and goals are central to a story.

- Main characters respond to the conflict as they try to achieve their goals, and this determines the plot.

Nonfiction is also a focus for retelling and requires the student to provide facts with details—the who, what, where, when, why, and how. This will include more information than a one- or two-sentence summary.

## DIFFICULTIES IN RETELLING

Students often experience stories as a random series of events. We need to focus their attention on the characters, and how their motives drive the plot: how characters respond to other characters and situations as they strive to achieve their goals or overcome their problems forms a chain of events or road map for a retelling. When students are confused, bring them back to the main character—his or her goals, what he or she says and does as a consequence, and how one thing leads to another (causal relationships).

Here are some suggestions to bolster the retellings in your classroom:

When students provide an incomplete, brief retelling, try the following.

- Make it concrete with retelling icons. To support the sequential nature of retelling, having something concrete in their hands makes all the difference for students. I attach magnetic strips to the back of the retelling icons (see Form 6.58) and have students place them vertically along the left side of their whiteboard. Students can slide them across one at a time as they retell each element. Having magnetic whiteboards for each student avoids the temptation to play around with the cards (not that your students would ever do that).

- Use the analogy of a phone. Model how a retelling is like a phone conversation in which you want the other person to know all the details about what just happened or something new you found out. Focus on the dialogue in the story or what the characters might have said to each other as an aid to recalling the events.

- Make connections, evaluate, and express opinions. Model how to embellish the retelling by integrating personal connections, questions, opinions, and inferences

- Incorporate sharing circles. As part of the daily literacy program, include time for students to share a book review or tell what they learned during independent practice time with three or four students. Allow one minute for each student to share, then pass the talking stick to the next student. Provide sentence stems as necessary and model the oral language that is required for this activity in a fishbowl format—have a group demonstrate for the class (after you have coached them) so that students can see what it looks and sounds like.

When students do not include key elements of the story, try the following:

- Front-load vocabulary for story elements. Students often lack sufficient expressive vocabulary for a detailed retelling, unless we introduce and discuss words representing key concepts before reading. Front-load the vocabulary for each element during the book introduction. Introduce any new vocabulary as you read the corresponding section of the text.

- Sort vocabulary by story elements. Select key vocabulary words from the text and write them on cards. Have students sort vocabulary word cards under the story elements (people, places, problem) before reading, predicting how the author will use the words in this text, and adjust any disconfirmed predictions after reading by moving the word card under the corresponding heading.

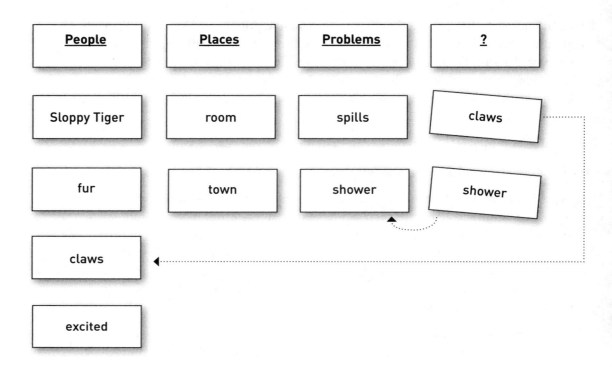

When students respond with a retelling that is not in logical sequence, encourage them to storyboard and to use graphic organizers (see page 272) on which they can sketch events and information in sequence, as a pictorial support to refer to during an oral retelling. These formats place less demand on students' writing skills, which are typically an area of concern for low-progress students, and are not as intimidating as a blank sheet of paper. You can also write "beginning," "middle," and "end" on three different-colored sheets of paper to help children think sequentially.

## SELECTING MATERIALS TO MODEL THE STRATEGY

Scaffold the retelling of fiction with short, highly structured texts with clear story element. For nonfiction, choose texts that are organized by headings and subheadings. Favorite read-alouds I use for modeling retelling include *Once Upon a Time ... the End* (humorous retellings of familiar folk tales) by Geoffrey Kloske (2005); *The Three Little Wolves and the Big Bad Pig* by Charlotte Zolotow (1993); and the *Paper Bag Princess* by Robert Munsch (1992). A reading series that includes a familiar central character throughout can also aid with retellings.

*Differentiating Reading Instruction for Success With RTI* © 2011 by Margo Southall • Scholastic Teaching Resources

# IDEAS FOR INTRODUCING AND DEMONSTRATING THE STRATEGY

Use the following think-aloud statements, strategy charts, and icons to help introduce and model how to retell.

### Think-Aloud Statements for Demonstration

Explain the purpose of the retelling strategy and use the interactive tools listed in the next section to give visual support to your think-aloud. For example, point to the I Can Retell retelling icons (Form 6.58 on the CD) and strategy chart (page 268) that depict each story element as you include each one in your retelling. Have students share what they noticed about your retelling with a partner or small group. With younger students, I use the simpler language of people, and places rather than the terms *character* and *settings*.

## Fiction Retelling

*When we are telling friends about something that happened to us, we tell them what took place and where, who was there, and how it happened. We offer enough detail to give them a picture in their minds, so they can understand what happened. Sometimes there might have been a problem, like something that got lost, that we had to solve. Before we stop talking, we always tell our friends how the situation ended.*

*As a reader, it also helps you understand a story when you can retell about all the people (characters), places (settings), and problems you encountered in your reading.*

## Nonfiction Retell

*If you are reading a book with lots of facts, retelling will help you remember them. We want to know what the book is about, where and when the events took place, how they happened, and why.*

## Icons

The I Can Retell icons (Form 6.58) represent each element of a fictional retelling. Copy onto cardstock or paste onto index cards. Display and point to these during demonstrations, as you share how you use this visual resource to help you compose a complete retelling that includes each element.

*The boy and the net is like the character and his goal—what he is trying to do.*

*The picture of the airplane is like the setting the author described in the story, which tells me where in the world the story takes place.*

*The lock is like the problem in the story that needs to be solved.*

*The comic strip is like the main event(s) in the story.*

*The key is like the solution for the problem.*

*The sunset is like the ending of the story.*

**I Can Retell Icons**
Form 6.58 on the CD

# I Can Retell

I can retell about...

people.

- what they do and say

- what they are like

- what their goal is

places.

- what it looks like

- how it feels there

problems.

- what the problem is

- how the people try to solve it

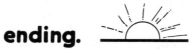

ending.

- how they finally solve the problem

- what happens at the end

Form 6.57 on the CD

*Differentiating Reading Instruction for Success With RTI* © 2011 by Margo Southall • Scholastic Teaching Resources

## Role-Play Puppets

The Role-Play cards (Form 6.59) represent a male storyteller (prince) and a female storyteller (princess) and can be made into puppets. To make the puppet, copy the form onto card-stock or paste onto index cards and attach to a craft or paint stick with Velcro. Hold up the character as you demonstrate the strategy, placing yourself in their role of storyteller. Students will be expected to do the same in turn-and-talk conversations during whole-class and small-group lessons.

> *My name is Reba/Reggie the Reteller, and my job is to tell you all about what I just read—who [what] it is about, where it happened, and what happened.*

## Strategy Chart

Refer to the statements and picture cues on the I Can Retell chart as you demonstrate the strategy and coach students to apply it during reading.

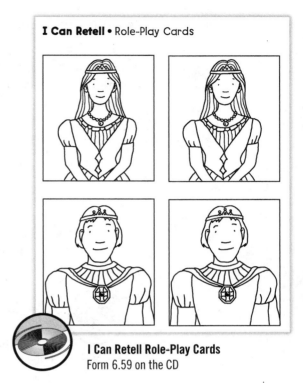

**I Can Retell** • Role-Play Cards

**I Can Retell Role-Play Cards**
Form 6.59 on the CD

## GUIDED PRACTICE IDEAS AND ACTIVITIES

The following activities provide fun, engaging practice with retelling.

### Hand Movements

- Students can rotate their hands over each other (like a wheel turning) to represent the movie-like nature of a retelling.
- Students can hold up each of their five fingers as they retell each of the five elements of the story: character, setting, goal/initiating events, problem/episodes, solution, resolution/ending.

### Hula-Hoop Sequence

Students step inside three hula-hoops as they tell the beginning, middle, and end of the story.

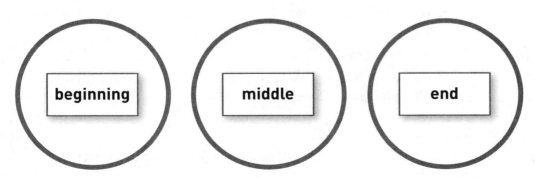

beginning    middle    end

### Role-Play Puppets

Provide students working in a small group with a craft-stick puppet like the one you used in the demonstrations. You can give students their own puppet or pass one around the table as each child, in turn, retells and/or adds to the retelling of the previous student.

**Can Retell Role-Play Cards**
Form 6.59 on the CD

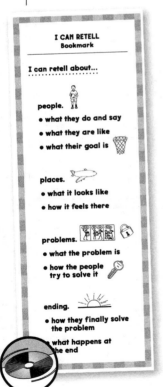

**I Can Retell Bookmark**
Form 6.60 on the CD

### Turn-and-Talk

Use these prompts to initiate focused turn-and-talk discussion.

*Tell your partner what you remember about the story. Use your bookmark to help you tell about each part.*

*Who was the most important character and why was he or she important? How does this character solve his or her problem in the story or achieve his or her goal?*

*Retell what happened.*

*Tell about this book as if you were talking to a kindergarten student or your little brother or sister.*

### Bookmarks

Students can use the I Can Retell bookmark (Form 6.60 on the CD) to guide their retellings.

*Differentiating Reading Instruction for Success With RTI* © 2011 by Margo Southall • Scholastic Teaching Resources

## Round-the-Table Retelling

Copy the I Can Retell icons (Form 6.58 on the CD) onto cardstock or paste them onto index cards. In small-group lessons, students participate in a round-the-table retelling using the cards. Before reading, give each student one card with a different story element. He or she is responsible for retelling that aspect of the text. Students may prepare by sketching and writing on their whiteboards during the reading (see also Southall, 2009)

## Retelling Cube

Copy the I Can Retell icons (Form 6.58 on the CD) and attach them to each side of a cube. Students roll the cube and retell the element showing on top. Students can make their own cubes by covering a tissue box with plain paper and drawing a different story element on each side: character, setting, problem, main event, solution, and ending

## Strategy Song

Students can make up songs about the characters, piggybacking on familiar tunes, such as the "Alphabet Song" or "Ladybird Fly Away Home."

| _____   _____ |
|---|
| Who (repeat 2 times) |
| _____ |
| Where |
| _____ |
| What |
| _____ |
| What |
| _____ |
| Ending |

*Goldilocks, Goldilocks*

*In the bears' house,*

*Eating all the porridge,*

*Trying out all the beds,*

*Run away home as fast as you can*

## Stories to Rap

In a shared or interactive format, write a retelling of the story or nonfiction text on chart paper, using short statements with clear divisions between each one. It does not have to rhyme. These statements can be cut apart for pairs of students to paste on a large sheet and illustrate. Display these in sequence on the wall to create a mural or wall story. Content reading can also be displayed this way.

*Once a girl called Goldilocks*

*Walked right into the three bears' house.*

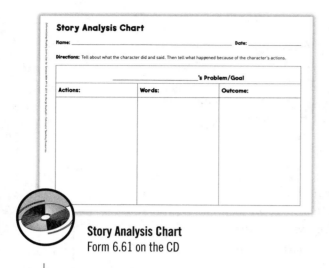

**Story Analysis Chart**
Form 6.61 on the CD

## Story Maps

After reading the beginning, middle, and end of a story—or simply at the end—complete a story analysis chart like the one at left. Using student input, state the character's problem/goal, his or her actions, what he or she said, and the outcome of the sequence of events.

## Storyboard It

The Storyboard It graphic organizer (Form 6.62 on the CD) provides a reference for you to model using a paper-size version chart, and for students to sketch the events in a story, like a comic strip. A storyboard is a grid that serves as a graphic organizer to reconstruct or construct a sequential story. Storyboarding is the way screenwriters plan movies. When we stop to fill in a frame at each stopping point or after reading, we can demonstrate this powerful tool for thinking about stories and writing in a sequential manner.

## Storyboard

**Title:** _____  **Author:** _____

| | |
|---|---|
| **1. Beginning**<br><br>[Introduce Main Character.] | **2. Setting: Place and Time**<br><br>[Describe setting.] |
| **3. Problem Begins**<br><br>[Describe problem.] | **4. Tries to Solve Problem**<br><br>[Describe attempt to solve.] |
| **5. Keeps trying to Solve Problem**<br><br>[Describe additional developments.] | **6. Begins to Solve the Problem**<br><br>[Describe events that led to the resolution.] |
| **7. Solves Problem**<br><br>[Describe resolution of problem.] | **8. Ending**<br><br>[Describe the ending.] |

It's best to use simple sketches (stick figures) with minimal text to visually represent a narrative structure. You can use this opportunity to discuss plotlines in narratives. In an eight-panel storyboard, the first frame is where we introduce the character. The second or third frame is where the problem arises or the adventure begins. The second-to-last frame contains the resolution of the problem or the conclusion of the adventure. The previous three frames typically depict the character's attempts to solve the problem.

Storyboards can be used for drafts and then rewritten to make a book with the same number of pages as there are panels on the board.

**Storyboard**
Form 6.62 on the CD

## The Story Builder

Label a chart with "Who," "What," "Where," and "When" (or "Characters," "Problem/ Adventure," "Setting," and "Time"). As you read aloud stories to the class, record the appropriate information under the four headings. Students write their own retelling using the elements displayed on the chart. You can also ask them to write their own version of the story, as in the updated versions of popular folktales. Cumulatively add to the chart over successive read-alouds so students can see the structure.

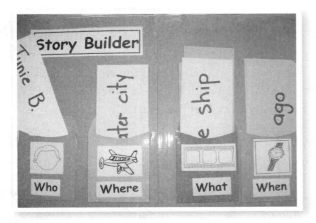

Students construct a story by mixing and matching elements from class read-alouds.

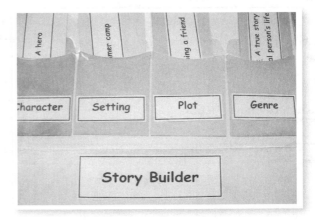

A more challenging story builder includes familiar plots and genres.

When students have had experience using this resource for retellings, I take it a step further by having them mix and match the story elements—placing the characters in different settings, with different problems and in different time periods/seasons. For example, students might write about how Junie B. would respond in a setting from an Arthur story, with a problem from an Amber Brown tale. Characters with any depth are difficult for young students to create—by giving them familiar characters and placing them in different situations, young readers gain insight into characters' traits—how and why they respond as they do. This activity fosters an understanding of the structure of a fictional text, and supports both comprehension and writing skills.

To make this same activity into one that students can use to generate their own retellings or versions of stories, label four 5" x 7" envelopes or library pockets "Who," "What," "Where," and "When." Attach these in a row to a file folder or posterboard. Create cards for each category using index cards, flash cards, or sentence strips (see photograph above). Print the names of characters, problems/events, places, times of day, seasons, and historical periods on the cards. You can color-code the cards for each of the four W's by using colored flash cards or by placing a colored sticker on each one.

Students build a complete sentence using picture-cued who, what, and where cards.

For a rebus format to support early literacy programs, paste or draw pictures of the story structure elements along with simple sight words onto the sentence strips or cards. I use clip art of story characters such as Froggie and Arthur from author websites and teaching resources for the different reading series.

## Story Structure Chart

Display the I Can Retell icons (Form 6.58 on the CD) for the Character, Setting, Problem, and Solution in a four-square chart. After the reading, point to each one as you ask students to orally retell the story using each of the elements as a guide. For nonfiction, use topic, fact 1, fact 2, and fact 3 in the chart.

### Story Structure Chart: Fiction

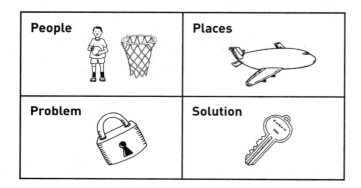

| People | Places |
|---|---|
| Problem | Solution |

### Story Structure Chart: Nonfiction

| Topic: | Fact 1: |
|---|---|
| Fact 2: | Fact 3: |

## Fiction Retelling Wall Story or Quilt

**Steps:**

1. Display the I Can Retell icons (Form 6.58 on the CD) in a large six-square chart (for a quilt effect) or a length of butcher or mural paper.

2. After the reading, point to each icon as you ask students to orally retell the story, using each of the elements as a guide.

3. Assign to groups of students one of the story elements to illustrate and label on art paper.

4. Scaffold students as they work by helping them locate the words they need from the text for their labels.

5. Encourage table group discussion on the information they will include on their illustration and label

*Differentiating Reading Instruction for Success With RTI* © 2011 by Margo Southall • Scholastic Teaching Resources

6. Tape the group work onto the six squares or in sequence to form a wall story or story quilt.

7. Refer to this chart as an anchor chart during subsequent read-alouds. Have partners, then individuals, create their own sequence of labeled illustrations.

**Retelling Quilt: Fiction**

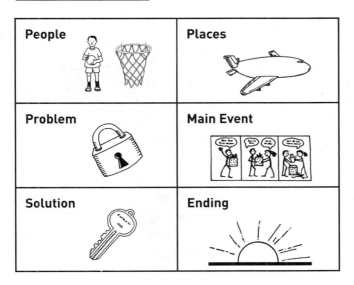

## Nonfiction Retelling Wall Story and Quilt

Students can construct a retelling of nonfiction reading material following a similar procedure as the one described above for fiction.

**Retelling Quilt: Nonfiction**

| | |
|---|---|
| Topic: | We already knew: |
| New Fact #1: | New Fact #2: |
| New Fact #3: | The most important thing we learned: |

## Text Mapping

Provide groups with photocopies of a story or pages taken from a magazine or comic book that you have taken apart. Groups or pairs will mark these up and arrange them in the correct sequence. Like storyboarding, this gives students greater access to the organization of the text, and by marking up each section, they can examine it in a way they could not in a book or magazine (see www.textmapping.org for more on this approach with textbooks and novels). Students use colored markers and highlighters to mark up the text in the following ways:

- Circling the headings and drawing a box around the related section
- Drawing a box around the illustrations
- Highlighting unfamiliar vocabulary in pink
- Highlighting important words, events, and information in different colors

### Story Pie

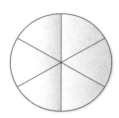

Give each group a round piece of paper or cardstock cut into six segments. Have students number the sections 1–6. Students discuss the story order, and each student is responsible for drawing and labeling—in cartoon format—one event or element. Students then sequence the slices of their story pie and share their retelling with the class. The slices can be pasted on a larger sheet of paper when complete.

## GUIDING PROMPTS

During independent reading, prompt students to retell what they have read so far, to identify the story elements, and to expand upon their retelling with details. Draw their attention to the motive of the character and his or her actions and reactions. You may also ask them to identify the message or theme.

*If you were telling the story to someone, what would you say?*

*Where does the story happen? Who has the problem?*

*What was the character's goal? What did he or she want? What stands in the way? How does the character solve the problem?*

*What can you tell me about ..? What more do you know?*

*What have you learned from this story?*

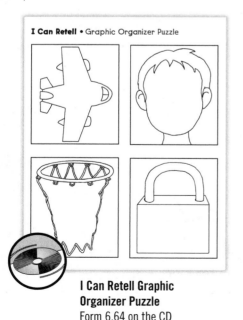

**I Can Retell** • Graphic Organizer Puzzle

**I Can Retell Graphic Organizer Puzzle**
Form 6.64 on the CD

## INDEPENDENT PRACTICE

These hand-on learning tasks provide all students access to the concept of retelling.

### Strategy Booklet

Students use the I Can Retell cover sheet (Form 6.63 on the CD) to create a booklet of retellings from their independent reading. The icons on the cover will remind them of what to include. You may provide students with sentence starters on a chart or photocopied sheet. They can also use reading notebook for the same purpose.

### I Can Retell Puzzle Graphic Organizer Puzzle

Using the I Can Retell Graphic Organizer Puzzle (Form 6.64 on the CD), students record the story elements inside the appropriate shape, cut them out, arrange as they choose, and paste the pieces on a sheet of paper.

## Retelling Paper Dolls

Students cut out two or three paper dolls and illustrate them to represent the main character and how he or she grew and changed in the story. Each one should bear a different expression to convey these changes. Another option is to make a doll for each of the main characters.

Students can hold these as they describe the character(s), their goals and problems or challenges, how their traits are reflected in their words, thoughts, and actions, how they changed as a result of events that took place and interaction with other characters (i.e., characters drive the plot). Or, if a series of different characters, how each character interacted with another and how this impacted the outcome of the story (cause and effect).

## Retelling and Summarizing Ropes

Copy the retelling icons onto cardstock, reducing them so they are no bigger than two inches square. Cut them apart, hole-punch and string together with braided yarn. Students can manipulate each picture cue in sequence as they orally retell the story.

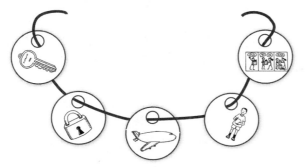

## Retelling Cube

Students cover a cube-shaped tissue box in plain paper and draw one of the story elements on each side, as it pertains to their independent reading: character, setting, problem, main event, solution, and ending.

## Flip-Flap Book

Students make a three-flap booklet to record the characters, the main event, and the ending. See template on Forms 6.10 and 6.11 on the CD.

# Summarizing

**Strategy Statement:** *I can sum it up.*

Summarizing requires students to identify which facts are most important, and even to determine the author's point of view. Giving the gist of a story in one or two sentences, using their own words, is truly challenging for students. We can scaffold this skill by discussing the topic and the author's purpose or big idea before students read a text. Then we can ask them to read and locate evidence to support the predicted purpose or big idea. Our end goal is for them to be able to perform this process themselves, but it requires demonstrations and guided practice over time. Synthesizing is an extension of summarizing that asks students to combine their connections, opinions, questions, and conclusions about a topic into one statement that represents all their thinking.

## DIFFICULTIES WITH SUMMARIZING

Summarizing presents students with a challenge because it requires a level of understanding beyond rote recall. Students may be adept at retelling everything they can remember about a text, but cannot identify the essential parts and limit their summary to those. They will need multiple exposures to determining big ideas and key details. Wherever possible, use picture cues to represent the big idea and add these cumulatively to a chart called "Big Ideas in Literature." For example, you might include photos that depict friendship, bravery, courage, conflict, survival, and so on.

**I Can Sum It Up
Bookmark**
Form 6.66 on the CD

## SELECTING MATERIALS TO MODEL THE STRATEGY

When too much text is covered in a lesson, students struggle to summarize. Demonstrate and guide practice with short, highly structured text. Informational text with supportive features, such as headings and captions, and fictional texts that include illustrations that support the big idea are helpful when teaching this strategy.

## IDEAS FOR INTRODUCING AND DEMONSTRATING THE STRATEGY

Clarify the concept of summarizing and how it differs from retelling using visuals, concrete materials, and role play.

| When students have difficulty summarizing, here are some ideas you can try: | When students rely on prior knowledge and do not integrate new information, try these ideas: |
| --- | --- |
| • Relate the principle of summarizing to personal experience by asking: *What happened to you today that was important? What do you bring to school each day that is important to remember?* | • Prompt students to adjust reading speed, going slower in parts that contain new information or important events. |
| • Use the concrete example of a funnel or strainer (see icons Form 6.67) to demonstrate the process of reducing a list of events or facts to only the most important: *Summarizing is like a vegetable strainer that drains away all the unimportant details and leaves the reader with what they need.* | • Have students record what they know on green strips of paper and new information on yellow strips. |
| • Prompt students after reading a short section of text to identify the subject and one thing the author would most want them to know. | • Ask students to stop and sketch each short section, cumulatively adding details to the same picture as they read on. |
| | • Sort the vocabulary before and after reading under the topic or chapter headings, subtopics, and subheadings for nonfiction and under the story elements for fiction. |

## Think-Aloud Statements for Demonstrations

Explain the summarizing strategy and how it helps us as readers:

*When we read a book that has a lot of information, we can't remember everything the author said. So it's important to remember what we absolutely have to know. Just like packing a suitcase for a holiday, we can only take what we really need. So we have to decide what is most important—and we use our own words to sum it up in one or two sentences.*

Pause and summarize the section of the text you just read aloud to students so they can hear the thinking processes they will need to use and internalize when summarizing:

*This was about ...*

*We learned ...*

*It's interesting that ...*

*What's important here is ...*

*What matters is ...*

# I Can Sum It Up

## I know...

## I learned...

## An important word is...

mammal

## An important fact is...

 Kangaroos are...

## This was about...

## Icons

Display the pictures on the I Can Sum It Up icons (Form 6.67 on the CD) as you explain the strategy. For an even more concrete analogy, bring in the actual items and connect the strategy to real-life applications. The analogy to a funnel, spaghetti strainer, school backpack, or suitcase that needs to be packed for a holiday (McGregor, 2007) all provide ways to demonstrate how our brain filters out what is and is not important to remember at the end of the reading—the big idea or "takeaway." Other objects include a flashlight that illuminates key words, facts, and events to form a summary (see Guided Practice activity).

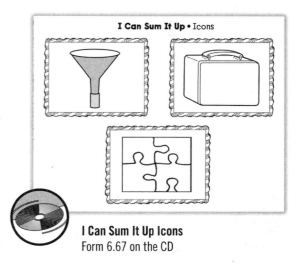

**I Can Sum It Up Icons**
Form 6.67 on the CD

> *Summarizing is like a funnel that only allows the "big ideas" in the text to make it through.*

> *Summarizing is like a suitcase that you pack with only the important things you need to take with you (there is only so much room and you can only take one).*

> *Summarizing is like putting all the pieces of the puzzle together to form a complete picture.*

## Role-Play Puppets

The summarizing role-play cards (Form 6.68 on the CD) engage students in the thinking process of summarizing by seeing these strategies through the eyes of a job-related function. Copy onto cardstock and attach to a craft stick with Velcro. Hold these up as you verbalize student thinking during a think-aloud.

For the summarizing strategy, we have a newspaper or television reporter whose job it is to provide the essential information for the reader or viewer to get the gist of it.

> *My name is Sam Summarizer. It is my job to sum up what has happened so far and tell what is most important to remember.*

## Strategy Chart

During demonstrations, refer to the I Can Sum It Up strategy chart (page 280 and Form 6.65 on the CD), using the language and picture cues to represent your thinking.

## GUIDED PRACTICE IDEAS AND ACTIVITIES

These shared experiences include all-student responses where students talk, move, write, and read as they master the concept of summarizing.

### What's the Difference Between a Retelling and a Summary?

Using a familiar text, demonstrate the difference between a retelling and a summary. Draw a two-column chart. Have students turn and talk and share all the events they can recall. Record these in the first column, discussing the sequence

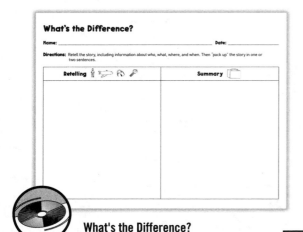

**What's the Difference?**

Name: _____ Date: _____

**Directions:** Retell the story, including information about who, what, where, and when. Then "pack up" the story in one or two sentences.

| Retelling | Summary |
|-----------|---------|
|           |         |

**What's the Difference?**
Form 6.69 on the CD

and resequencing students' contributions as necessary. Read through the retelling and identify what is most important that the author wants us to remember—what was the big idea, the main point the author wished to make? Underline a few words that contain essential points. For example, in the story of Goldilocks and the Three Bears, a chart might look like the one below.

The graphic organizer What's the Difference? (Form 6.69 on the CD) can be used for students to practice this with another familiar story or their own independent reading.

| Retelling | Summary |
|-----------|---------|
| Once upon a time a girl called <u>Goldilocks</u> was walking in the forest when she found a <u>house</u> where <u>three bears</u> lived.<br><br>Goldilocks was hungry and tired so she ate their <u>porridge</u> and went to sleep in one of the beds.<br><br>When the bears came home they found her asleep on the bed. She woke up and saw the bears looking at her. Goldilocks was so <u>scared</u> that she <u>ran</u> all the way <u>home</u>. | A girl called <u>Goldilocks found a house</u> where <u>three bears</u> lived and tried out their furniture and food. When they came back home Goldilocks was so <u>scared</u> that she <u>ran home</u>. |

### Rhyme

Read this together and discuss the definition of a summary. The words from the Strategy Chart and bookmark are in bold print.

*When **I sum it up***
*I get to the gist,*
*Use **an important word,***
*Not a long list*

*To say what **I learned.***
***I can sum it up***
*Get right to the core,*
*Tell me what it **was about***
*And nothing more.*

## Actions

Provide another connection to the reading brain by having students use muscle movements to represent strategy use.

● Students can pretend to write a text message on a cell phone.

● Students can hold up ten fingers, saying a word for each finger to make a ten-word summary.

● Students can pretend to use a lasso to round up the most important events or facts; tighten the lasso to reduce the number of words in a retelling to a brief summary. (Ozckus, 2009).

## Role-Play Puppets

Students use the puppets in the same way you modeled in demonstrations (see page 281), holding them up as they verbalize their summary or important information to compose a collaborative summary.

**I Can Sum It Up Role-Play Cards**
Form 6.68 on the CD

## Text Messages Versus Cell Phone Conversations

Highlighting the differences between a text message and a cell phone conversation may help our techno-savvy students grasp the difference between a summary and a retelling. In a text message you have to reduce the whole story or information to a brief synopsis.

Read an excerpt of a text students are familiar with and ask them how it might be summarized into a text message. They can write their summaries on whiteboards to hold up and share. Record student suggestions and use their ideas to write one text message that sums up important information—the gist of the passage. The graphic organizer Text Message Summary (Form 6.70 on the CD) can be used for this activity and to follow independent reading.

### From Retelling to Summary Card Game

Compose a retelling with 20–30 words. Provide a deck of playing cards and have students pick a card and subtract the number of words from the original summary. For example, if the retelling is 20 words and a student picks the 8 of hearts, the class or group will now compose a 12-word summary. Once students become familiar with this, have them pick a card and summarize the story in that many words. Face cards are worth 10. This can be a partner activity with students writing it on their whiteboards and sharing with the group. Scaffold by displaying the key vocabulary.

### Is It Interesting or Important?

When reading longer texts, and especially informational texts, students may see every event or fact as important. It is helpful to model how to sort out what is interesting and what is important (Harvey & Goudvis, 2007). The graphic organizer Interesting or Important? (Form 6.71 on the CD) fosters an understanding of this distinction.

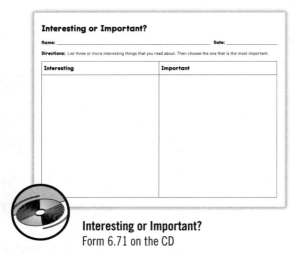

**Interesting or Important?**
Form 6.71 on the CD

- Record the facts for the retelling of an informational text on large sticky notes, or have table groups write them. Place them in the first column, or record them on a chart using student input.

- Ask students to determine one or two facts or points that they consider to be most important. You can place a star on these, or put a sticky note next to them if using a chart.

- Read and reread the facts during this discussion, modeling the process of determining importance. Disagreements are welcome opportunities for learning. Use these important facts to write a one- or two-sentence summary.

### Going on a Trip Game

Have students imagine they're going on a trip and can take only one item with them—the most important item from the reading. Have students shuffle the cards and collaboratively sort them under the headings Important and Interesting. Students will move items between the columns as they discuss and prioritize.

| Interesting | Important |
|---|---|
|  |  |

### Note Repeated Words and Phrases

When reading informational text, draw students' attention to repeated words and those that represent big ideas. With the focus on the rate of reading in fluency assessments, your students may be reading as fast as they can and need to be cued to

*Differentiating Reading Instruction for Success With RTI* © 2011 by Margo Southall • Scholastic Teaching Resources

slow down when they encounter important events, lists of facts, and new information in expository texts. Chunking the text into sections and cumulatively retelling, and then summarizing this retelling (see chart on page 282) gives students time to process, clarify any areas of confusion, and revisit concepts they may have neglected.

## Nonfiction Summary Chart

After reading, use student input to collaboratively complete a six-frame chart, or have students work in groups to complete a square and then display the finished squares as a six-frame or linear sequence (see Nonfiction Wall Story, page 275).

| We Know | We Learned |
|---|---|
| **An Important Word** | **An Important Fact** |
| **Another Important Fact** | **This Was About** |

## Telling Board

To help develop summarizing skills, give students three minutes to draw three key points. Remind them to use simple stick figures to convey what's important. The graphic organizer Sketch Summary (Form 6.72 on the CD) can be used for this activity and for a follow-up to independent reading.

### Turn-and-Talk

Have student pairs take turns summing up the reading for their partners.

## Sticky Flags

- **Interesting and Important:** Mark sticky flags with "I" for important and "i" for interesting for students to place on the outside margin of text as they read.

- **Important Information:** Distribute two or three sticky notes for students to mark what they consider the most important information in the text. These can be moved as students prioritize what is most important. Have students explain their choices. These can be shared in pairs and contributed to the writing of a group summary.

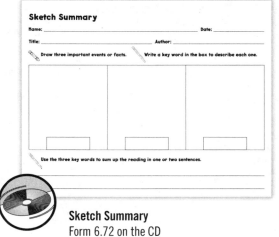

**Sketch Summary**
Form 6.72 on the CD

## GUIDING PROMPTS

Coach students during reading by providing focusing questions:

*If you were telling someone about _____ and you had to say it in a text message—one or two sentences—what would you say? Which pieces of information would you use?*

*If you only had ten seconds to tell a friend about this, what would you tell him or her that would sum it up?*

*Think about your reason for reading this. What are you trying to find out? Look for words that will help you to sum it up.*

## INDEPENDENT PRACTICE

The following activities provide fun, engaging practice with summarizing skills.

### Strategy Booklet

Make a strategy booklet using the cover on Form 6.73 on the CD and the graphic organizers on Forms 6.69–6.72 and 6.74 on the CD. Staple these together for students to complete for each section or after they complete their independent reading.

### Graphic Organizers

The following graphic organizers can be introduced in Guided Practice and then used as a response to independent reading:

- What's the Difference? (Form 6.69 on the CD)
- Text Message Summary (Form 6.70 on the CD)
- Interesting or Important? (Form 6.71 on the CD)
- Sketch Summary (Form 6.72 on the CD)

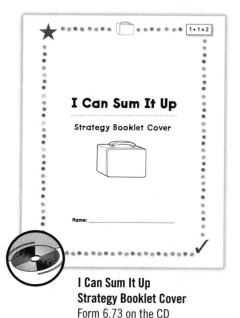

**I Can Sum It Up
Strategy Booklet Cover**
Form 6.73 on the CD

**What's the Difference?**
Form 6.69 on the CD

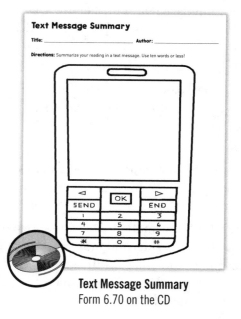

**Text Message Summary**
Form 6.70 on the CD

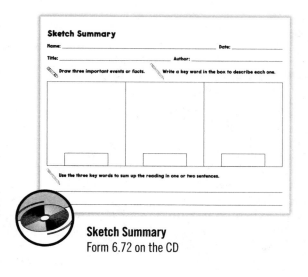

**Sketch Summary**
Form 6.72 on the CD

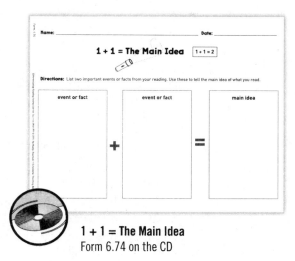

**1 + 1 = The Main Idea**
Form 6.74 on the CD

Following is an additional graphic organizer for independent practice.

- 1 + 1 = The Main Idea (Form 6.74 on the CD): Students record events or facts in the columns that add up to the main idea.

## Color-Coded Strip Summary

Students write the topic sentence or summary beginning on a strip of green paper, three events or facts with details on a strip of yellow paper, and the concluding sentence or ending on pink paper. These can be pasted in sequence and stapled together.

## Sticky Flags

Students use these with their independent reading, following the directions detailed in the guided practice activities (page 285).

## Sketches and Concept Murals

Build upon the Telling Board activity on page 285. When reading informational text, students can create a series of three to six images depicting pertinent facts. Concepts from social studies and science can be represented in sketches.

## Captions

Provide students with magazine photos and illustrations and have them write captions on sticky notes and label them.

## Flip-Flap book

Make two-flap booklets; see template on Form 6.10 on the CD. Students write what is important on the top flaps and record interesting details about each important point underneath.

# Integrating Multiple Strategies

As we model strategies and guide student practice, we keep in mind our end goal—that our students acquire sufficient understanding of each strategy and are able to call on them in any order or combination during reading to better understand the text. As you listen in as students discuss what they just read, you will hear that different students used different strategies, even as they read the same page or paragraph. And this is just what we want—for our students to flexibly apply the strategies we teach in a way that works for them.

We must be sure to show students that they ultimately will decide which strategy to use when, and that they can use more than one at a time. After you have focused on a strategy and students have had guided practice opportunities with it, be sure to continue modeling it in tandem with other strategies that you're teaching so students see how it can be applied in various situations and in conjunction with other strategies.

Students complete a four-square reciprocal teaching chart.

## Difficulties With Integrating Multiple Strategies

When it comes to teaching our low-progress readers, we might stay in the driver's seat for a long time—posing strategic questions and prompting for specific strategies—but there comes a time when we step back (still scaffolding as needed) and allow students to choose the strategic actions that help them understand best. At this stage, they are no longer passive readers who are spoon-fed which strategy to use and when, but more active readers able to independently integrate information from multiple sources to self-monitor for meaning.

One well-researched model of integrated strategy use that I have found effective with students of all ages and levels of proficiency, but especially low-progress readers, is reciprocal teaching. Within this format, students, in turn, assume responsibility for one of four strategies—predicting, questioning, clarifying, and summarizing—during a small-group lesson. In whole-class lessons you can use student input to create a four-square chart, pausing during reading to add examples of student thinking under each strategy heading. Students can also complete a four-square chart as a table group or in pairs. Several teacher resources and articles have given new life to this format, assigning characters and icons to each strategy so that students can "get into" the thinking behind the strategic action (Oczkus, 2003, 2009; Marcell, DeCleene & Juettner, 2010). The role-play resources and formats included in this section are designed to be used in a similar way.

## IDEAS FOR INTRODUCING AND DEMONSTRATING THE STRATEGY

### Think-Aloud Statements for Demonstrations

Read, pause, and model the use of different strategies for different sections of text, or more than one at a time; refer to the think-aloud statements for all the previous strategies.

### Strategy Charts

Once you've taught the strategies individually, you may introduce integrated strategy charts, such as those on pages 290–291 (Forms 6.75 and 6.76 on the CD), that provide a visual reference for each of the strategies we have examined in this chapter. The first chart uses the student-friendly language. The second uses more formal terminology for the strategies; use it as an alternative to the first chart for older and more advanced students.

### Role-Play Puppets

Use the various puppets you've used to introduce the comprehension strategies in this chapter to help students integrate strategies as they read. Select each one in turn as you demonstrate the corresponding strategy. Emphasize that you choose a strategy based on the situation and what you need to do to understand the text.

## GUIDED PRACTICE IDEAS AND ACTIVITIES

### Role-Play Puppets and Strategy Role Student Prompt Cards

Using the puppets you created for each of the strategies, invite students to imagine that the strategy workers now come together to interact with one another, so that students can experience the contribution each one makes to their understanding. The Strategy Role Student Prompt Cards (Form 6.77 on the CD) are designed to support this discussion. Copy the cards onto cardstock or paste onto index cards. Students can refer to these sentence starters as necessary. Allow each student to assume the thinking role of each strategy character at different points in the reading, or over successive lessons. You can also provide students with a set of the prompt cards secured with an O-ring to enable them to flexibly select the card that represents their strategic thinking.

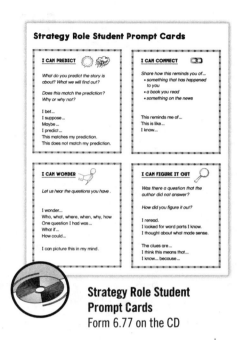

**Strategy Role Student Prompt Cards**
Form 6.77 on the CD

# Integrated Strategy Chart #1

## I can...

predict.

connect.

wonder.

figure it out.

stop and fix.

picture it.

retell.

sum it up.

# Integrated Strategy Chart #2

## I can...

predict.

connect.

question.

infer.

clarify.

visualize.

retell.

summarize.

Form 6.76 on the CD

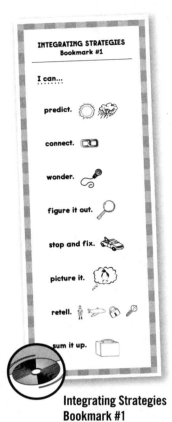

**Integrating Strategies Bookmark #1**
Form 6.78 on the CD

### Integrating Strategies Bookmarks

The student bookmarks on Form 6.78 on the CD also provide a visual and tactile tool for students to verbalize their strategy use; they can "think-pinch-share" the strategies that reflect the way they processed information and developed their understanding.

### I Can Code My Thinking Strategy Chart

Help students integrate their strategy use by teaching them simple notations to describe the kind of thinking they're doing. For instance, they can use a star to indicate they've learned something new, a tick mark to indicate information they already know, or question marks to indicate confusions. Coding their reading this way helps students track their thinking and makes them aware of the strategies they're applying.

Copy and display the I Can Code My Thinking strategy chart (see page 293 and Form 6.79 on the CD). Introduce the codes one or two at a time, then cumulatively. During a read-aloud, pause and invite students to name the strategies they're using. Draw the code that represents the strategy on the left side of a chart, then record what the student said alongside it in a short statement. This models how we can interact with the text using multiple strategies, and marks their thinking so they can retrieve it for sharing orally or in writing.

Once you've introduced the strategy chart, you may want to give students their own copies so they have the codes at their fingertips during reading.

**Comprehension in Action:** *Sebastian Gets the Hiccups* by Jenny Feely (2001)

| | |
|---|---|
| 😊 | I tried blowing into a paper bag, too. It didn't work and the bag blew up. |
| **?** | How can you rub your tummy and pat your head at the same time? |
| 😊 | If I stand on my head I get dizzy. |
| 🧩 🧩 | Is Isabella his sister or a friend? I am puzzled about who she is. |
| 💡 | I figured out that she is probably his sister, because everyone in the story so far is in his family. |
| 😊 | I would feel angry too if someone came up to me and shouted "Boo" like that. |

*Differentiating Reading Instruction for Success With RTI* © 2011 by Margo Southall • Scholastic Teaching Resources

# I Can Code My Thinking

I know... ✔

This reminds me...

I wonder... ?

I learned... ★

I am puzzled...

Aha! Now I get it.

Students code the text with the strategy that represents their thinking.

## I Can Code My Thinking Sticky Flags

Print the codes from the I Can Code My Thinking strategy chart on sticky flags for students to place in the text during reading. You can store these along the edge of index cards. Provide each student with a card that contains only the flags with the strategies you wish them to use. You can give students more than one sticky flag for the same strategy, if that is your focus—for example, you might wish to give them three question flags. Students share the thinking spots they have marked with the group and then replace the sticky flags back on the card for you to collect and reuse in another lesson.

## Coded Cube

Prepare a cube using the codes for the I Can Code My Thinking strategy chart (page 293), placing a different strategy on each side. Students roll the cube and use the code to guide their response—to generate a question, share a connection, and so on at different points in the reading.

## Squeezable Strategy Manipulatives

Squeeze 'n' Reads are a set of foam shapes labeled with reading strategies that are (see list of Resources on page 296). Distribute the squeezable foam shapes to students during small-group lessons, selecting the appropriate strategy at each discussion point. Students can pass these around the table to provide a tactile cue and supporting prop for verbalizing their strategy use. For example, they may hold on to the brain-shaped manipulative when discussing inferencing, or the Band-Aid shape when discussing clarifying strategies.

## INDEPENDENT PRACTICE

Authentic comprehension requires students to integrate multiple strategies during independent reading.

## Strategy Booklet

**Integrating Strategies Strategy Booklet Cover**
Form 6.80 on the CD

Make a mixed strategy booklet using the cover on Form 6.80 on the CD and selected graphic organizers from all of the strategies in this chapter. Add blank pages so that students can also write responses to independent reading using prompts from the Strategy Role Student Prompt Cards (Form 6.77 on the CD), Strategy Placemats (see below and Forms 6.85 and 6.86 on the CD), the My Thinking Boxes graphic organizer (Form 6.81 on the CD), and/or My Strategy Sheets (Forms 6.82-6.84 on the CD). Staple these together for students to complete as a tangible record of their thinking

## Strategy Placemats

You can copy both Strategy Placemat #1 and #2 (Forms 6.85-6.86 on the CD) onto both sides of a piece of cardstock so students will have sentence starters for all strategies at their fingertips. Distribute to students during small-group lessons and make available during writing in response to independent reading tasks.

**Strategy Placemat #1**
Form 6.85 on the CD

**Strategy Placemat #2**
Form 6.86 on the CD

**My Strategy Sheet #3**
Form 6.84 on the CD

## Graphic Organizers

- **My Thinking in Boxes** (Form 6.81 on the CD): Students select a quote from the book that stands out to them, record a question they have about it, and summarize what it means in one sentence. Then they draw a pencil sketch that represents their thinking.

- **My Strategy Sheet #1, #2, and #3** (Forms 6.82-6.84 on the CD): Students record their strategic thinking that correlates to each strategy. These strategy sheets consist of four, six, and eight strategies, so are increasingly more challenging.

## Sticky Flags

Students use coded sticky flags in the same way as in the guided practice lessons, now using them with independent reading. They may write their responses in their reading notebooks.

**My Thinking in Boxes: Q and S**
Form 6.81 on the CD

# Resources for Differentiated Comprehension Instruction

### Websites for Vocabulary Definitions and Pictures

Google.com – googlescholar, search images
http://innovativocab.wikispaces.com

www.visuwords.com
www.wordsmith.org/
www.visualthesaurus.com/
www.vocabularya-z.com

### Comprehension Websites

View and print strategy charts from: www.mrsbunyi.com

Find comic strip stories with question in a game-like format:
www.Professorgarfield.com

Find think-aloud examples and strategy prompts at:
http://reading.ecb.org

### Comprehension Strategy Manipulatives

"Squeeze 'n' read" sets of foam pieces that represent
comprehension strategies are available from:
www.s-cook.org

### Books for Read Aloud Demonstrations by Strategy

### Making Connections

*17 Things I'm Not Allowed to Do Anymore* by Jennifer Offill
*Hooway for Wodney Wat and Listen Buddy* by Helen Lester
*What Are You So Grumpy About?* by Tom Lichtenheld

### Inferring

*The Story of Jumping Mouse* by Steptoe
*Squids Will Be Squids* by Jon Scieszka
*Shortcut* by David Macaulay
*No, David!* and *David Goes to School* by David Shannon
  (picture supported inferences)

### Asking Questions

*Two Bobbies* by Kirby Larson and Mary Nethery
*The Lotus Seed* by Sherry Garland
*Charlie Anderson* by Barbara Abercrombie
*The Stranger* by Chris Van Allsburgh
*An Angel for Solomon Singer* by Cynthia Rylant
All of David Weisner's books

### Visualization

*Here We All Are* by Tomie de Paola
*A Bad Case of Stripes* by David Shannon
*Knots on a Counting Rope* by Bill Martin Jr.
*An Octopus is Amazing* by Patricia Lauber

### Retelling and Summarizing

*Once Upon a Time ... the End* by Geoffrey Kloske
Magic School Bus series by Joanna Cole
*The Paper Bag Princess* by Robert Munsch
*The Three Little Wolves and the Big Bad* Pig by Charlotte Zolotow
and Eugene Trivias

### Vocabulary Enrichment

*Max's Words* by Kate Banks
*Miss Alaineus: A Vocabulary Disaster* by Debra Frasier
*The Boy Who Cried Fabulous* by Leslea Newman
*The Boy Who Loved Words* by Roni Schotter
*Thesaurus Rex* by Laya Steinberg
*Things That Are Most in the World* by Judi Barrett
*Donovan's Word Jar* by DeGross
*A Particular Cow* by Mem Fox

### Words with Multiple Meanings

Amelia Bedelia series by Peggy Parish
Commander Toady series by Jane Yolen
*The Dove Dove* by Marvin Terban
*Baby Buggy, Buggy Baby* by Harriet Ziefert
*A Chocolate Moose for Dinner* by Fred Gwynne
*A Little Pigeon Toad* by Fred Gwynne

### Wordplay Books

*Antics* by Cathi Hepworth
*Eight Ate: a Feast of Homonym Riddles* by Marvin Terban
*In a Pickle and Other Funny Idioms* by Marvin Terban
*Knock, Knock! Who's There?* By Tad Hills
*Superdupers: Really Funny Real Words* by Marvin Terban
*Once There Was a Bull...(frog)* by Rich Walton
  (compound words)
*There's an Ant in Anthony* by Bernard Most
  (finding familiar parts in multisyllabic words)

*Differentiating Reading Instruction for Success With RTI* © 2011 by Margo Southall • Scholastic Teaching Resources

# CD Contents List

## CHAPTER 2

| Form # | Title |
|---|---|
| 2.1 | Profile as a Reader |
| 2.2 | Profile as a Learner |
| 2.3 | Student Reading Goals, Observations, and Instruction |
| 2.4 | Planning for Group Instruction |
| 2.5 | Observation Rubrics |
| 2.6 | Observing Student Responses |
| 2.7 | Recording Student Talk |
| 2.8 | Class Profile |
| 2.9 | Monitoring Progress with Instructional Text Levels |
| 2.10 | Student Instructional Log |
| 2.11 | Intervention Group Log |
| 2.12 | Student Survey |
| 2.13 | My Reading Goals |
| 2.14 | Intervention Plan |

## CHAPTER 3

| Form # | Title |
|---|---|
| 3.1 | Center Tracking Form |
| 3.2 | Choice Board |
| 3.3 | Choice Board |
| 3.4 | Choice Board |
| 3.5 | Bulletin Board Statements: 3 Headers – Word Solving, Fluency, and Comprehension |
| 3.6 | Bulletin Board Statements: Word Solving |
| 3.7 | Bulletin Board Statements: Word Solving; Fluency |
| 3.8 | Bulletin Board Statements: Fluency |
| 3.9 | Bulletin Board Statements: Comprehension |
| 3.10 | Bulletin Board Statements: Comprehension |
| 3.11 | Bulletin Board Statements: Comprehension |
| 3.12 | Bulletin Board Statements: Comprehension |

## CHAPTER 4

| Form # | Title |
|---|---|
| 4.1 | Developmental Progression of Phonics Knowledge |
| 4.2 | Assessment Record: Word Study |
| 4.3 | Folder Labels: Word Solving |
| 4.4 | Sound and Say Strategy Chart |
| 4.5 | Chunk the Words Strategy Chart |
| 4.6 | I Can Use What I Know Strategy Chart |
| 4.7 | Build and Blend Dominoes: *a* |
| 4.8 | Build and Blend Dominoes: *e* |
| 4.9 | Build and Blend Dominoes: *i* |
| 4.10 | Build and Blend Dominoes: *o* |
| 4.11 | Build and Blend Dominoes: *u* |
| 4.12 | Lesson: Hearing and Recording Sounds in Sequence: Initial and Final Sounds |
| 4.13 | Sounds in Sequence: Initial & Final Sounds |
| 4.14 | Sounds in Sequence: Medial Sounds |
| 4.15 | Sounds in Sequence: Blends & Digraphs |
| 4.16 | Lesson: Cumulative Blending With CVC Words |
| 4.17 | Lesson: Cumulative Blending With Initial Consonant Blends |
| 4.18 | Lesson: Cumulative Blending From the Medial Vowel |
| 4.19 | Lesson: Word Building With Medial Vowels |
| 4.20 | Lesson: Word Sorting for Medial Vowels |
| 4.21 | Cut and Sort |
| 4.22 | Lesson: Five-Step Guided Word Sort |
| 4.23 | Five-Step Lesson Guide |
| 4.24 | Lesson: Six-Step Guided Word Sort |
| 4.25 | Six-Step Lesson Guide |
| 4.26 | I Can Use Words I Know |

# CD Contents List (continued)

*Differentiating Reading Instruction for Success With RTI* © 2011 by Margo Southall • Scholastic Teaching Resources

# CD Contents List (continued)

# References

Allington, R. L. (2009). *What really matters in response to intervention.* Boston: Pearson.

Allington, R. L. (2005). *What really matters for struggling readers: Designing research-based programs.* (2nd ed.). Boston: Pearson

Applegate, A. J., Applegate, M. D., & Turner, J. D. (2010). Learning disabilities or teaching disabilities? Rethinking literacy failure. *The Reading Teacher,* Vol. 64, (3), 211–213.

Applegate, M. D., Quinn, K. B., & Applegate, A. J. (2006). Profiles in comprehension. *The Reading Teacher,* Vol. 60, (1), 48-57.

Archer, Anita. Adding zip and zest: Explicit Teaching of Strategies and Concepts. Keynote presentation, Maryland International Reading Association Conference, Hunt Valley, MD, April 14-, 2010.

Bear, D. R., Invernizzi, M., Johnston, F., & Templeton, S. (2010). *Words their way letter and picture sorts for emergent spellers.* (2nd ed.). New York: Prentice Hall.

Bear, D. R., Invernizzi, M., Templeton, S., & Johnston, F. (2008). *Words their way: Word study for phonics, vocabulary, and spelling instruction.* (4th ed.). Upper Saddle River, New Jersey: Pearson.

Beck, I. L. (2006). *Making sense of phonics: The hows and whys.* New York: Guilford Press.

Beck, I, & Hamilton, R. (2000). *Beginning reading module.* Washington, DC: American Federation of Teachers.

Beck, I, L., & McKeown, M. G. (2001). Text talk: Capturing the benefits of read aloud experiences for young children. *The Reading Teacher,* 55, 10–35.

Beck, I., McKeown, M., & Kucan, L. (2002). *Bringing words to life: Robust vocabulary instruction.* New York: Guilford.

Blair, T.R., W.H. Rupley, & W. Nichols. (2007). The effective teaching of reading: Considering the "what" and "how" of instruction. *The Reading Teacher,* Vol. 60, (5) 442–438.

Blevins, W. (2006). *Phonics from A to Z: A practical guide.* 2006. (2nd ed.). New York: Scholastic Inc.

Blevins, W. (2001). *Teaching phonics and word study in the intermediate grades: A complete source book.* New York: Scholastic.

Boushey, G, & Moser, J. (2006). *The daily five.* Portland, ME: Stenhouse.

Carnine, D. W., Silbert, J., & Kame'enui, E. J.; & Tarver, S. G. (2009). *Direct reading instruction.* (5th ed.). Upper Saddle River, NJ: Prentice Hall.

Christensen, C. A., & Bowey J. A. (2005). The efficacy of orthographic rime, grapheme-phoneme correspondence, and implicit phonics approaches to teaching decoding skills. *Scientific Studies of Reading,* 9, 327–349.

Clay, M. (2006). *An observation survey of early literacy achievement.* Portsmouth, NH: Heinemann.

Clay, M. (2005). *Literacy lessons: Designed for individuals, part two.* Portsmouth, NH: Heinemann.

Clay, M. (2001). *Running records for classroom teachers.* Portsmouth, NH: Heinemann.

Clay, M. (1997). *Reading recovery: A guidebook for teachers in training.* Portsmouth, NH: Heinemann.

Cunningham, P. (2009). *Phonics they use: Words for reading and writing.* (5th ed.). Boston: Allyn & Bacon.

Cunningham, P., (2000). *Sequential, systematic phonics they use.* Greensboro, NC: Carson-Dellosa.

Cunningham, P., & Stanovich, K. E. (1998). The impact of print exposure on word recognition. In J. Metsala & L. Ehri (Eds.), *Word recognition in beginning literacy* (pp. 235–262). Mahwah, NJ: Erlbaum.

Dewitz, P., Jones, J., & Leahy, S. (2009). Comprehension strategy instruction in core reading programs. *Reading Research Quarterly,* 44 (2), 102–126.

Dorn, L. J., & Saffos, C. (2011). *Interventions that work: A comprehensive intervention model for preventing reading failure in grades K–3.* Boston: Allyn & Bacon.

Dorn, L. J., & Saffos, C. (2001). *Shaping literate minds.* New York: Stenhouse.

Dorn, L. J., & Henderson, S. C. (2010). The comprehensive intervention model: A systems approach to RTI. In M. Y. Lipson,, & K. K. Wixson (Eds.), *Successful approaches to RTI: Collaborative practices for improving K–12 literacy.* Newark, DE: International Reading Association, pp. 88–133.

Dunn, M.W. (2007). Diagnosing reading disability: Reading Recovery as a component of a response-to-intervention assessment method. *Journal of Learning Disabilities* 5(2), 31-47.

Fisher, D., & Frey, N. (2010). *Enhancing RTI: How to ensure success with effective classroom instruction and intervention.* Alexandria, VA: ASCD.

Frey, N., & Fisher, D. (2009). *Learning words inside and out: Vocabulary instruction that boosts achievement in all subject areas.* Portsmouth, NH: Heinemann.

Fountas, I. C., & Pinnell, G. S. (1996). *Guided reading: Good first teaching.* Portsmouth, NH: Heinemann.

Fountas, I. C., & Pinnell, G. S. (2005). *Leveled books: Matching texts to readers.* Portsmouth, NH: Heinemann.

Fountas, I. C., & Pinnell, G. S. (2008). *The benchmark assessment system.* Portsmouth, NH: Heinemann.

Ganske, K. (2000). Word journeys: *Assessment-guided phonics, spelling and vocabulary instruction.* New York: Guilford.

Ganske, K. (2003). *Word sorts and more: Sound, pattern and meaning exploration K–3.* New York: Guilford.

Gaskins, I. W. (2005). *Success with struggling readers: The benchmark school approach.* New York: Guilford.

Gaskins, I. W., Linnea E. C., Cress, C., O'Hara, C., & Donnelly, K. (1997). Procedures for word learning: Making discoveries about words. *The Reading Teacher,* Vol. 50, 312-327.

Gregory, A. E., & Cahill, M. (2010). Kindergartners can do it, too! Comprehension strategies for early readers. *The Reading Teacher,* Vol. 63 (6), 515–520.

Gunning, T. G. (2006). *Assessing and correcting reading and writing difficulties.* (3rd ed.). Boston: Allyn & Bacon.

Haager, D., Klingner, J., & Vaughn, S. (2007). *Evidence-based reading practices for response to intervention.* Baltimore: Brookes Publishing.

Harvey, S., & Goudvis, A. (2007). *Strategies that work: Teaching comprehension to enhance understanding.* (2nd ed.). Portland, ME: Stenhouse.

Howard, P. J. (2001). *The owner's manual for the brain: Everyday applications from mind-brain research.* Atlanta: Bard Press.

International Reading Association (2010). Response to intervention: Guiding principles for educators. Newark, DE. Retrieved from http://www.reading.org/Libraries/Resources/RTI_brochure_web.sflb.ashx

Jensen, E. (2005). *Teaching with the brain in mind.* (2nd ed.). Alexandria, VA: Association for Supervision and Curriculum Development (ASCD).

Joseph, L.M. (2000). Developing first graders' phonemic awareness, word identification and spelling: A comparison of two contemporary phonic instructional approaches. *Reading Research and Instruction*, 39 (2), 160–169

Juel, C., & Minden-Cupp, C. (2000). One down and 80,000 to go: Word recognition instruction in the primary grades. *The Reading Teacher*, Vol. 53, No. 4, 332-335.

Johns, J. L., & Lenski, S. D. (2000). *Improving reading: Strategies and resources.* Dubuque, IA: Kendall-Hunt.

Johnson, P. (2006). *One child at a time: Making the most of your time with struggling readers K–6.* Portland, ME: Stenhouse.

Johnston, P. (2000). *Running records: A self-tutoring guide* (book and audiotape). Portland, ME: Stenhouse.

Johnston, P. (2004). *Choice words: How our language affects children's learning.* Portland, ME: Stenhouse.

Keene, E. O., & Zimmerman, S. (2007). *Mosaic of thought: The power of comprehension strategy instruction.* (2nd ed.). Portsmouth, NH: Heinemann.

Kingner, J. K., Vaughn. S., and Boardman, A. (2007). *Teaching reading comprehension to students with learning difficulties.* New York: Guilford.

Kosanovich, M,. Ladinsky, K., Nelson, L., & Torgesen, J. (2006). *Differentiated reading instruction: Small group alternative lesson structures for all students.* Florida Center for Reading Research. Retrieved from www.fcrr.org

Kuhn, M. (2004). Helping students become accurate, expressive readers: Fluency instruction for small groups. *The Reading Teacher*, Vol. 58 (4) 338–344.

Kuhn, M., & Stahl, S. (2003). Fluency: A review of developmental and remedial strategies. *The Journal of Educational Psychology.* 95, 1–19.

Larson, L. C. (2010). Digital readers: The next chapter in e-book reading and response. *The Reading Teacher*, Vol. 64 (1), pp.15–22.

Lipson, M. Y., & Wixson, K. K. (2010). *Successful approaches to RTI: Collaborative practices for improving K–12 Literacy.* Newark, DE: International Reading Association.

Lovett, M, W., Lacerenza L., & Borden, S. L. (2000). Putting struggling readers on the PHAST track: A program to integrate phonological and strategy-based remedial reading instruction and maximize outcomes. *Journal of Learning Disabilities*, 33(5), 458–476.

Marcell, B., DeCleene, J., & Juettner, M. (2010). Caution! Comprehension under construction: Cementing a foundation of comprehension strategy usage that carries over to independent practice. *The Reading Teacher*, Vol. 63 (8), 687–691.

Marzano, R. J. (2004). *Building background knowledge for academic achievement.* Alexandria, VA: Association for Supervision & Curriculum.

Marzano, R. J., Pickering, D. J. (2005). *Building academic vocabulary for student achievement: Teacher's manual.* Alexandria, VA: Association for Supervision and Curriculum Development.

Massi, J. (2007.) Tier 1: A guide for Title 1 directors. Presentation at West Virginia Title 1 Directors Conference. June 17-18, Morgantown, West Virginia.

McCandliss, B., Beck, I., Sendak, R., & Perfetti, C. (2003.) Focusing attention on decoding for children with poor reading skills: Design and preliminary tests of the Word building intervention. *Scientific Studies of Reading*, 7, 75–104.

McCarthy, P. A. (2008). Using sound boxes systematically to develop phonemic awareness. *The Reading Teacher*, 62(4), pp. 346-349.

McGregor, T. (2007). *Comprehension connections: Bridges to strategic reading.* Portsmouth, ME: Heinemann.

Mesmer, H. A., & Griffith, P. L. (2006). Everybody's selling it—But just what is explicit, systematic phonics instruction? *The Reading Teacher*, Vol. 59, No. 4. 366-376.

McKeown, M. G., & Kucan, L. (eds.). (2010). Bringing reading research to life. *The Reading Teacher*, 55 (1), 10–19.

McKeown, M. (2010). Robust vocabulary affects comprehension. Presentation at Maryland International Reading Association Conference Hunt Valley, MD, April 16, 2010.

Minskoff, E. (2005). *Teaching reading to struggling learners.* Baltimore, MD: Paul H. Brookes Publishing.

Moats, L. (2000). *Speech to print: Language essentials for teachers.* Baltimore: Brookes.

Moss, B. (2005). Making a case and a place for effective content area literacy instruction in the elementary grades. *The Reading Teacher*, 59(1), 46–55.

National Institute of Child Health and Human Development (2000). *Report of the National Reading Panel. Teaching children to read: An evidence-based assessment of the scientific literature on reading and its implications for reading instruction.* (NIH – 00 – 4769). Washington, DC: Government Printing Office.

Neuman, S. B. (2006). The knowledge gap: Implications for children of poverty: Differential effects of adult mediation and literacy-enriched play settings on environmental and functional print tasks. *American Educational Research Journal*, 30, 95–122.

O'Connor, R. E. (2007). *Teaching word recognition: Effective strategies for students with learning disabilities.* New York: Guilford.

Oczkus, L. (2008). *Interactive think-aloud lessons.* New York: Scholastic.

Oczkus, L. (2003). *Reciprocal teaching at work.* Newark, DE: International Reading Association.

Pinnell, G., & Fountas, I. (2009). *When readers struggle: Teaching that works.* Portsmouth, NH: Heinemann.

Prescott-Griffin, M., Witherell, N. L. (2004). *Fluency in focus.* Portsmouth: Heinemann.

Rasinski, T. (2010). *The fluent reader.* (2nd ed.). New York: Scholastic.

Rasinski, T., & Hamman, P. (2010). Fluency: Why it is "Not Hot." *Reading Today*, August/September. International Reading Association.

Richek, M. (2001). *Vocabulary strategies that boost your students' reading comprehension: Video resource guide.* Bureau of Education and Research, WA.

Rubin, H. (2003). *Differentiating literacy instruction.* The Stern Center for Language and Learning Symposium, New Hampshire.

Scanlon, D. M., Anderson, K. L., & Sweeney J. M. (2010). *Early intervention for reading difficulties: The interactive strategies approach.* New York: Guilford.

Shaywitz, S. (2003). *Overcoming dyslexia: New and complete science-based program for reading problems at any level.* New York: Knopf.

Schirmer, B. R. (2010). *Teaching the struggling reader.* Boston: Pearson.

Shea, M. (2000). *Taking running records.* New York: Scholastic.

Sibberson, F., & Szymusiak, K. (2008). *Day-to-day assessment in the reading workshop.* New York: Scholastic.

Southall, M. (2009). *Differentiated small-group reading lessons.* New York: Scholastic.

Southall, M. (2007). *Differentiated literacy centers.* New York: Scholastic.

Sprenger, M. (2008). *Differentiation through learning styles and memory.* (2nd edition.). Thousand Oaks, CA: Corwin Press.

Stahl, S. A., Heubach, K. M., & Cramond, B. (1997). Fluency-oriented reading instruction. *Reading Research Rep. No. 79.* Athens, GA: National Reading Research Center.

Stead, T. (2006). *Reality checks: Teaching reading comprehension with nonfiction.* Portland, ME: Stenhouse.

Taylor, B. M., & Pearson, P. D., Clark, K. F., & Walpole, S. (1999). Effective schools/accomplished teachers. *The Reading Teacher,* Vol. 53, No. 2.

Taberski, S. (2000). *On solid ground.* Portsmouth, NH: Heinemann.

Torgesen, Joseph. 2005. Preventing reading disabilities in young children: Requirements at the classroom and school level. University of Florida. Florida Center for Reading Research. Presentation for the International Dyslexia Association. Retrieved from www.fcrr.org

Vaughn, S., & Roberts, G. (2007). Secondary interventions in reading: Providing additional instruction for students at risk. *Teaching Exceptional Children,* 39(5), 40–46.

Vaughn, S., Bos, C. S., Shay, J., & Schumm, S. (2002). *Teaching exceptional, diverse, and at-risk students in the general education classroom.* (3rd ed.). Boston: Allyn & Bacon.

Walpole, S., & McKenna, R. (2009). *How to plan differentiated reading instruction.* New York: Guilford.

Walpole, S., & McKenna, R. (2007). *Differentiated reading instruction.* New York: Guilford.

Weaver, C. (2002). *Reading process and practice.* (3rd ed.). Portsmouth, NH: Heinemann.

Williams, C., Phillips-Birdsong, C., Hufnagel, C., Hungler, D., & Lundstrom, R. P. (2009). Word study instruction in the K–2 classroom. *The Reading Teacher,* 6(27), pp. 570–578.

Wolf, M. (2007). *Proust and the squid: The story and science of the reading brain.* New York: HarperCollins.

Wolf, M. (2000). Naming-speed processes and developmental reading disabilities. *Journal of Learning Disabilities.* Vol. 33, (4), July/August, pp. 322–324.